The Political Papacy

The Political Papacy
John Paul II, Benedict XVI, and Their Influence

Edited by
CHESTER GILLIS

Paradigm Publishers
Boulder • London

Copyright © 2006 Paradigm Publishers

Published in the United States by Paradigm Publishers, 3360 Mitchell Lane, Suite E, Boulder, CO 80305 USA.

Paradigm Publishers is the trade name of Birkenkamp & Company, LLC, Dean Birkenkamp, President and Publisher.

Library of Congress Cataloging-in-Publication Data

Gillis, Chester, 1951–
   The political papacy : John Paul II, Benedict XVI, and their influence
/ Chester Gillis.
   p. cm.
   Includes bibliographical references and index.
   ISBN 1-59451-181-0 (hc : alk. paper)
   1. John Paul II, Pope, 1920–2005—Political activity. 2. Benedict XVI,
   Pope, 1927– —Political activity. 3. Popes—Political
activity—History—20th century. I. Title.
   BX1878.5.G55 2005 *2006*
   282.092—dc22
                                                                    2005027854

Designed and Typeset by Hoffman-Paulson Associates

10 09 08 07 06   1 2 3 4 5

Contents

Introduction: Understanding the Political in the Papacy

Even the most casual observer would probably agree that popes function as political figures as well as spiritual leaders. Historically, some have been more politically inclined and active than others, but all have had influence on societies, cultures, and public policies. During the earliest development of the church, their influence affected a relatively small community of believers. Nevertheless, in the view of Roman overlords, these believers posed a threat to Roman rule—a perception that resulted in persecution. As the numbers of Christians increased, so did papal influence. With the rise of Constantine in the early fourth century C.E., the church gained recognition from the state, thus enhancing its influence.

Since that time, popes, regardless of their personal piety or lack thereof, have played important roles in the social, cultural, and political order. In the Middle Ages and the Renaissance, they crowned kings. This power underscored both the divine right of kings and the church's authority. They also had the power to influence culture. For example, Julius II commissioned Michelangelo to paint the Sistine Chapel. Despite the fact that Julius mistreated this distinguished artist, enduring art resulted. Popes owned principalities, advised monarchies, established moral codes, governed educational institutions, served as patrons of music and art, and fought wars—all in the name of the church. Their decisions and the directions they took influenced the religious, social, cultural, and *political* landscape. Until the twentieth century, the Vatican owned considerable land—holdings that made it an economic and political power.

Some popes apprenticed themselves for the role of supreme pontiff by virtue of their membership in the papal diplomatic corps, representing the Holy See in various parts of the world. For example, Pius XII (Eugenio Pacelli) served as Papal Nuncio to Germany and as Vatican Secretary of State before becoming pope in 1939. Others learned their skills from papal mentors, as in the case of Joseph Cardinal Ratzinger, who, when he headed the Vatican Congregation of the Doctrine of the Faith, served as one of John Paul II's closest confidants.

Some pontiffs, however, have had more political influence than others. John Paul II counts among these. A pious man nominated for sainthood soon after his death, he understood and capitalized on the political nature of his office. His biography, in part, explains his political interests. Karol Wojtyla grew up in Poland, then a country occupied by the Nazi regime. Following World War II, he and his fellow Poles suffered under communist rule. They longed for independence and freedom but chafed under an oppressive foreign regime. In the communist era, many Polish people collaborated with their Russian overlords, causing division and mistrust. The Catholic Church walked a fine line between resistance and capitulation.

Growing up in pre–World War II Poland, Wojtyla befriended ostracized Jews, who were fellow Poles unfairly singled out for punishment by a racist Nazi regime. In his view, his acts were likely more humanitarian and Christian than political, but they contributed to a political philosophy that opposed oppression wherever it occurred and championed national self-determination and human rights—dispositions that carried over to his papacy.

Benedict, only seven years younger than his predecessor John Paul II, also grew up under the Nazi regime, and, since he was a German citizen, his experience of oppression was more direct. Forced to join Hitler's youth corps when he was fourteen years old, Joseph Ratzinger experienced the horrors of a dictatorship early in his life. Again unwillingly, he served briefly in Hitler's army and then deserted. How could such experiences not shape the view of totalitarianism and absolute political power for these future popes?

Once elected, all pontiffs recognize that they have the responsibility to make pronouncements with political implications since silence might mean a lost opportunity. At the same time, they must do so thoughtfully and carefully, often balancing the church's diplomatic needs and the gospel's demand to be prophetic. What a pope says is important because, as the leader of more than one billion Catholics, he commands the most significant international religious voice in the world. What he says is reported in the press all over the world. And what he says goes beyond pious platitudes. By his pronouncements, he attempts to influence public policy, other religions, governments, believers, and nonbelievers alike.

When a pope speaks out against war, stem-cell research, abortion, same-sex marriage, capital punishment, or contraception, the press often describes these as social issues, and indeed they are. However, in the church's view these constitute not just social issues but also *moral* issues. The church does not treat them simply as matters of social preference but as matters of right and wrong. Most people recognize the moral implications of social policy, and that is why such issues stir so much controversy.

However, pronouncements are not always heard, or heeded, by Catholics or others. Many Catholics disagree with the church's official teachings on a range of concerns. In many instances, despite the church's best efforts to disseminate its teachings, some Catholics (and others) do not know what the church teaches on a number of issues. In other cases, they may know, for example, that the Vatican condemns artificial contraception, but they practice birth control. They may know of the pope's opposition to capital punishment, but they fear criminals and want the worst of them put to death. They understand that the church considers abortion a mortal sin, but they want to protect a woman's right to choose. They read that the church opposes same-sex marriage and homosexual activity, but they have friends who are gay and are reluctant to condemn them. The church opposes war except as a last resort, and John Paul II and Benedict XVI both objected to the Iraq war, but their protests went unheeded by the U.S. government and many Americans.

One of the ironies of the political papacy is that popes are not chosen by popular election. Rather, they achieve the office by an arcane election process called a conclave, during which a very small, all-male group of peers (cardinals) selects one of its own. Once elected, popes never have to stand for election again since their reign ends only with their death. They command no armies, though they have an elite group known as the Swiss Guard dedicated to their protection. They have no parliaments or congresses, though they collaborate with a worldwide constituency of bishops, all of whom answer to the pope. They oversee a sizable budget, the funds for which are derived from contributions, not taxes. Most of these financial resources are not under the direct control of the Vatican but are in the jurisdiction of dioceses and parishes, with much of the money dedicated to maintenance of buildings and personnel, and a significant portion underwriting works of charity. Popes meet with heads of state and are usually considered peers by the world's most powerful political figures. By a variety of mechanisms, they lobby leaders and governments, and are lobbied in kind. Though spiritual leaders, they know that their positions on political and social policies and practices will be carefully noted by those who make laws or govern nations.

Anyone who is elected pope, even the most spiritual of men, quickly realizes that the office has political implications, or he risks being irrelevant or ineffective. A pope who does not seize the opportunity to influence leaders, nations, and peoples misses a dimension of his office. The forgiveness of sins, the blessing of children, the devotion to Christ, a life of piety, the teaching of the faith, and service to the faithful all consume a good deal of the pope's time and energy. But so does his support of policies that reflect the church's values and his opposition to those that run counter to its teaching.

By virtue of his position, therefore, the pope is a political figure. Whether a given pope emphasizes this dimension of his papacy depends upon his understanding of the office, his personal temperament, the time in which he lives, and his willingness or reluctance to exercise his power in this domain. Some popes have been proactive in international politics. Others have left much of this work to Vatican diplomats and curial officers. But for the pope and the Vatican, politics is inescapable. The church has a stake in the world, and the secular world must acknowledge religious figures and institutions as influential. One would be hard-pressed to find a more powerful religious institution than the Catholic Church, with its one-billion-plus Catholics and four-thousand-plus bishops worldwide.

Popes are expected to uphold the tradition and teachings of the church. Sometimes this requires a vigorous defense of the church's positions. This may include the necessity to confront a corrupt or repressive political leader or regime. Where human rights are being ignored or trampled upon, the pope has a moral obligation to speak out against such injustices. In the case of John Paul II, some-times this meant going directly to the oppressor's territory to do so, as in the case of his visit to Fidel Castro in Cuba. Other times, it meant meeting with controver-sial leaders at the Vatican, as in the case of Yasser Arafat. On special occasions, it has included addressing the United Nations.

However, there have been instances in which the church's voice has been sub-dued in the face of evil. For example, some argue that because of the potential risks to innocent people, Pius XII, during World War II, did not condemn the Nazi regime as publicly and forcefully as many would have liked. Others think that it was a lack of courage that led to less-than-bold diplomatic efforts to stop Hitler. Politi-cal scientists and historians, not to mention ordinary citizens, debate the prudence, morality, and effectiveness of political papal decisions in every era, including recently under John Paul II and currently under Benedict XVI. When, in the sum-mer of 2005, Benedict condemned violence and terrorism in several venues but neglected to mention the suicide bombers who have plagued Israel, he was imme-diately criticized by the Jewish community. The pope, new to the office, quickly made amends to the Jewish community and no doubt realized how closely his words would be scrutinized.

In his travels, John Paul II was welcomed, almost always enthusiastically, to scores of nations. Although praising leaders and nations for the good that they do, he never shied away from condemning practices that the church considered harm-ful or sinful, from abortion to consumerism to communism. Whether he was addressing corrupt regimes in the developing world or what he considered to be immoral practices in the developed world, he spoke his mind. Some believe that the failed assassination attempt on his life in 1981 was designed to silence him for polit-ical reasons. Popes have enemies. The stronger and more vocal the pope, the more formidable his enemies.

Yet, for all of their statements and positions taken, how effective are these spiritual leaders at changing the political landscape? This, no doubt, is difficult to measure. In some instances, however, observers agree that popes have had a major influence on politics. One such case was John Paul II's confrontation with commu-nism. Having grown up under the oppression of communism in Poland, he worked skillfully and tirelessly to topple it, first as bishop, then as cardinal, and finally as pope. Of course, no one can reasonably claim that John Paul II alone defeated com-munism in Eastern Europe and the Soviet Union. At the same time, no one can deny that he had a significant role in its demise. In the present day, Benedict clearly has an interest in public acknowledgment of Christianity's historic role in the devel-opment of Europe. Though many of the architects of a potential European consti-tution do not want to include the history of Christianity in such a document, Benedict will continue to press for its acknowledgment even as he attempts to revive the largely moribund faith of contemporary Europeans.

In 2005, when the Spanish parliament debated whether to recognize same-sex marriage, a Roman Catholic group presented the members of parliament with a 600,000-signature petition opposing the legislation. Before the vote, the church endorsed a "pro-family" demonstration in Madrid, and Benedict XVI condemned gay marriage as an expression of "anarchic freedom" that threatens the future of the family. Legalization of same-sex marriage is but one example of a social policy with moral implications. The church believes that it has a right and an obligation to express disapproval of policies it considers immoral. Nevertheless, as in the case of Spain, a heavily Catholic country, the church does not always prevail. The Spanish parliament approved the measure.

The political reach of the church extends far beyond the Vatican. Even a cursory examination of political activity in the United States reveals that the church, particularly via bishops, weighs in on numerous social and political issues. The church often assumes the role of moral guardian in American society. Making rules and pronouncements designed to bind Catholics, the church also attempts to influence the larger culture by providing moral norms and guidelines, for example, in its marshaling of a well-organized and funded pro-life effort. In practice, some Catholics ignore some of the norms proposed, and some non-Catholics resent the church for "meddling" in political policy and personal life as it attempts to set the moral compass for American society. But moral concerns represent a central element of the church's mission and teaching.

Illustrative of John Paul II's concern that religion have a place in public discourse is the pope's charge to the Honorable Lindy Boggs as Ambassador to the Holy See on December 16, 1997:

> It would truly be a sad thing if the religious and moral convictions upon which the American experiment was founded could now somehow be considered a danger to free society, such that those who would bring these convictions to bear upon your nation's public life would be denied a voice in debating and resolving issues of public policy. The original separation of church and state in the United States was certainly not an effort to ban all religious conviction from the public sphere, a kind of banishment of God from civil society.[1]

No moral issue has divided the Roman Catholic Church in the United States as much as the controversy about abortion. Even characterizing it as a moral issue is a signal that it should be considered an ethical-moral-religious concern rather than a "social" or "personal" issue, as many political analysts describe it. On this issue the bishops line up staunchly behind the Vatican. Abortion is, at the same time, an intensely private matter and a widely debated public issue. Over this ethical conundrum, private morality and public morality collide in a battle that has divided the nation as well as affected the church. The institutional church, via the hierarchy and the offices of the U.S. Catholic Conference, attempts to influence public policy; the church joins its protest with the protests of evangelical Christians in an alliance that some call unholy, and individual bishops and priests have made it the focal point of their ministry. The stances on abortion are as divisive as they are decisive. Reacting to the 1973 Supreme Court ruling in *Roe vs. Wade* that legalized abortion, the U.S. bishops issued a "Pastoral Plan for Pro-Life Activities" in

1975 in order to coordinate Catholic efforts to counter the Court's decision. In 1995, in his encyclical *Evangelium Vitae,* John Paul II stated that the church's teaching on abortion

> is unchanged and unchangeable. . . . This doctrine is based upon the natural law and upon the written word of God, is transmitted by the Church's Tradition and taught by the ordinary and universal Magisterium. No circumstance, no purpose, no law whatsoever can ever make licit an act which is intrinsically illicit, since it is contrary to the law of God which is written in every human heart, knowable by reason itself, and proclaimed by the Church.[2]

At the pope's summer residence, Castel Gandolfo, Italy, John Paul II addressed George W. Bush on July 23, 2001, about the right to life, including a warning about stem-cell research:

> Another area in which political and moral choices have the gravest consequences for the future of civilization concerns the most fundamental of human rights, the right to life itself. Experience is already showing how a tragic coarsening of consciences accompanies the assault on innocent human life in the womb, leading to accommodation and acquiescence in the face of other related evils such as euthanasia, infanticide, and, most recently, proposals for the creation for research purposes of human embryos, destined to destruction in the process. . . . America can show the world the path to a truly humane future in which man remains the master, not the product, of his technology.[3]

Sometimes the church warns its own followers, as is the case in the Vatican's 2002 document issued by the Congregation of the Faith (then headed by Cardinal Ratzinger) entitled "The Participation of Catholics in Political Life." It states:

> Christians must recognize that what is at stake is the essence of the moral law, which concerns the integral good of the human person. This is the case with laws concerning *abortion* and *euthanasia.* . . . Such laws must defend the basic right to life from conception to natural death. In the same way, it is necessary to recall the duty to respect and protect the rights of the *human embryo.* Analogously, the *family* needs to be safeguarded and promoted, based on monogamous marriage between a man and a woman, and protected in its unity and stability in the face of modern laws on divorce: in no way can other forms of cohabitation be placed on the same level as marriage, nor can they receive legal recognition as such. The same is true for the freedom of parents regarding the *education* of their children; it is an inalienable right recognized also by the Universal Declaration on Human Rights. In the same way, one must consider *society's protection of minors* and freedom from *modern forms of slavery* (drug abuse and prostitution, for example). In addition, there is the right to *religious freedom* and the development of an *economy* that is at the service of the human person and of the common good, with

respect for social justice, the principles of human solidarity and subsidiarity. . . . Finally, the question of *peace* must be mentioned. Certain pacifistic and ideological visions tend at times to secularize the value of peace, while, in other cases, there is the problem of summary ethical judgments which forget the complexity of the issues involved. Peace . . . demands the absolute and radical rejection of violence and terrorism and requires a constant and vigilant commitment on the part of all political leaders.[4]

Benedict angered Chinese government officials in September 2005 when he invited Chinese bishops, including those not approved by the Chinese government, to a meeting at the Vatican. China severed ties with the Vatican in 1951 and has a tense relationship with the Vatican because the state controls the church in China. The Vatican nevertheless appoints bishops whom the government does not approve, creating tensions between the two powers and making it difficult for those bishops to function.

Many of the selections included in this collection are the words of John Paul II and Benedict XVI themselves, written during the course of their papacies (all of Benedict's, with the exception of "War Service and Imprisonment," being recent) and delivered to a wide variety of audiences—some to church hierarchy, some to the laity, some to leaders and followers of other religions, some to world leaders, some to the world at large. These selections allow the reader to encounter papal views directly. Other selections are observations and evaluations by a range of figures from journalists to theologians to political scientists.

There are, of course, many other instances of papal political activity that are not included in this book. The editing process necessitated selecting a representative sample of the political activity of these two important popes. Benedict XVI's long tenure as head of the Congregation for the Doctrine of the Faith, though primarily dealing with internal theological matters, nevertheless had political implications as, for example, his writings on homosexuality and other religions clearly attest. However, I have elected to include only his papal pronouncements since these represent his views as pope, which, though likely consistent with his previous views, now carry more importance.

Some of these documents are short, but they are included to demonstrate the range of issues that have political implications and the diverse audiences to which the statements are directed. They may also make the reader aware that the pope regularly makes statements that have political implications in different parts of the world. He is, after all, a world figure directing a universal church. This may mean weighing how a statement will likely be received in one cultural/geographic context versus another before issuing it. Some statements, of course, are targeted to a particular national or regional audience, but the content of all statements must be consistent with church tradition and teaching.

John Paul II never shied away from controversy. Although he tailored his comments to the regional or national audience he was addressing (often in person), he spoke prophetically, confronting Catholics and others with a message that was sometimes quite unpopular. Thus, he described Western societies as being in the grip of a culture of death; he condemned euthanasia, abortion, and capital punishment along with capitalism and consumerism. The church not only condemns social policies with which it disagrees; it also lobbies proactively for legislation that favors the poor and promotes justice. Thus, John Paul II challenged rich, developed nations to reach out to the developing world. He advocated debt relief for poor nations that were weighed down with such excessive debts that they used much of their gross national product to service the debt, leaving them little chance for economic growth. In his message to the "Jubilee 2000 Debt Campaign," John Paul II wrote:

> Debt relief is . . . urgent. It is, in many ways, a precondition for the poorest countries to make progress in their fight against poverty. This is something which is now widely recognized, and credit is due to all those who have contributed to this change in direction. We have to ask, however, why progress in resolving the debt problem is still so slow. Why so many hesitations? Why the difficulty in providing the funds needed even for the already agreed initiatives? It is the poor who pay the cost of indecision and delay.[5]

Siding with the poor is a political act. Although not claiming the competence to offer complex technical economic strategies, the pope could hardly stand on the sidelines and allow nations, mostly from the Northern Hemisphere, to control the lives of Southern Hemisphere dwellers.

John Paul II, perhaps emboldened by his experiences with Solidarity in his native Poland, defended work for every individual as a God-given right, along with the right of workers to form legitimate unions. In his 1981 encyclical *Laborem Exercens* ("On Human Work"), the pope wrote, "[U]nemployment, which in all cases is an evil, when it reaches a certain level, can become a real social disaster." John Paul II echoed the positions of his predecessors. Leo XIII defended workers in his 1891 encyclical *Rerum Novarum* ("On the Rights and Duties of Capital and Labor"), and Pius XI confirmed this in his Depression-era 1931 encyclical *Quadragesimo Anno* (commemorating the fortieth anniversary of Leo XIII's *Rerum Novarum*), which claimed that "the opportunity to work be provided for those who are willing and able to work." John XXIII, in his 1963 encyclical *Pacem in Terris* ("Peace on Earth"), stated, "[I]t is clear that human beings have the natural right to free initiative in the economic field and the right to work"; and Paul VI also urged a new economic order in his 1967 encyclical *Populorum Progressio* ("Development of Peoples"). Taking a stance on the side of workers is a political act, but one grounded in a moral conscience.

In recent decades, the church has engaged in dialogue with other religions as well as with other Christian communities. In this book, relations between the church and the Jewish and Muslim communities are highlighted. These entries are selected examples that illustrate the importance of relations of the church with all religions and, therefore, with cultures and governments as well. These discussions require sophisticated theology and careful rhetoric. The church can afford neither to ignore its non-Christian neighbors nor to sacrifice its doctrinal and dogmatic claims to accommodate differences. A globalized world demands respectful relations between religions. Today, the pope must address not only Catholic believers but other believers as well. How he handles these dialogues is watched closely by leaders and followers of other religions and by political figures around the world. For example, Benedict XVI met with Jordan's King Abdullah in September 2005, in part to discuss interreligious dialogue, since relations between religions is of importance to both leaders. Negotiating those relationships skillfully rests with the pope, who sets the tone and direction for diplomatic relations.

Popes must regularly balance diplomacy with prophecy. How John Paul II and Benedict XVI have done that can be discerned in these texts. How well they have done it is for the reader to assess.

ACKNOWLEDGMENTS

I wish to thank my colleague James Walsh, S.J., for his close reading of the text; Linda Ferneyhough of the Georgetown Theology Department for her editing assistance; Eric Mittereder, a Georgetown College student who assisted in the research for this book; and Dean Birkenkamp, Melanie Stafford, and Beth Davis of Paradigm Publishers, who with professionalism, competence, and courtesy kept this project on track.

Chester Gillis

NOTES

1. http://www.vatican.va/holy_father/john_paul_ii/speeches/1997/december/documents/hf_jp-ii_spe_19971216_ambassador-usa_en.html.

2. http://www.vatican.va/edocs/ENG0141/_INDEX.HTM.

3. http://www.vatican.va/holy_father/john_paul_ii/speeches/2001/documents/hf_jp-ii_spe_20010723_president-bush_en.html.

4. www.vatican.va/roman_curia/congregations/cfaith/documents/rc_con_cfaith_doc_20021124_politica_en.html.

5. http://www.vatican.va/holy_father/john_paul_ii/speeches/1999/september/documents/hf_jp-ii_mes_23091999_jubilee-2000-debt-campaign_en.html.

1. John Paul II and Benedict XVI

Jo Renee Formicola
The Political Legacy of Pope John Paul II

I. INTRODUCTION

As pope of the Catholic Church, Pope John Paul II was the unquestioned spiritual leader of over one billion adherents. So powerful was his religious position that he was recognized as infallible when speaking on matters of faith and morals. As the head of the Vatican State as well, John Paul will be remembered as a formidable geopolitical actor, one who used his considerable influence to infuse moral values into the global political arena.

Pope John Paul II was committed to four basic goals: the protection of the autonomy of the church, respect for human dignity, religious engagement and reconciliation with numerous states, and a concern for social, economic, and political justice. The nuances of these commitments, their translation into church policy, and their eventual infusion into the global political consciousness attest to the pontiff's Christian ideology and often militant evangelization for a higher order of politics during his papacy.

II. A LIFE OF SERVICE AND LEADERSHIP

Karol Wojtyla, the first Polish pope, was born in 1920 and grew up in Wadowice. The son of a former military officer and a frail mother, he had an older brother and many friends. But when the future pope was only nine years old, his mother died and his older brother soon left for medical school, leaving him alone with only his father. They were very close; the father enjoyed cooking, sewing and even playing

1

soccer with his son in their living room.[1] John Paul later recounted that "Sometimes I would wake up during the night and find my father on his knees . . . his example was in a way my first seminary."[2] Only a few years later, John Paul's brother died of scarlet fever while an intern during the epidemic, thus drawinsg him even closer to his father.

In 1938, both moved to Krakow where the younger Wojtyla attended the Jagellonian University. After only one year of study, the Nazis invaded Poland, imprisoned Jewish professors and forced the university to close. The future pope, then, had to work in a quarry to support both himself and his father.

When possible, Wojtyla participated in the underground theatre. Stephan Sephia, the archbishop of Krakow and supporter of "UNIA," another theatre group known for its moral opposition to the Nazis, noticed the young actor. Sephia began to mentor Wojtyla who was soon studying secretly in the clandestine seminary supported by the archbishop. Returning from work one day, however, the future pope found his beloved father dead and from that point on, all his efforts were dedicated to his vocation.

In 1946, after the liberation of Poland by the Soviets, Karol Wojtyla was ordained a priest. He studied in Rome where he earned a doctorate in theology,[3] and on his return to Poland was assigned to a small parish. Later he served as a priest and a faculty member at the Jagellonian University. There, he received another Ph.D. in ethics in 1954. Four years later, he was appointed auxiliary bishop of Krakow.

Wojtyla attended Vatican II as part of the Polish hierarchical delegation. In Rome, he came to know many influential members of the church, particularly Pope Paul VI with whom Wojtyla shared similar pro-life views. The pontiff appointed Wojtyla to positions in his inner circle, enabling the Polish prelate to make many trips to the Vatican as well as to other parts of the world. He was also invited to give a Lenten religious retreat to the most powerful cardinals in the church, at the behest of Pope Paul VI. This gave him entrée to those who would choose the next pope.

Wojtyla also continued his upward ecclesiastical climb in Poland, being named archbishop of Krakow. When Pope Paul VI died, the rumor mills mentioned Wojtyla as a possible successor, but as a conservative in a world of post–Vatican II liberals, it seemed unlikely. Indeed, the College of Cardinals elected Pope John Paul I, a liberal Italian, instead, thus making the possibility of a conservative Polish pope appear highly unlikely in the future. But the death of the new pope only a month later seemed like a message from the Lord[4] to some church leaders, and revealed how closely divided the College of Cardinals must have been at its earlier conclave. To the astonishment of the world, Karol Wojtyla, the conservative Pole, was elected Pope John Paul II in 1978.

III. BEHIND JOHN PAUL'S POLITICS

Pope John Paul II's political legacy is one that was impelled by his theological beliefs. Central to his understanding of politics was the religious notion of "imago dei," the belief that each individual is made in the image and likeness of God and therefore, worthy of dignity and respect. A profound commitment to this credo gave religious and political meaning to the pope's commitment to advance social justice, economic development, and human rights around the world.

He interpreted his primary papal obligation as the responsibility to protect the autonomy of the church throughout the world so that its priests could carry out Jesus' mission: to teach, preach, and sanctify its adherents. Thus, all John Paul's political efforts were external manifestations of the religious engagement of the Vatican with other states to protect church freedom. In 1979, the pope began his pontificate by urging priests to be pastors rather than politicians.[5] Particularly in Latin America where the clergy had been calling for the church to bring about the political and economic transformation of society based on Marxist principles, John Paul opposed liberation theology. He rejected the involvement of priests in partisan politics and the interpretation of Christianity based on a Marxist catechesis. Instead, he called for a positive vision of change in Latin America, one implemented by evangelization, or preaching, and based on the principles of Christ rather than Marx.

The pope's life experiences were also critical to his politics. Having grown up under the Nazis and later having served as a priest under the Communists, John Paul knew firsthand what repression meant. In one of his earliest speeches at the United Nations, he reached out to the diplomats to end political abuses and to view any threat to human dignity as a "form of warfare against humanity."[6] Noting that he had come "from the country, on whose living body Auschwitz was at one time constructed,"[7] he carried the genocide of the Jews with him always. During the first decade of his leadership, the pope traveled to numerous states, and when necessary castigated dictators who repressed the rights of those in their care. Fernando Marcos, General Wojciech Jaruselski, Daniel Ortega, Jean-Claude Duvalier, Jean Bertrand Aristide, and Sese Seko Mobuto were but a few who drew his open criticism and militant evangelization.

IV. RELIGIOUS ENGAGEMENT:
A MEANS TO REFORM AND RECONCILIATION

Pope John Paul II recognized that the religious engagement of states by the holy see could also be used as an opening to establish new Vatican political relationships. Using a policy of outreach,[8] he started discussions on religious freedom with a number of states and was eventually able to draw some of the East European states into negotiations on a broader range of social and economic issues.

For example, the pope's theological concern for freedom of religion and his own experience with communist limitations on Catholic practice[9] led him to seek ways to eradicate communism. In 1984, the Vatican and the United States entered into diplomatic relations, with Ronald Reagan and John Paul cooperating to defeat their mutual atheistic enemy, first in Poland, then in the rest of Eastern Europe.

Thus, when Mikhail Gorbachev recognized the need for a state restructuring on the basis of new values, particularly *perestroika* and *glasnost,* the pope agreed to support his reforms in 1989. This led to a *detente* between them, and as a political by-product, created an ideological symbiosis between the U.S. and the Vatican, as well as the USSR and the holy see. Based on a higher order of political values, these relationships with the two superpowers allowed the pope enough latitude to both support and/or oppose their policies based on their commitment to the common good.

Pope John Paul II also sought to create other meaningful alliances between the Vatican and the plethora of emerging states after the fall of communism. The Vatican was one of the first to recognize Poland, the pope having also supported the trade union Solidarity earlier in its fight for existence within the Soviet-dominated governmental structure. This action gave immediate diplomatic legitimacy to Poland and followed with the recognition of Hungary, Czechoslovakia, and the other emerging states in Eastern Europe by the holy see.

The need to reconcile the church with the Jews was also part of John Paul's own personal spiritual and political agenda. In 1987, he called together a symposium of theologians to examine the conscience of the church, particularly on the matter of church silence during the Holocaust. As a result of this institutional introspection, the church apologized for the lack of Roman Catholic action to stop the mass killing of Jews during World War II, and stressed the common heritage of Christians and Jews. Seizing upon the shift in attitude and theology, John Paul used both as a basis for religious engagement with Israel. It led to the establishment of diplomatic relations in 1994 and a Vatican promise to work against anti-Semitism. The new relationship was further solidified when the pope called on the entire church to repent for its former anti-Jewish behavior, when he sought public forgiveness for church inaction during World War II, and when he visited Yad Vashem, the memorial to the victims of the Holocaust. There, the pope expressed the church's sincere and abiding desire for reconciliation with the Jews and the State of Israel.[10]

At the same time, the pope engaged other states in the Middle East to work for peace. The Vatican's political position was predicated on the internationalization of Jerusalem, a homeland for the Palestinians, and a greater respect for the human dignity of all those who lived in the region. In March 2000, Pope John Paul II visited Jordan, Israel, and the Palestinian Autonomous Territories. In Jordan, he reached out and preached for reconciliation and peace among Muslims, Jews, and Christians. In Israel, he met with political leaders pledging solidarity with the Jews, professing sorrow for the Holocaust, and meeting with a series of ecumenical leaders. Journeying to Bethlehem and also the refugee camp at Dheisheh, the pope criticized the suffering of the Palestinians. Calling their treatment "degrading,"[11] he appealed for greater international solidarity and the political will to change their situation. "Your torment," he said, "is before the eyes of the world. And it has gone on too long."[12]

V. "THE THIRD WAY": A NEW CHRISTIAN APPROACH
TO ECONOMICS, HUMAN RIGHTS, AND SOCIAL JUSTICE

Pope John Paul II's theology was also at the basis of his attempt to bring social justice to the Third World. His numerous trips to Central and South America were tied to calls for respect for human rights and economic development. In almost every state in the Western Hemisphere, the pope evangelized on the basis of the *magisterium,* or the traditional social teachings of the church, rather than on the ideological principles of either the left or the right. John Paul called this new economic and political approach to relations with developing states the "third way."

In a trilogy of encyclicals,[13] he characterized a new, "authentic" capitalism as one based on a Christian model. In his view, this included a new understanding of private property, respect for the value of work and the dignity of the laborer, the importance of economic development for peace, the need for debt relief for economically disadvantaged states, and an option for the poor. In short, John Paul called on First World states to share their wealth with those in the developing world. He supported World Bank and IMF attempts to implement debt reduction, political movements to bring about a greater privatization of state economic holdings, and bringing debtor states into the process of globalization.

Translated politically, John Paul believed that the "third way" should be implemented by "authentic," democratic principles as well. These included the development of political structures built on a judicial framework that would respect and promote freedom, dignity and a broad decision making role for citizens. Government, according to the pope, was to be oriented toward the common good, balanced by subsidiary powers, and able to be replaced when and if it did not perform its appropriate duties. Most critically, to the pope, the political process in the "third way" was expected to allow the spiritual mission of religion to go unimpeded, to respect superior universal values, and to implement them.

VI. A UNIQUE MEANS OF GEOPOLITICAL ACTION:
PROPHETIC POLITICS

Pope John Paul II will be remembered politically for moving the Catholic Church in a new geopolitical direction. Always concerned with the church's obligation to carry out its spiritual mission to teach, preach and sanctify its adherents, he also embraced a broader moral goal: to implement transcendent values in the global arena. Thus, it is safe to say that the pope's understanding and use of geopolitical power were always tied to a transcendent objective: the creation of moral change in the world that could transform the social, political, and economic structures in the world for the common good.

His method was simple: evangelization, that is, the use of militant teaching of truth to power. John Paul used his religious platform to contrast the message of

Jesus with the actions of repressive regimes. He often mentioned leaders by name or their policies in practice. Using open diplomacy, he also practiced "prophetic politics." The pope called for a higher order of political behavior based on an objective, divine criticism that was dedicated to seeking creative economic and political solutions for the good of all.[14] In short, he challenged political leaders to work toward transcendental values, i.e, charity, peace, and justice based on the principles of Jesus Christ.

VII. THE LEGACY

As a result of John Paul's papacy, the Vatican has become a major actor in the geopolitical arena by working for moral change in the world. The pontiff broadened the diplomatic involvement of the holy see in the international arena and created new alliances. These include the religious engagement with Russia and its former satellites, the United States, African and Asian nations, the Middle East, and most developing states. Some relations have been pursued on the basis of religious reconciliation, particularly those with Israel and Palestine, and others were carried out for religious openings, especially those with atheistic states such as Cuba and China. As a result, the holy see now has diplomatic relations with more than 190 states, a political situation unheard of during the church's two-thousand-year history.

Pope John Paul II was also responsible for bringing the moral dimension into the international arena and infusing transcendent principles into global thought on matters of social justice, human rights, and economic development. He leaves a more involved and powerful Vatican, one that questions geopolitics, one that argues for social justice as it reaches out to developing states, and one that challenges the self interested policies and wealth of the First World.

NOTES

1. Tad Szulc, *Pope John Paul II, The Biography* (New York: Pocket Books, 1995), 65.

2. Pope John Paul II, *Gift and Mystery* (New York: Image Books, 1999), 20.

3. Due to financial reasons, the degree was actually conferred by the Jagellonian University in 1948 rather than the Angelicum University in Rome.

4. George Weigel, *Witness to Hope* (New York: HarperCollins, 1999), 252.

5. In 1979, at a meeting of the Latin American Conference of Bishops at Puebla, Mexico, Pope John Paul II stressed that "your chief duty is to be teachers of the truth." See *Opening Address at Puebla, 28 January 1979,* Part I. It was followed up one year later with a speech in Kinshasha, Zaire, by the pope entitled *Be Pastors, Not Politicians,* 4 May 1980, Section 9. In it, he stressed that "the priest must reveal himself to be a man of discernment and an authentic teacher of the faith."

6. Pope John Paul II, "Transcript of Pope John Paul's United Nations Address," *New York Times,* 3 October 1979, B4.

7. Ibid.

8. Building on a policy of "ostpolitik," begun by his predecessors, John XXIII and Paul VI, he attempted to gain allies in Eastern Europe and the Third World early in his papacy.

9. As both an academician and a cleric in Poland before his accession to the papacy, Pope John Paul II had to deal with the Soviet take-over of his homeland on many levels. As a professor, he had been subject to the new rules of the reorganized Ministry of Education under the Communists. It had imposed a curriculum that included Marxist-Leninist philosophy, removed other courses such as those taught by Wojtyla, changed tenure and promotion regulations, and instituted new licensing requirements to teach in state universities. The future pope lost this teaching position at a state university controlled by the Communists. As a cleric, he also faced political problems. Appointed as the auxiliary bishop of Krakow in 1958, he became a political target for the Krakow community Presidium within a year. He was pulled into the political tensions between the church and the state because he had participated in meditation days with lawyers, physicians, teachers, and students. This was one of the reasons why he emerged as a vocal and viable opponent of communism in Poland.

10. In his remarks he said: "I have come to Yad Vashem to pay homage to the millions of Jewish people who, stripped of everything especially of their human dignity, were murdered in the Holocaust. . . . As bishop of Rome and successor of the Apostle Peter, I assure the Jewish people that the Catholic Church, motivated by the Gospel of law and truth and love and by no political considerations, is deeply saddened by the hatred, acts of persecution and displays of anti-Semitism directed against the Jews by Christians at any time and in any place. The church rejects racism in any form as a denial of the image of the Creator inherent in every human being. . . . Let us build a new future [on] the mutual respect required of those who adore the one Creator and Lord and look to Abraham as our common father in faith. See Pope John Paul II, "Text of Speech at Yad Vachem," *New York Times,* 23 March 2000, A6.

11. Remarks of John Paul II, "Visit to the Refugee Camp of Dheisheh," 22 March 2000, available at www.vatican.va.

12. Alessandra Stanley, "Vatican and PLO Sign Pact Guaranteeing the Church's Rights," *New York Times,* 22 March 2000, A5.

13. See Pope John Paul II's encyclicals: *Laborem Exercens* (1981), *Sollicitudo Rei Socialis* (1987), and *Centesimus Annus* (1991).

14. For a deeper description of "prophetic politics" see, for example, Neal Riemer, *The Future of the Democratic Revolution: Toward a Prophetic Politics* (New York: Praeger, 1984).

&

John L. Allen Jr.

Who Is Joseph Ratzinger?

Though Cardinal Joseph Ratzinger had been a known quantity in the Catholic world since the Second Vatican Council, 1985 was the year that made him a star. In that year, his book-length interview with Italian journalist Vittorio Messori, titled in English *The Ratzinger Report,* became a publishing sensation around the world. Ratzinger's tart diagnoses of the problems facing the Church made him into a hero for Catholic conservatives, who had wondered if anyone in Rome saw the same crisis they did, and a lightning rod for the Church's liberal wing, a symbol of what they saw as a reactionary desire to "turn back the clock" on Church reform. Public discussion of the book was intense. During the 1985 Synod of Bishops, called to take stock of Vatican II twenty years after its close, Cardinal Godfried Danneels became so sick of answering questions about *The Ratzinger Report* during a press conference that he snapped, "This is not a synod on the book, it's a synod on the council!"

From that year on, Ratzinger occupied a place all by himself in the pantheon of Catholic celebrities.

As proof of the point, when Ratzinger turned seventy in 1997, two of the biggest secular publishing houses in Germany brought out new editions of his books, his picture appeared on the front cover of the largest mass-market news-magazine in Italy, and virtually every newspaper and TV network in Europe prepared extensive profiles to mark the occasion. Just by virtue of having a birthday, Ratzinger was news.

By the standards of the normally shadowy world of the Roman Curia, Joseph Ratzinger, as the Vatican's top doctrinal official, was not just a star, but a mega-star. After being elected pope, the Italians quickly dubbed him "Papa-Razi," a play on the term paparazzi for those photographers who trail celebrities around, and the term has a curious fittingness for the preexisting celebrity status of Benedict XVI. He's perhaps the first pope of modern times who truly needs no introduction.

In that sense, offering a biographical sketch here of the new pope almost seems an exercise in redundancy. Still, as William Wordsworth once put it, "the child is father of the man," and so a brief overview of Ratzinger's life, especially his experiences in Nazi Germany and his later career as one of the most promising Catholic theologians of his generation, will be helpful in approaching the question of what kind of pontificate he is likely to lead.

In this regard, we are helped by the fact that Ratzinger himself has outlined the story of his life, at least prior to being made a bishop, in his 1997 memoir *Mile-stones.* This slim volume is required reading for anyone seeking to understand the mind of the new pope. Moreover, there is Pope Benedict's own prodigious literary output to draw upon, both as a theologian and a cultural critic. Prior to his election as pope, Cardinal Karol Wojtyla of Krakow, widely regarded as one of the more thoughtful members of the College of Cardinals in his day, had written three major books: *The Acting Person, Sign of Contradiction,* and *Love and Responsibility.* Pope Benedict, on the other hand, has written more than fifty books, along with a seemingly infinite series of journal articles, popular essays, and lectures, which range from the late 1950s up to just days before the conclave.

Given the abundance of this primary material, only the briefest of profiles is offered here, just enough to situate the Pope in time and place as a sort of backdrop to the coming drama of his pontificate. Doing so is perhaps especially important with respect to what is likely to be the characteristic struggle of his papacy—the battle against what he called a "dictatorship of relativism," and to recover the Christian roots of Europe.

CHILDHOOD

Joseph Aloysius Ratzinger was born on April 16, 1927, on Holy Saturday, in a small Bavarian town called Marktl am Inn, just across the border from Austria and the city that enchanted his youth, Salzburg. He was the youngest of three children in a lower-middle-class Bavarian household, and his parents were named Joseph and Mary. Joseph was a policeman, while Mary stayed at home during some periods of her life, and worked as a cook in bed-and-breakfast establishments in others.

Joseph's sister, Maria, was born in 1921, and his older brother, Georg, in 1924. Georg, like Joseph, became a priest (they were ordained the same day in 1951), and also like his brother has a passion for music. Georg went on to be a choir conductor. Maria spent most of her adult life as a caretaker for the brothers, especially Joseph; when Joseph was a professor, and later a senior churchman, she looked after his office and household. Maria died in November 1991, in the Roman apartment in the Piazza Leonina she shared with her brother, while Georg is retired in Regensburg.

In Bavaria, Ratzinger grew up in a homogeneous, deeply practicing Catholic environment. While his mother was the new pope's primary catechist, his father was deeply faithful as well, sometimes attending as many as three Masses on Sunday. In *Milestones,* Ratzinger recounts fond memories of his mother teaching him devotional practices, and of the deep impression that the Easter liturgies made on his religious imagination. It does not seem that the Pope ever seriously contemplated any other career than the priesthood (though he said at one point he considered working as a house painter); unlike his predecessor, Karol Wojtyla, he was never tempted by the theater or other walks of life. He also does not seem to have had any serious romantic relationships as a young man, though when asked at a press conference in Germany for the launch of *Milestones* why he didn't discuss any girlfriends in the book, he jokingly replied that "I had to keep the manuscript to one hundred pages."

As a young man, the Pope developed a lifelong love of music, especially Mozart, that native son of Salzburg whose melodies became the sound track of Pope Benedict's life. Of Mozart, he said in 1996: "His music is by no means just entertainment; it contains the whole tragedy of human existence." The Pope himself became an accomplished pianist, and in an interview published in the 1980s said he tried to get in at least fifteen minutes a day at the keyboard playing Mozart and Beethoven. Brahms, he sighed, is too difficult. His brother Georg was the conductor of the famed Regensburg choir, which had the honor of performing at the closing session of the Second Vatican Council. The new pope's musical tastes are not "catholic," however, in the sense of universal; he is not a fan of rock and roll, which he once called "a vehicle of antireligion." One strains to imagine Pope Benedict, like John Paul II did in 1997, tapping his toes to a performance by Bob Dylan, or being dubbed by U2's Bono as "the first funky pontiff."

NATIONAL SOCIALISM

The main historical shadow that hung over Ratzinger's youth was the rise of National Socialism in Germany. He was six when Hitler came to power in 1933, and was eighteen when the Second World War ended in 1945. The Nazi period thus coincided with the formative period of his life, and his reflections on that experience continue to exert influence on his theological and political outlook today.

First, to clarify the relationship of the Ratzinger family, and the new pope specifically, with respect to National Socialism, it can be said with crystal clarity that the Ratzingers were not "pro-Nazi." The father on more than one occasion expressed criticism of the Brownshirts, and concern about the potential implications of those views for himself and his family triggered a series of relocations to progressively less significant Bavarian assignments, until in 1937 he retired and the family moved to the Bavarian city of Traunstein. Ratzinger has written that his family belonged to a political tradition in Bavaria that looked to Austria and to France rather than to Prussia, and that therefore had little sympathy for Hitler's form of German nationalism.

In *The Ratzinger Report,* Ratzinger disassociated his cultural roots from Hitler and the Nazi movement: "The poisonous seeds of Nazism are not the fruit of Austrian and Southern German Catholicism, but rather of the decadent cosmopolitan atmosphere of Vienna at the end of the monarchy."

In 1941, when Joseph Ratzinger was fourteen, membership in the Hitler Youth became compulsory, and both he and Georg were enrolled. Yet Joseph did not attend activities, and as he recalls in *Milestones,* a sympathetic teacher in the high school in Traunstein allowed him to qualify for a reduction in tuition even though he did not have the mandatory Hitler Youth registration card.

In 1943, after Joseph had entered the seminary, he and his entire class were conscripted into the German army, spending most of his time as part of an anti-aircraft battalion guarding a BMW plant outside Munich.

In a 1993 interview with *Time,* Ratzinger said he never fired a gun "in anger" during his military service, and eventually deserted. He ended up in an American prisoner-of-war camp, and was eventually released to continue his studies for the priesthood.

On the basis of this record, it seems clear that while Ratzinger did not take part in active resistance to the Nazi regime, he was by no means a supporter of the Nazis either. He and his family opposed Hitler.

(I pointed all this out on CNN after the Pope's election, in response to rumblings in the British press about Ratzinger's "Nazi past." My comments earned a kind of immortalization from Jon Stewart of the *Daily Show,* who said of the Hitler Youth controversy: "To be fair, membership in that group was compulsory; and as Ratzinger's biographer John Allen has noted, Ratzinger's tenure in the group was brief and unenthusiastic, as evidenced by his basement full of unsold Hitler Youth cookies.")

The brutality of the Nazi regime once touched the Ratzinger family personally. A cousin with Down's syndrome, who in 1941 was fourteen years old, just a few months younger than Ratzinger himself, was taken away in that year by the Nazi authorities for "therapy." Not long afterward, the family received word that he was dead, presumably one of the "undesirables" eliminated during that time. Ratzinger revealed the episode on November 28, 1996, at a Vatican conference organized by the Pontifical Council for Health Care. He cited it to illustrate the danger of ideological systems that define certain classes of human beings as unworthy of protection.

Perhaps more important than these biographical details is how Benedict XVI looks back on the Nazi period today, especially in the context of the lessons to be drawn for institutional Christianity. First of all, Pope Benedict is proud of the resistance offered to National Socialism by the Church. In *Milestones,* he writes:

> Despite many human failings, the Church was the alternative to the destructive ideology of the brown rulers; in the inferno that had swallowed up the powerful, she had stood firm with a force coming to her from eternity. It had been demonstrated: The gates of hell will not overpower her. From our own experience we now knew what was meant by "the gates of hell," and we could also see with our own eyes that the house built on rock had stood firm.

In *The Ratzinger Report,* he echoed the same point: "It is well known," he said, "that in the decisive elections in 1933 Hitler had no majorities in the Catholic states." The Nazi assault on the Catholic Church is inarguable; some twelve thousand priests and male religious were victims of persecution and harassment during the Hitler era, representing 36 percent of the diocesan clergy at the time.

As a historical matter, the extent of this resistance offered by the Church, and its impact on the course of events, is still a subject of debate. Ratzinger is obviously aware that some Catholics backed the regime, but he sees them as exceptions to an overall pattern of opposition. The point here is not to resolve those controversies, but to understand how the new pope remembers them.

Ratzinger has been critical of the way some Christian denominations in Germany, especially those he regarded as more "liberal," were corrupted by National Socialist ideology. In a 1986 lecture in Toronto, he said that "liberal accommodation . . . quickly turned from liberality into a willingness to serve totalitarianism." In *The Ratzinger Report,* he said that many Protestant churches were more easily co-opted by the Nazis because the idea of nationalism and a national church was more attractive to them, having decoupled themselves from the concept of a transnational institutional Christianity with a strong teaching office.

The Pope's conclusion, on the basis of these experiences, is that only a form of Christianity clear about its core beliefs, and equally clear about its system of authority, will have the inner strength to stand up against alien forces attempting to seduce or hijack it. While the threat posed by hostile cultural currents is not as clear today—because in Europe at least there are no Brownshirts burning churches or rounding people up in the middle of the night—the risk remains, especially in the form of rampant materialism and relativism in the West. The Church, he believes, must be equally vigilant to be sure it is not gradually assimilated to the prevailing cultural ethos. A system of theology decoupled from the institution or its authorities, Pope Benedict worries, leaves itself prey to other powers, which can manipulate that theology to sap the Church's strength from within.

RATZINGER THE THEOLOGIAN

After ordination in 1951, the young Joseph Ratzinger pursued a career as a theologian, teaching in a succession of German universities that were among the most vital and productive centers of theological energy of the time: Freising, Bonn, Münster, and, in 1966, Tübingen. These were the places where much of the intellectual scaffolding that would support the reforms of the Second Vatican Council was erected. So indebted was Vatican II to the German theological contribution, in fact, that one of the most famous early books about the council, by Fr. Ralph M. Wiltgen, was entitled *The Rhine Flows into the Tiber.*

Ratzinger was present for all four sessions of the Second Vatican Council as the *peritos,* or theological expert, for Cardinal Josef Frings of Cologne, Germany, whom Ratzinger had met and befriended while teaching at Bonn. Broadly speaking, Frings was part of the progressive majority at the council that spoke in favor of greater collegiality among the bishops, liturgical reform, greater ecumenical and interreligious openness, and a more transparent style of governance within the Church.

Ironically, Ratzinger was the principal ghostwriter of a speech Frings gave on the floor of the council on November 8, 1963, that denounced the "methods and behavior" of the Holy Office, today the Congregation for the Doctrine of the Faith, as "a cause of scandal to the world." Less than two decades later, Ratzinger was the prefect of that office himself, drawing some of the same kind of criticism he had once helped express. More than one critic accused Ratzinger of having come down with "scarlet fever"—that is, the ambition for high ecclesiastical office—though defenders point out that Ratzinger's career did not follow the traditional track of someone seeking a bishop's miter.

What changed between the Ratzinger of 1963 and the Ratzinger of 1981, the year he moved to Rome at John Paul's invitation to head the doctrinal office?

Ratzinger himself has long insisted, as he did in an interview with *Time* magazine in 1993, that his positions have not changed, but rather the context has. There's undoubtedly truth to that assertion. To speak in generalities, at least two currents were in play within the progressive majority at Vatican II: one, known as *ressourcement,* or a "return to the sources," looking to recover earlier stages of Christian tradition; another known as *aggiornamento,* or "renewal," looking to reconcile the Church with the modern world. One impulse, in other words, looked back, another looked forward. Ratzinger, under the influence of figures such as Augustine, Romano Guardini, and Hans Urs von Balthasar, was always more comfortable in the *ressourcement* camp. As the *aggiornamento* group gained dominance in the immediate post–Vatican II period, he worried that too much of the tradition was being squandered based on an uncritical reading of the goodness of "the world."

In *The Ratzinger Report,* he put the point this way: "I have always tried to remain true to Vatican II, to this *today* of the Church, without any longing for a *yesterday* irretrievably gone with the wind, and without any impatient thrust toward a *tomorrow* that is not ours."

At the same time, there's little question that on some issues, from the theological status of national bishops' conferences to liturgical reform, the later Ratzinger has struck more traditional and "conservative" notes. Though it is overly simplistic to express this in terms of a shift from "Ratzinger the liberal" to "Ratzinger the conservative," nevertheless something did change in his thought in the critical years since 1965, at the close of Vatican II, when Paul VI made him archbishop of Munich.

The pivotal point seems to have come in 1968, with the student revolutions that swept across Europe, including Tübingen, where Ratzinger was teaching. More troubling still, those uprisings often had the explicit support of sectors within the Catholic Church, which tended to identify Marxist socialism with Catholic social teaching. This was deeply troubling for Ratzinger, who felt he had already lived through one ruinous attempt at the ideological manipulation of the Christian faith in Nazi Germany, and therefore felt himself obliged to resist another. In the lengthy interview with German journalist Peter Seewald that became 1997's *Salt of the Earth,* Ratzinger said of this period: "Anyone who wanted to remain a progressive in this context had to give up his integrity."

The new pope himself has not shrunk from describing his attitude toward the postconciliar period in terms of the need for a "restoration," saying in *The Ratzinger Report:* "If by 'restoration' we understand the search for a new balance after all the exaggerations of an indiscriminate opening to the world, after the overly positive interpretations of an agnostic and atheistic world, then a restoration understood in this sense (a newly found balance of orientation and values within the Catholic totality) is altogether desirable and, for that matter, is already in operation in the Church."

Yet it would be a mistake to regard the story line of this stage of Ratzinger's life as centering on the revision of his previous positions. This was also the most creative period of his career as a theologian, resulting in the production of significant books that rank among the most impressive theological output of the era. Pride of place goes to his 1968 book *Introduction to Christianity,* a contemporary presentation of Christian faith. The book was no legalistic manual stuffed with rules and regulations; it was a meditation on faith that reached into the depths of human experience, a book that dared to walk naked before doubt and disbelief in order to discover the truth of what it means to be a modern Christian. Many found it exhil-arating. Another significant tide from this period is *Eschatology: Death and Eternal Life* (1977), which Ratzinger himself once called "my most thorough work, and the one I labored over the most strenuously." In it, Ratzinger argues for the need to "detach eschatology from politics," to never construe the Reign of God with some this-worldly social or political order. This, he argues, does not mean disengagement from politics, but rather a relativization of politics that sets limits to power and ulti-mately upends totalitarianism.

ARCHBISHOP OF MUNICH

After relocating to Regensburg to continue his theological career, a new twist came in 1977, when Paul VI named Ratzinger archbishop of Munich and then, just weeks later, made him a cardinal. Suddenly Ratzinger found himself at the pinnacle of the career ladder in the Catholic Church, despite never having served in a chancery, never having worked in the Vatican, and never having served as a diocesan bishop. It was a daring choice by Paul VI to elevate a thinker rather than a bureaucrat; the Pope obviously felt that, given the way the winds were blowing in Western Europe, and especially Germany, the Church had to do more than "business as usual" in order to mount a credible response. Upon his appointment, the future pope chose as his epis-copal motto *Cooperatores Veritatis,* "coworkers of the truth," reflecting a concern for objective truth that runs through his thought and career.

The Pope's brief stint as archbishop is of interest because it marks his only direct experience as a pastor prior to being elected the Bishop of Rome in the con-clave of 2005. How those years look depends to a great extent upon whom you ask.

As archbishop, Ratzinger played a minor role in the decision by Pope John Paul II to strip Hans Küng, his old colleague from Tübingen, of his license to teach Catholic theology. He also blocked Johann Baptist Metz, another erstwhile col-league, from an appointment at the University of Munich in 1979 (a right he enjoyed under the Bavarian concordat of 1924). Many in the theological commu-nity complained that Ratzinger had forgotten his roots, such as famed German Jesuit Karl Rahner, who called the move an "injustice and misuse of power." Some of the priests in the Munich archdiocese also complained that Ratzinger was aloof and did not communicate well with them, although others dispute this. Defenders of Ratzinger recall him as a devoted shepherd, whose actions only made the Ger-man press when they had some disciplinary connotation; his gentleness with ordi-nary believers and his simplicity, they say, remained largely hidden.

As a footnote to the Metz episode, Ratzinger appeared at a 1998 symposium to mark Metz's seventieth birthday. Metz described that appearance in an interview with the *National Catholic Reporter* as "a gesture of reconciliation towards the theo-logical community."

Ratzinger's appointment as a cardinal in 1977 also meant that he was on hand to take part in the two conclaves of 1978, which elected John Paul I and John

Paul II. In the interregnum leading to the second conclave of 1978, Ratzinger warned in a newspaper interview against the "Marxist presuppositions" underlying liberation theology in Latin America, which he said opened the door for "ideological struggle." At the same time, he said, the reality of social injustice, coupled with what he termed a "pushy Americanism" demanding conversion to free-market principles, created a real basis for social protest. Some Vaticanologists believe Ratzinger played a role in the election of the cardinal of Krakow, Karol Wojtyla, as John Paul II; prior to both conclaves, Ratzinger made some short lists of *papabili* himself.

In November 1980, Ratzinger was responsible for organizing John Paul II's trip to Munich. Also in 1980, John Paul appointed Ratzinger as the relator, or chairman, of the Synod of Bishops on the Family, and in that capacity he won high marks as a listener and synthesizer of the bishops' concerns, despite the fact that in his own speeches at the synod he strenuously defended traditional positions on birth control and other issues of sexual morality. His professorial capacity to bracket off his own views and listen to those of others, coupled with his reputation as an eminent theologian, made it little surprising when John Paul called Ratzinger to Rome in 1981 to take over the Congregation for the Doctrine of the Faith, becoming the first truly first-rate theologian to become the pope's top doctrinal authority since St. Robert Bellarmine in the sixteenth century.

RATZINGER IN THE VATICAN

In many ways, Ratzinger's twenty-four years at the Congregation for the Doctrine of the Faith are so well-documented as to make reviewing them here unnecessary.

Critics remember Ratzinger as the driving force behind some of the most controversial aspects of the pontificate of John Paul II, including the disciplining of theologians such as Fr. Charles Curran, an American moral theologian who advocates a right to public dissent from official Church teaching; Fr. Matthew Fox, an American known for his work on creation spirituality; Sr. Ivone Gebara, a Brazilian whose thinking blends liberation theology with environmental concerns; and Fr. Tissa Balasuriya, a Sri Lankan interested in how Christianity can be expressed through Eastern concepts.

Ratzinger also reined in a series of bishops seen as unacceptably progressive, including Archbishop Raymond Hunthausen of Seattle, Washington, reproached by Rome for his tolerance of ministry to homosexuals and his involvement in progressive political causes, and Bishop Dom Pedro Casaldáliga of Sao Félix, Brazil, criticized for his political engagement beyond the borders of his own diocese.

It was Ratzinger who in the mid-1980s led the Vatican crackdown on liberation theology, a movement in Latin America that sought to align the Roman Catholic Church with progressive movements for social change. Ratzinger saw liberation theology as a European export that amounted to Marxism in another guise, and brought the full force of Vatican authority to stopping it in its tracks.

Ratzinger sought to redefine the nature of bishops' conferences around the world, insisting that they lack teaching authority. That campaign resulted in a 1998 document, *Apostolos Suos,* that some saw as an attack on powerful conferences such as those in the United States and Germany that to some extent acted as counterweights to the Vatican. He also expanded the borders of "infallibility" to include such disparate points as the ban on women's ordination and the invalidity of ordinations in the Anglican Communion under the umbrella of a de facto infallibility as part of the "ordinary and universal magisterium of the Church."

It was Ratzinger who, in a famous 1986 document, defined homosexuality as "a more or less strong tendency ordered toward an intrinsic moral evil." In the 1990s, Ratzinger led a campaign against the theology of religious pluralism, insisting that the traditional teaching of Christ as the lone and unique savior of humanity not be compromised. This effort culminated in the 2001 document *Dominus Iesus,* which asserted that non-Christians are in a "gravely deficient situation" with respect to Christians. The same effort led to critical notifications on the work of two Jesuit theologians, Jesuit Fr. Jacques Dupuis of Belgium, and Fr. Roger Haight of the United States.

Despite Ratzinger's reputation as a stellar theologian, critics also say that occasionally he can be sloppy, relying on misleading assessments by aides and consultors. English Presbyterian writer John Hick, for example, pointed out in 1997 that in a public lecture criticizing his work, Ratzinger erroneously identified him as an American, and cited page numbers in one of his books that had nothing to do with the matter under discussion. In the Dupuis case, Ratzinger's office prepared a highly critical notification that it asked Dupuis to sign, only to have Dupuis defenders object that once again the citations were incorrect and the statements attributed to Dupuis were, in fact, nowhere to be found in his book. Ratzinger took the point, and a milder version of the notification was drafted.

This track record means that some in the Catholic theological community, especially on the more liberal wing, are not great Ratzinger admirers. A Jesuit who followed the Dupuis case closely, asked for his thoughts on the possibility of a Ratzinger papacy days before the conclave opened, said tersely: "It fills me with dread."

Ratzinger also has a reputation for making occasionally provocative comments that stir controversy. He once called Buddhism an "autoerotic spirituality," and in *Salt of the Earth* was critical of Islam: "Nor must we forget that Islam was at the head of the slave traffic and by no means displayed any great regard for the blacks. And above all Islam doesn't make any sort of concession to inculturation," he said. He later added, "One has to have a clear understanding that it is not simply a denomination that can be included in the free realm of a pluralistic society."

Ratzinger has also said on many occasions that the Church of the future may have to be smaller to remain faithful, referring to Christianity's short-term destiny as representing a "creative minority" in a world largely hostile to its message. He has also used the image of the "mustard seed," suggesting a smaller presence that nevertheless carries the capacity for future growth as long as it remains true to itself.

Such views have drawn criticism in some quarters for being excessively pessimistic. The English Catholic writer Eamonn Duffy, for example, said in 1985 of Ratzinger's judgment about the contemporary world: "The 'world' is not entirely inhabited by hedonistic bourgeois materialists, any more than it is by abortionists, pornographers or concentration camp commandants. The 'world' is the place where ordinary men and women live and must find their salvation."

Finally, Ratzinger has insisted that his primary responsibility in the doctrinal office is not primarily to make life easy for theologians, but to protect the right of the 1.1 billion Roman Catholics in the world to have the faith presented to them fully and accurately. As he put it in 1997, "Those who, as it were, can't fight back intellectually have to be defended against intellectual assault on what sustains their life." He has suggested that theological "creativity," as it has come to be understood, may be partly to blame for the decline in Catholic religious practice in some quarters: "Theologians should ponder to what extent they are to blame for the fact that increasing numbers of people seek refuge in narrow or unhealthy forms of religion. When one no longer offers anything but questions and doesn't offer any positive way to faith, such flights are inevitable," he said.

All these positions, and many others, have made Ratzinger a polarizing figure, at least within center-left circles in academia and ecclesiastical life. Fr. Charles Curran, one of Ratzinger's targets for his views on sexual morality and theological dissent, blames Ratzinger for artificially shutting down theological discussion.

"The problem is that he has too readily identified the truth with what the magisterium has taught at a given moment," Curran said in 1999. "The Holy Office cannot have a copyright on what it means to be Catholic."

Yet Ratzinger's fans, and they are many, insist that focusing only on the public controversies associated with his tenure leaves two essential pieces of the picture out of focus: the personal qualities of the man, and the abiding concerns upon which the specific battles he's waged are based.

As for Ratzinger's personal side, those who have worked with him insist that he is not the bruiser that a quick rehearsal of his public record, like the one above, might suggest.

"He is an extraordinarily refined, calm, and open-minded person," said Archbishop William J. Levada of San Francisco, who worked on Ratzinger's Vatican staff in the early 1980s. "He can listen and synthesize a group of people's thought and find much of value in almost anything that is said. He has the uncanny ability to articulate those things we meant but forgot to say," Levada told the *National Catholic Reporter* in February 1999. Obviously the respect is mutual, since the new pope named Levada his successor at the Congregation for the Doctrine of the Faith on May 13, 2005.

That graciousness is reflected in the fact that, as prefect of the doctrinal congregation, Ratzinger on many occasions has accepted invitations to dialogue with intellectuals of other faiths and of none, often in very public settings, and has always come off as open, willing to concede points when they were well articulated and cogent, and never defensive or arrogant. On October 25, 2004, for example, he took part in a colloquium with Italian lay thinker Ernesto Galli della Loggia, a conservative nonbeliever, at Rome's Palazzo Colona. In his opening remarks, Ratzinger called contemporary society "truly ill," and said that humanity's moral capacity has not kept pace with its technological skill. In such a context, he argued, there is an urgent need for religious believers and secularists of goodwill to join forces in an attempt to revivify moral reasoning.

"I've come with this realization of needing to make common cause," Ratzinger said.

During the discussion, Galli della Loggia challenged Ratzinger, objecting to what he called the Church's tendency to blur "life" with "personhood," saying he agreed that an embryo is life but not that it is a person, and not all the same moral categories apply.

Ratzinger readily conceded the point.

"I think a use of the word 'life' that sometimes substitutes 'person' is mistaken," he said. "After all, a plant is life."

At the end of the evening, the audience roundly applauded Ratzinger's stamina and openness, and most scored him the winner of the exchange.

A similar event took place in a jam-packed Roman theater in 2000, when Ratzinger agreed to an exchange with Italian philosopher Paolo Flores d'Arcais, a self-described atheist. Many in the crowd of several hundred people arrived skeptical of the Vatican's "enforcer" but were gradually won over by his charm, quick wit, and willingness to listen to the other party. When Flores drew cheers for suggesting that sometimes nonbelievers have done a better job of living gospel values than believers, Ratzinger said: "I'm satisfied with the applause. It's good for both of us to be self-critical, to reflect anew."

Admirers say Ratzinger's kindness is not just hauled out for public display at this sort of event, but is a fundamental quality of the man. After his election as pope, for example, Ratzinger went by his apartment in the Piazza Leonina to pick up whatever personal effects he wanted to collect. The apartment is on the same floor with the apartments of three other cardinals, and as he left, Pope Benedict rang the doorbells of the other three apartments to thank the startled religious women who act as the household staffs for the cardinals for being such good neighbors during his years in that location. (As a footnote, many of these sisters are Americans, members of the Mercy Sisters of Alma.) Those who know the new pope well say it was a vintage gesture.

The devotion Ratzinger inspires among his staff at the Congregation for the Doctrine of the Faith is also the stuff of legend. When he visited the office shortly after his election, he was accompanied by the secretary of state, Cardinal Angelo Sodano, and the *sostituto,* or "substitute," Archbishop Leonardo Sandri, both men known for maintaining rather formal and distant relationships with subordinates. One staff member at the congregation described the two as "stunned" by the outpouring of affection for the new pope from his former aides; most staffers, when introduced to the Pope, choked back tears. One said he was literally unable to speak when his turn came, and had to content himself with later writing a note to Pope Benedict trying to describe his emotions.

Further, defenders insist, the positions articulated by the Congregation for the Doctrine of the Faith over these twenty-four years are not the personal musings of Joseph Ratzinger, but represent the collective judgment of the staff of the congregation, as well as the other cardinals who are its members. Ratzinger himself made this argument in *Salt of the Earth:* "I would never presume to use the decisions of the Congregation to impose my own theological ideas on the Christian people. . . . I see my role as that of coordinator of a large working group," he said. "When the Cardinals meet, we never make decisions if the consultors aren't in substantial agreement, because we say that if there are markedly different opinions among good theologians, then we can't declare by some higher light, as it were, that only one is right. Only when the advisory team has come to at least a large degree of unanimity, a basic convergence, do we make decisions as well."

This point was made by Washington's Cardinal McCarrick after Pope Benedict's election.

"The Congregation for the Doctrine of the Faith is not just Ratzinger going into his office, closing the door, and writing documents," he said. "Everything he does has to be in continuity with the tradition of the Church."

To some degree, therefore, Ratzinger admirers, including many of the cardinals who elected him pope, believe that he has unfairly shouldered the public blame for a quarter-century for conclusions that virtually any prefect of the doctrinal office would have been obliged to reach. Behind the scenes, they argue, he has sometimes had a moderating effect, such as his widely rumored intervention during the drafting of the 1993 encyclical *Veritatis Splendor* to argue that the Church's teaching on birth control, because it is not directly a matter of divine revelation, cannot be declared formally infallible.

As for Ratzinger's core concerns, which presumably will extend to his new role as Pope Benedict XVI, admirers insist that he has no interest in choking off theological debate simply for the sake of exercising power, or for offending constituencies who may find some of his public pronouncements painful, such as homosexuals or women who feel called to the Catholic priesthood. He is not, they say, by nature a head-knocker.

Instead, they argue, the underlying passion of Ratzinger's life has always been truth. No doctrine, Ratzinger believes, can truly liberate, and no theological discussion is truly free, if it leads human beings into false conceptions of the meaning and purpose of their lives. In that sense, Ratzinger sees no contradiction between doctrinal and pastoral imperatives—the best pastoral service the Church can offer, he believes, is to tell someone the truth. Drawing on his own experience of National Socialism in Germany, Ratzinger argues that he has witnessed the ruin that lies on the other side of wrong ideas, false doctrine. Insisting upon the capacity of the human intellect to attain truth, and that this truth is offered in its fullest form in the Christian gospel, is, he believes, the only secure basis of authentic humanism.

"A lot of people read everything I may say as part of a mechanism that basically wants to keep mankind in tutelage and not as a genuine, honest, intellectual attempt to understand the world and man," Ratzinger said in *Salt of the Earth.*

For this reason, Ratzinger's admirers have long scoffed at characterizations of him as a kind of "control freak."

"I do not believe any credible case could be made for him as an authoritarian," Dominican Fr. Augustine Di Noia told the *National Catholic Reporter* in 1999. At the time, Di Noia was the chief theological adviser for the U.S. bishops conference; later, he would come to Rome to serve as Ratzinger's undersecretary in the Congregation for the Doctrine of the Faith, a position he holds today.

"Faith is not the suppression of intelligence, but its exaltation," Di Noia said in 1999. "The fundamental divide between dissenting or revisionist theologians and the mode of John Paul II and Ratzinger lies along this fault. Ratzinger is stating points which would have been totally noncontroversial even fifty years ago," Di Noia said. On the rare occasions when he has had to rein someone in, Di Noia said, it is because "a clear line in the sand" was crossed.

A FINAL CASUALTY

Just two weeks after Benedict's pontificate began, a final casualty was claimed in the battles fought during his tenure at the Congregation for the Doctrine of the Faith, one last echo of the controversies rehearsed above. Fr. Thomas Reese, S.J., editor of the respected Jesuit-run *America* magazine, resigned after the congregation asked the Jesuit authorities to remove him as editor, capping five years of largely hidden tensions between Ratzinger's office, the Jesuit order, and Reese himself.

Ironically, Reese got the news just days after returning to New York from Rome, where he covered the conclave that elected Ratzinger as Pope Benedict XVI.

Over the course of a five-year exchange between the doctrinal congregation and the Jesuits, the congregation had raised objections to various editorial choices at *America* under Reese's leadership, including:

- An essay exploring moral arguments for the approval of condoms in the context of HIV/AIDS;
- Several critical analyses of the doctrinal congregation's September 2000 document *Dominus Iesus,* on religious pluralism;
- An editorial criticizing what *America* called a lack of due process in the congregation's procedures for the investigation of theologians;
- An essay about homosexual priests;
- A guest essay by Congressman David Obey (D., Wis.), challenging suggestions that the Church should refuse Communion to Catholic politicians who do not vote pro-life.

In each case, defenders note, while these contributions in some respects challenged official Church positions, they were published as part of *America*'s broader coverage of the topic, which always included substantial contributions making the opposing argument.

The formal correspondence about Reese's fate was carried on between the Congregation for the Doctrine of the Faith and the superior general of the Jesuits, Fr. Peter-Hans Kolvenbach of Holland, with the content then relayed to Reese's Jesuit superiors in the United States. Although critics of Reese both in the United States and Rome have occasionally accused him of an "antihierarchical" mentality, supporters noted in their responses to the congregation that over his seven years as editor, *America* routinely published weighty pieces by prominent members of the hierarchy, at one stage including Ratzinger himself.

In February 2002, the Congregation for the Doctrine of the Faith proposed creating a three-member commission of American bishops to act as "censors" for *America,* though in the end this never came to pass. Throughout the back-and-forth discussions, the congregation told the Jesuits that it was acting in response to concerns from bishops in the United States. Whatever the source, the tensions did not diminish, and by early spring of 2005 it was clear that Reese would have to go. A letter requesting that he be removed was dated in mid-March. Observers speculate that had someone other than Ratzinger been elected pope, Reese might have waited to see how policy would develop, but given Ratzinger's victory, Reese believed he saw the handwriting on the wall. He elected to take a sabbatical in California while considering his next move.

Reese's departure will be seen as puzzling in some quarters, given that *America* has long been seen as a moderate, though clearly left-leaning, sophisticated publication that tried to steer between extremes. Perhaps, some speculated, Reese's high profile in the American media as a commentator on Church affairs was a factor in making him a "target," though if so, the intervention seemed destined to be futile. Reese was already widely cited in the press prior to taking over at *America* in 1998, and presumably the notoriety of having been "fired by the new pope" will do little to reduce his visibility. Others concluded that it was *America's* reputation for intelligent, nuanced commentary that made it a "threat."

Defenders of the Congregation for the Doctrine of the Faith, on the other hand, argued that it is not unreasonable to expect a publication sponsored by a religious order, and with a member of that order as editor, to uphold the teaching of the Church.

Whatever one makes of the debate, it should be emphasized that the pressure for Reese's removal dates from the end of Ratzinger's term at the doctrinal office, and it may be unfair to treat it as a sign of where Benedict's pontificate will go. Further, despite the fact that the buck at the congregation stopped on Ratzinger's desk, it is unclear to what extent he was personally involved in the deliberations surrounding Reese. Still, the fact that the congregation targeted Reese and *America* will be troubling to some trying to discern where Benedict XVI may want to take the Church. If *America* is not safe, some observers in the Catholic Church will wonder, who is?

A COMPLEX MAN

This, then, is the complex man who has become Pope Benedict XVI: a serious intellectual, an ardent defender of the faith, a man with deep doubts about the health of contemporary culture, willing to use the disciplinary tools of the teaching office when a matter of faith is at stake, but also a man of deep kindness and humility, someone capable of stirring remarkable love and devotion in those close to him, a man with a reputation for being both tough and collegial, erudite yet concerned with the common person. Given these facets of his history and personal character, which sometimes rest in uneasy tension with one another, his promises to be a fascinating pontificate.

2. *The Battle with Totalitarian Regimes*

John Paul II

Was God at Work in the Fall of Communism?
(Excerpt)

By your question you confirm that in *the fall of Communism* the action of God has become almost visible in the history of our century. We must be wary of oversimplification. What we refer to as Communism has its own history. It is the history of protest in the face of injustice, as I recalled in the encyclical *Laborem Exercens*—a protest on the part of the great world of workers, which then became an ideology. But *this protest has also become part of the teaching of the Church.* We need but recall the encyclical *Rerum Novarum,* from the end of the last century. We add: this *teaching is not limited to protest, but throws a farseeing glance toward the future.* In fact, it was Leo XIII who in a certain sense predicted the fall of Communism, a fall which would cost humanity and Europe dearly, *since the medicine*—he wrote in his encyclical of 1891—*could prove more dangerous than the disease itself!* The pope said this with all the seriousness and the authority of the Church's Magisterium.

And what are we to say of the *three children from Fatima* who suddenly, on the eve of the outbreak of the October Revolution, heard: "Russia will convert" and "In the end, my Heart will triumph. . . !" They could not have invented those predictions. They did not know enough about history or geography, much less the social movements and ideological developments. And nevertheless it happened just as they had said.

Perhaps this is also why the pope was called from "a faraway country," perhaps this is why it was necessary for the assassination attempt to be made in St. Peter's Square precisely on May 13, 1981, the anniversary of the first apparition at Fatima—so that all could become more transparent and comprehensible, so that the voice of God which speaks in human history through the "signs of the times" could be more easily heard and understood.

This, then, is the Father who is always at work, and this is the Son, who is also at work, and this is the invisible Holy Spirit who is Love, and as Love is ceaseless creative, saving, sanctifying, and lifegiving action.

Therefore, it would be simplistic to say that Divine Providence caused the fall of Communism. In a certain sense Communism as a system fell by itself. It fell as a consequence of its own mistakes and abuses. *It proved to be a medicine more dangerous than the disease itself.* It did not bring about true social reform, yet it did become a powerful threat and challenge to the entire world. But *it fell by itself, because of its own inherent weakness.*

"My Father is at work until now, so I am at work" *(John* 5:17). The fall of Communism opens before us a *retrospective panorama of modern civilization's typical way of thinking and acting,* especially in Europe, where Communism originated. Modern civilization, despite undisputed successes in many fields, has also made many mistakes and given rise to many abuses with regard to man, exploiting him in various ways. It is a civilization that constantly equips itself with power structures and structures of oppression, both political and cultural (especially through the media), in order to impose similar mistakes and abuses on all humanity.

How else can we explain the increasing gap between the rich North and the ever poorer South! Who is responsible for this! Man is responsible—man, ideologies, and philosophical systems. I would say that *responsibility lies with the struggle against God, the systematic elimination of all that is Christian.* This struggle has to a large degree dominated thought and life in the West for three centuries. *Marxist collectivism is nothing more than a "cheap version" of this plan.* Today a similar plan is revealing itself in all its danger and, at the same time, in all its faultiness.

God, on the other hand, is faithful to His Covenant. He has made it with humanity in Jesus Christ. He cannot now withdraw from it, having decided once and for all that the destiny of man is eternal life and the Kingdom of Heaven. *Will man surrender to the love of God, will he recognize his tragic mistake?* Will the Prince of Darkness surrender, he who is "the father of lies" *(John* 8:44), who continually accuses the sons of men as once he accused Job (cf *Job* 1:9ff)? It is unlikely that he will surrender, but his arguments may weaken. Perhaps, little by little, humanity will become more sober, people will open their ears once more in order to hear that word by which God has said everything to humanity.

And there will be nothing humiliating about this. Every person can learn from his own mistakes. So can humanity, allowing God to lead the way along the winding paths of history. God does not cease to be at work. *His essential work will always remain the Cross and the Resurrection of Christ.* This is the ultimate word of truth and of love. This is also the unending source of God's action in the sacraments, as well as in other ways that are known to Him alone. His is an action which passes through the heart of man and through the history of humanity.

~

CARL BERNSTEIN
John Paul II and the Fall of Communism

On Monday, October 16, 1978, ninety-nine cardinals out of one hundred and eight gave the archbishop of Kraków their vote. They had done the unimaginable: They had chosen a pope from a country subject to the Soviet Union, a country with a Marxist and atheist government. He was the first non-Italian pontiff in 450 years, a young pope, at the age of fifty-eight. Outside of Poland and the Sacred College, few knew much about this Slav who had become shepherd to a flock of eight hundred million Catholics.

Amid the silence the voice of the cardinal president could be heard asking: "Do you accept? What name will you take?"

Wojtyla accepted. The tension vanished from his face, which took on a solemn expression. Not only did he say "Yes," as tradition demanded, with a clear voice, but he added: "With obedience in faith to Christ, my Lord, and with trust in the Mother of Christ and of the Church, in spite of the great difficulties, I accept."

Now to express his commitment to the legacy of the last three popes and his affinity to Albino Luciani, he took as his name John Paul II.

~

In Warsaw, an officer flung the door open and, ignoring both protocol and discipline, shouted: "Comrade General, sensational news! Wojtyla's been elected pope."

The man at the desk had a pale, almost ghostly white face. Hidden behind dark glasses, his eyes were invisible. The back brace he was snapped into made him sit stiffly. In his olive-green uniform he looked like a mannequin. He thanked the adjutant correctly and acknowledged the message: In two hours members of the Politburo and other state officials would meet in extraordinary session.

Jaruzelski seemed almost overwhelmed with ambiguity: How to handle this news from Rome? Wojtyla as pope meant trouble. Relations between the cardinal of Kraków and the Communist authorities had been strained. Yet the general allowed a wave of patriotism to sweep over him. For the first time in the thousand-year history of Catholic Poland, a son of the motherland was ascending the loftiest throne in the world. It was as if this day—October 16, 1978—had conferred a magnificent prize on the entire nation. Perhaps a bit of the splendor would shine on the government too, undoing the sense of defeat and indignity that scarred the national conscience. Poland had once been a European power, but that had been a long time ago.

The streets of Warsaw were filling up with people on their way to church to pray and light votive candles. Their joy seemed close to rapture—as if Easter, Christmas, and Independence Day had all come at once. Government-controlled Polish radio and television had incongruously broadcast the historic news in the form of a brief bulletin. Since the party hadn't issued any official response, no one had dared flesh out the report with so much as a thumbnail biographical sketch of the new pope.

Yet across the capital the bells were booming like an autumnal cloudburst, as each church rang out in celebration of the news. Jaruzelski thought the choice of a pope from Kraków was a master stroke. From the great cathedral on the Wawel Hill and his episcopal palace, Wojtyla had systematically and ostentatiously ignored the party hierarchy. With philosophical contempt, he had denied any legitimacy to Marxist-Leninist ideology; and with his considerable influence on the Catholic intelligentsia, he had built up a front of spiritual resistance to the country's political leadership. Indeed, Wojtyla's election was dangerous. Jaruzelski was worried that the Polish Church would become a model for all of Eastern Europe, that its influence, hitherto held within the borders of Poland, would now reach Christians in the USSR.

Jaruzelski felt swamped by confusion. He picked up the phone and tried to get some guidance—and commiseration—from the chief Communist overseer of the Catholic Church in Poland, Stanislaw Kania, head of the party's Administrative Department.

"What is there to build on?" Kania asked tentatively. He conceded, of course, that past relations with the archbishop of Kraków offered little ground for optimism. But Communist rhetoric required that every negation be followed by an affirmation. The Church of Rome, he declared, had learned the value of cooperating with the Communist authorities. "We can expect the Holy See to stick to the path of reconciliation, of *Ostpolitik*." But that wasn't enough to calm the assembled leaders, now beset with visions of a grand conspiracy. Was a Polish pope a threat to the socialist system in Poland? That was the crucial question.

"What if the new pope decides to come to Poland?" one of the ministers asked Kania. The weight of the question settled oppressively over the entire room.

The government, warned the minister of internal affairs, has to focus immediately on the risk of a wave of pilgrimages by the Polish faithful to Rome. "Those trips alone might pose a danger to the stability of Poland."

In the very first hours of his pontificate, the election of the first pope from a socialist country had raised the specter of destabilization. Suddenly the Vatican had become an ominous, unknown quantity to the Communist world.

≈

The first day of John Paul II's triumphant return to his homeland on June 2, 1979, had left the Communist authorities in Warsaw and Moscow shaken. More than a million Poles had converged on the airport road, on Victory Square and in the Old City during the first hours of his visit. Students had taken up the crucifix as the symbol of resistance to the regime. Just as disturbing to the Polish authorities were the pope's words in private to First Secretary Edward Gierek. In the course of their meeting in the Belweder Palace John Paul II had voiced his hopes for the kind of agreement between Church and state that Gierek himself badly wanted. But the pope had laid down a list of conditions designed to convince a Communist power that it would have to make unprecedented concessions if it was to coexist peacefully with the Church.

Gierek had spoken about international detente. The pope replied that "peace and rapprochement among peoples had to be based on the principle of respect for the objective rights of the nation," among which he included its right to "shape its own culture and civilization."

Gierek had spoken about Poland's security obligations and its position in the international community—a clear allusion to the alliances of COMECON (the Council for Mutual Economic Assistance) and the Warsaw Pact, both of which were thoroughly dominated and run by the Soviet Union. John Paul II had responded that "all forms of political, economic, or cultural imperialism contradict the needs of the international order." The only valid pacts could be those "based on mutual respect and on the recognition of the welfare of every nation." His boldness took the Communist leader by surprise. Gierek was disposed to reach a generous settlement on the place to be assigned the Church in Polish society for its religious activities. The pope wanted an acknowledgment that the Church "serves men and women in the temporal dimension of their lives," that is, in the social and political spheres. All this was deeply disturbing to the hierarchy of the Polish Party and— more significant—to the men in the Kremlin.

The next day, Pentecost, June 3, John Paul II arrived in the city of Gniezno like a modern incarnation of the Spirit, by helicopter. The million people who had turned out in Warsaw proved not an exception, just a prelude. Enormous throngs awaited him in the field where his helicopter touched down. "We want God," they chanted, taking up the same cry as the crowds in Warsaw the previous day.

By Sunday evening, June 3, John Paul II had already succeeded, through the prophetic vehemence of his speeches, in challenging the ideology of the regime, the role of the state, the nature of Poland's alliance with the Soviet Union, and the geopolitical arrangements in Europe resulting from the Second World War. General Jaruzelski, who was following the pope's moves from a command center in the Ministry of Defense, could see that his comrades in the Polish Politburo were extremely disturbed, even fearful—both of the responses the pope was eliciting and of reaction from the Kremlin. The party hierarchy didn't like the crowds' attitudes, which struck them as "beyond normal behavior," almost cult-like. Worse, many passages in the pope's speeches went dangerously beyond the expectable tame religious formulas. Gierek, the party secretary, and Premier Piotr Jaroszewicz were already expressing their concerns about "destabilization."

To make matters worse, every gesture, every allusion of the pope was imme-diately rebroadcast throughout the world by the more than a thousand journalists who had come to Poland to follow the story. In turn, echoes of the trip from the outside world were having negative reverberations in the USSR, Czechoslovakia, and East Germany, whose leaders eyed Warsaw's every move with suspicion and skepticism.

From the third day on, his trip began to look more and more like a tri-umphant pilgrimage by the pontiff among his people—and an enthusiastic march of millions of Poles toward the pope, their compatriot. All the regime's precautions for limiting the impact of his visit proved futile. On the contrary, every restriction was turned into formidable counterpropaganda against the regime. The roadblocks set up by the police eighteen miles from Czestochowa to screen the pilgrims served only to remind Poles of the vexations inflicted on them by the totalitarian system. The restrictions imposed on television programs—people in Warsaw or Poulah were barred from seeing what anyone in Czestochowa could see—only increased the desire for the free flow of information. The tricks in TV camera coverage, which during religious celebrations tended to show only the pope and persons next to him at the altar, instead of the vast crowds, only added to the drama of his words and the shouted responses from the unseen masses.

An enormous billboard, hung on the walls by the Catholic students of Lublin, summed up the general feeling: "Holy Father, we want to be with you, we want to live a better life with you, we want to pray with you." When the pope met the min-ers from Silesia, the underground monthly *Glos* commented: "The millions of working people gathered to meet the pope would seem to prove that the official the-sis of the natural atheism of the working class and its progressive de-Christianiza-tion is utterly false." The dissident journal added prophetically: "At present the authorities are afraid that the pope, who used to be a worker himself, and whose sensitivity to exploitation is well known, might act as a spokesman for the Polish working class." In the face of the intense expectations focused on his person, John Paul II was careful to act with great calm and balance, avoiding confrontational tones. Speaking freely with a group of a thousand university students from Lublin in a closed-door meeting, the pope said: "The cause of Christ can also be furthered or harmed by the choice of a worldview diametrically opposed to Christianity. Everyone who makes this choice with innermost conviction must have our respect." Some students were perplexed by these remarks. By way of explaining his thoughts the pope added: "There is a danger for both sides, both for the Church and for the others, in the attitude of the person who makes no choice at all." Thus, in keeping with his philosophical vocation, John Paul II had returned to preach personal com-mitment and respect for those who think differently.

On the penultimate day of his trip, the pope chose a meeting with workers near the monastery of Mogila, in the Nowa Huta district, to seize ground tradi-tionally claimed by the Communists and deliver a direct blow to Communist ide-ology. "Christianity and the Church have no fear of the world of work," he proclaimed. "They're not afraid of any system based on work. The pope isn't afraid of the workers." Many times, of course, popes had feared worker movements. John Paul II recalled his personal experience working in the rock quarry and the Solvay factory during the Nazi occupation; and he extolled the Gospel as a guide for the problems of work in the contemporary world. Amid an ecstatic crowd, waving thousands of flags and banners, the pontiff defiantly declared that people couldn't be demeaned as a mere means of production. "Christ will never approve of it," he exclaimed. "Both the worker and the employer must remember this, both the system of labor and the system of remuneration must remember this. The state, the nation, and the Church must all remember this."

The audience cheered and applauded frenetically. For the workers this was pouring oil on the flames. They were already outraged at the government's latest price increases and eager for higher salaries, and they remembered the regime's violence against the workers' protest in 1976 at Ursus and Radom. Now the Polish leadership took the rebuff, powerless to fight back. In the final analysis the requests made of the pope by the government were having no effect at all. Not on John Paul, not on the people. Monitoring his speeches day by day, General Jaruzelski noted both the force of the pope's words and the subtlety of his approach: John Paul II was not only addressing the present state of affairs, "he was consolidating hope and courage" for future struggles, for the long term.

A similar thought occurred to Wiktor Kulerski, who would join the ranks of Solidarity activists barely a year later. "We're living in a different country," he told himself as the pope traveled around Poland. "Communism doesn't matter anymore, because nobody submits to it." Kulerski felt that the pope's stay in Poland was a moment of relief, a moment to gather one's energies: "The pope is here, and he's beyond the reach of the Communists. He can say and do the things we can't. They can't get him. People repeat the pope's words, and they know that he's their bulwark."

On June 10, more than a million faithful arrived at the meadow at Blonie on the edge of the city. Merely to draw a million people was incredible, even revolutionary in a country of the socialist bloc. That day was chosen to honor St. Stanislaw during the papal trip, and it turned into a celebration of the new power of John Paul II as, brandishing Christ like a battle standard, he announced that the nine hundredth anniversary of the death of St. Stanislaw would be a turning point for the nation and the Church.

That was all the crowd needed; they understood perfectly. As he left, the pope could bestow a new blessing on his people. He could entrust them with a new mission. "You must be strong, dearest brothers and sisters!" he cried. "You must be strong with the strength that flows from faith! You must be strong with the strength of faith!"

For one last time he addressed—without naming them, but in a way obvious to everyone—the peoples behind the iron curtain. "There is no need to be afraid. The frontiers must be opened. There is no imperialism in the Church, only service." Catching sight of a group of pilgrims from Czechoslovakia, he insisted: "Oh how I would wish that our brothers and sisters, who are united to us by language and the fortunes of history, could also have been present during the pilgrimage of this Slavic pope. If they are not here, if they are not here in this vast expanse, they are surely in our hearts." The pope and the Slavic nations versus the Soviet empire. The battle lines were now drawn. In his native land, almost one out of every three citizens had been able to see him in person.

～

On Thursday, August 14, 1980, Pope John Paul II spent the day in the papal villa at Castel Gandolfo, twenty miles from the Vatican. The air in the Alban hills was more breathable than in the scorching streets of Rome. Ever since the late 1600s the villa had been a refuge for popes during the hottest months of the year.

That Thursday, the pace at Castel Gandolfo was more languid than usual. It was the eve of the Assumption, *ferragosto,* the summer's most sacred holiday for Italians, when everything stops running, even the buses.

While the pope worked in his study, Lech Walesa, a square-shouldered, unemployed electrician with a distinctive mustache, was clambering up a steam shovel at the Lenin Shipyard in Gdansk, Poland. All summer the workers at the shipyard had declined to join the strikes that were sweeping the country. But on this morning, some of them formed into an unruly procession within the gates, demanding pay raises and the rehiring of the shipyard's crane operator—a defiant critic of management who had been transferred to a job outside Gdansk.

Poland's economy was devastated. Millions of factory workers across Poland were by now thoroughly disgruntled. The spontaneous strikes that had begun in July had spread to more than 150 enterprises. The government was reacting with the usual promises of change and salary increases—so far without violence. This time the protests continued. The sun was setting on the decade of Gierek. The country now found itself mired in debt; productivity was sinking; basic items like spare parts for industrial equipment were in short supply. Bankruptcy loomed.

The workers in the naval shipyard, the most important in Poland, where police in 1970 had killed forty-five striking employees, had shown little enthusiasm for a new confrontation. The director of the Gdansk shipyard, Klemens Giech, was promising a pay raise if workers would go back on the job, and many were ready to agree. But Walesa, who had scaled the yard's twelve-foot high chain-link fence that morning, now stood next to the shipyard manager atop the steam shovel and denounced his offers.

He was a popular figure who had taken part in the uprisings of 1970 that had brought down Gomulka. After the bloody repression of the demonstrations in Radom and Ursus in 1976, he had devoted himself to creating an independent labor union, and he had often been arrested for these activities. Now he called for a sit-down strike: To protect themselves from security forces, workers would lock themselves inside the factory. The crowd heeded his call.

The truth was that the strikes that shook Poland in the summer of 1980 were not merely strikes. They were political insurrections—"counterrevolution," as Brezhnev correctly put it. This movement, like all historic social revolutions, united a constellation of formidable political forces—labor, the intelligentsia, and the Church—that had never before come together so decisively.

In the previous economic crises, which had ended in violence, the workers had been disorganized and had lacked any national forum for expressing their grievances. In 1980, though there was still no centrally organized political opposition, there was a loose alliance of forces prepared to challenge the whims of an imperious state. These were the Workers Defense Committees (known by the acronym KOR) that had been formed by intellectuals to assist workers arrested or fired after the violent crackdown in 1976; the Catholic Intellectual Clubs (KIK); and the bishops who, backed by the Polish pope, now tentatively preached a gospel of human rights as well as of salvation.

On Saturday, August 16, the workers again seemed inclined to call off their strike, in exchange for the promise of a 1,500-zloty raise and a guarantee that a monument would be built at the shipyard to honor the victims of December 1970. But Walesa, emboldened by these concessions, issued a sixteen-point list of demands, the most important of which was government recognition of free trade unions. His proposal was not especially popular, and a day later, when management offered a heftier pay raise, many older workers filed out of the yard, giving up the strike. This was perhaps Walesa's greatest moment: Circling the yard in a small motorized vehicle, he rallied the workers back to the cause. When the strike finally resumed in full force on the 18th, Walesa issued a new, more radical list of twenty-one demands, including alleviation of censorship and the release of political prisoners. It showed the hand of KOR advisers who had infiltrated the shipyard.

All negotiations were broadcast by loudspeaker through the yard, so word of the strike and the workers' audacious new demands spread rapidly across the Baltic seacoast. That day work stopped in 180 more factories from Gdynia, Gdansk, and Sopot on the coast to Tarnow (near Kraków) and Katowice in Silesia. Now the avalanche was unleashed.

At Castel Gandolfo, John Paul II received confidential reports on the events in Poland from Monsignor Dziwisz, his Polish secretary, and from his Secretariat of State, which was in touch with the Polish episcopate. Breaking habit, Wojtyla eagerly watched television reports of the sensational events in his homeland. With him was Sister Zofia Zdybicka, his ex-student who was staying at the summer residence as a guest. Sister Zdybicka, like the pope, was a philosopher, and first as a student, then as a teacher, finally as a friend, she had often discussed such matters as the nature of Marxism and the destiny of man with Karol Wojtyla. "This," she declared as she watched the TV news, "is a lesson for the whole world. Look at the contradiction: The workers are against communism." The pope readily agreed, but at first he seemed less confident, less enthusiastic. "Except that the world doesn't understand anything," he replied. "The world doesn't get it." He said this three times. He didn't seem entirely surprised by the remarkable doings in Poland. Sister Zdybicka remembered being with the pope on another occasion when he had told a visiting professor from the Catholic University in Lublin, "You have to be ready."

Ready for what? she and the professor had wondered, but now she thought she understood. This was what the pope had been waiting for.

Walesa, said the pope, had been sent by God, by Providence. On the screen they watched Walesa and the workers praying. "So serious, so young, those intent faces," she noted. In his lapel Walesa wore a pin with a picture of the Black Madonna of Czestochowa. On Sunday and now on Monday, mass was celebrated by the strikers in the shipyard, led by Walesa's parish priest, Father Henryk Jankowski, of St. Brygida's in Gdansk.

Photos of the pope and large pictures of the Black Madonna were posted on the gates of the shipyard. John Paul noted with ironic satisfaction that Western politicians, especially those on the left, were amazed that throngs of strikers were flocking on bended knee around improvised outdoor confessionals and that they had chosen religious symbols for their battle standards. Sister Zdybicka sensed that the pope saw the hand of God lifted up against the Communists, as the workers turned their rulers' weapons against them.

Spontaneous demonstrations were now breaking out along the coast under the leadership of the Inter-Factory Strike Committee in solidarity with the strikers at the Lenin Shipyard. Workers all over the country, spurred into action by KOR, were joining forces with the Catholic intelligentsia, while secular-minded intellectuals too were making common cause with the Church.

John Paul II kept silent for a week. Like the heads of the European community who cautioned Gierek and the Polish leadership not to take repressive measures, like U.S. President Jimmy Carter, and like Moscow, which was trying to figure out how the Polish Communist Party could maintain control of the country, the pope was prudent.

On Wednesday, August 20, as the strike movement threatened to provoke long-term political paralysis, the pope said two brief prayers with a group of Polish pilgrims in St. Peter's Square: "God, grant through the intercession of Mary that religion may always enjoy freedom and that our homeland may enjoy security. . . . Lord, help this people, and always defend it from every evil and danger."

"These two prayers," said the pope, "show that all of us here in Rome are united with our compatriots in Poland, with the Church in Poland, whose problems are so close to our heart."

Thus did the pope do something that old Cardinal Wyszynski couldn't and wouldn't do: He publicly blessed the strike. This was a turning point. Now the bishop of Gdansk, Lech Kaczmarek, presented Walesa and the other fourteen members of the strike committee with medals of Pope John Paul II.

Walesa, in turn, sent a reassuring message to Moscow and the Polish Communists: "Our struggle is about unions; it's not a political effort. . . . We have no intention of calling into question Poland's international alliances."

With the world's attention focused on the extraordinary events in Poland, President Carter privately wrote to the pope that the United States shared the aspirations of the Polish workers and that it would use its diplomatic channels to urge Soviet restraint.

On August 23, the pope sent the primate of the Polish Church a delicately nuanced letter: "I am writing these brief words to say how especially close I have felt to you in the course of these last difficult days." Then, after the affectionate flourishes and invocations of the Madonna, the letter gave a precise political order: "I pray with all my heart that the bishops of Poland . . . can even now help this nation in its difficult struggle for daily bread, for social justice, and the safeguarding of its inviolable rights to its own life and development." Bread, social justice, independent development. With these words the pope gave his complete support to the strikers' goals. The Church, observed the Catholic writer Stefan Kisielewski, with only a touch of oversimplification, was managing the first democratic strike in the history of Poland.

That evening the government made a historic concession, agreeing to enter into direct negotiations with the strike committees in Gdansk, Gdynia, and Szczecin.

With the beginning of negotiations, which turned into a dramatic weeklong test of strength, a group of advisers made an appearance alongside Lech Walesa. The group included intellectuals, professors, and members of the Polish Academy of Sciences. Two of its leaders were closely associated with Wojtyla: Tadeusz Mazowiecki, editor of the Warsaw Catholic periodical *Wiez,* and historian Bronislaw Geremek. With the arrival of this group, the strategic leadership of the movement—eventually to be known as Solidarity—passed largely into the hands of the Church. Now the Black Madonna in Walesa's lapel was a sign that Solidarity had taken its inspiration directly from Karol Wojtyla.

On August 27, at the pope's instigation, the Polish bishops approved a document that explicitly claimed "the right to independence both of organizations representing the workers and of organizations of self-government." The pope's will had become the national will. Now the government had little choice but to give in. Walesa knew he had the pope's backing.

On August 31, the historic Gdansk accords were signed, ratifying the establishment of the first independent union behind the iron curtain. The accords set the standard for subsequent agreements that would be made throughout Poland as the Solidarity movement swept the land. Free trade unions, wage increases, health care improvements, curtailment of censorship, release of political prisoners—virtually everything was now negotiable.

At the signing ceremonies for the accords, Walesa dramatically pulled an oversized, brightly colored pen out of his pocket. TV cameras recorded the moment: The pen was a souvenir from John Paul's trip to Poland, and on it was a picture of the pope.

～

The attempt to murder the pope on May 13, 1981, remains one of this century's great mysteries. The pope's response to the shooting and its aftermath has only deepened the mystery.

Nonetheless, many of the pope's closest aides and acquaintances became convinced that the Soviets or their allies, notably the Bulgarian regime, were behind the attempt. An informal group meeting in the Vatican, which included Secretary of State Casaroli, argued secretly that the Soviets wanted the pope killed because his death seemed to be the only way to decapitate Solidarity. With the pope dead, this reasoning went, Solidarity could have been smothered by the Polish authorities without the Soviets incurring the lasting international opprobrium that military intervention by the Warsaw Pact would have brought.

"Surely the assassination was not an isolated attack," Casaroli stated publicly in January 1995.

Cardinal Achille Silvestrini, who was Casaroli's deputy at the time, says, "It was clear to us that it was not a random accident . . . not simply the act of a mad-man. It was something aimed at a goal, there was something behind the killer. . . . We have to keep in mind the situation in Poland and Eastern Europe at that time. If the assassination attempt had succeeded, it would have been the gravestone for Poland and for those who were challenging the control of the [Soviet] system." But Silvestrini is skeptical about the Bulgarian scenario and believes the trail heads somewhere else in the former communist East.

No illuminating documents relating to the assassination attempt have been found in either Bulgaria or Moscow since the fall of communism—though Western intelligence professionals ridicule the notion that a paper trail to the Kremlin might exist.

Many facts about the attempt on the pope's life are contradictory or open to interpretation, and the failure of intelligence agencies around the world to tackle the case immediately and pool their knowledge has helped make it impossible to piece together a definitive record.

≈

On May 17, 1981, four days after the shooting of Wojtyla, President Reagan, who had only partially regained his strength but seemed in the midst of a vigorous recovery, made his first trip since being shot: to deliver a long-scheduled commencement address at the University of Notre Dame—*Our Lady*—in South Bend, Indiana.

By now, Reagan's speechwriters knew his priorities: As on the day he was shot, Reagan again turned his thoughts to the pope and the Evil Empire. Wearing a black academic gown and a black mortarboard with a yellow tassel, the president looked out over a vast audience; he could see that it included a small number of students wearing white armbands and white mortarboards to protest administration policies in El Salvador and budget cuts that hurt the poor. Then the president of the United States made his own prophecy:

The years ahead will be great ones for our country, for the cause of freedom and for the spread of civilization. The West will not contain communism, it will transcend communism. We will not bother to denounce it, we'll dismiss it as a sad, bizarre chapter in human history whose last pages are even now being written.

He was deadly serious, though the reporters traveling with him mistook his words for mere rhetoric and blind hope. But he had confided to his wife and his closest aides that he was certain this was why he and the pope had been spared. The previous day, in Kraków, 300,000 people had attended an open-air mass to pray for their former archbishop John Paul II and for the recovery of Cardinal Wyszynski, whose grave illness had been announced by the episcopate the day after the pope was shot. Reagan continued:

> It was Pope John Paul II who warned last year, in his encyclical on mercy and justice, against certain economic theories that use the rhetoric of class struggle to justify injustice: that "in the name of an alleged justice the neighbor is sometimes destroyed, killed, deprived of liberty or stripped of fundamental human rights." For the West, for America, the time has come to dare to show to the world that our civilized ideas, our traditions, our values are not—like the ideology and war machine of totalitarian societies—a facade of strength. It is time the world knew that our intellectual and spiritual values are rooted in the source of all real strength—a belief in a supreme being, a law higher than our own.

Not only had he quoted the pope, but in the religious cadences of his rhetoric, Ronald Reagan had begun to sound like the pope.

∼

By mid-October of 1981, the situation in Poland was on the brink of chaos. No one seemed to be in control of the country; uncompromising factions in both the Polish Communist Party and Solidarity were demanding harsh, almost apocalyptic action. Riots and clashes between civilians and security forces were spreading. The Polish economy was in ruins, and the crisis was aggravated by hundreds of strikes, by everyone from coal miners to transport workers. In the stores, even toothpaste and soap had disappeared from the shelves.

At the stroke of midnight, tanks and soldiers stationed across the country moved into the streets and forests as Operation X got under way. At six a.m., Jaruzelski addressed the nation on television.

"Citizens and lady citizens of the Polish People's Republic! I turn to you as a soldier and chief of government! Our motherland is on the verge of an abyss." By the time he read his prepared statement, thousands were already in jail. The prisoners, he said, were guilty of "growing aggressiveness and an attempt to dismantle the state. How long will our outstretched hand be met with the fist?" he asked.

For the foreseeable future, the nation would be governed by a Military Council of National Salvation. The new rules of governance, ending sixteen months of hope and excitement, suffering and disappointment, were pasted on lampposts, street corners, and trees throughout the cities and across the countryside. They had been printed months before—in the Soviet Union.

The civil society that Solidarity had been building brick by brick under the protection of the Church was gone. In its place was a declaration of a "state of war."

A nightly curfew was in effect indefinitely. Except for those of the military and security forces, every telephone in Poland was dead (even at local Communist Party headquarters) and would remain so for a month. All civilian communications with the outside world were severed. All schools except nursery schools were closed, as were theaters and movie houses. Except for religious services, public gatherings were now illegal. Travel outside one's city of residence could only be undertaken with official permission. All mail was subject to censorship. "Tourism, yachting, and rowing . . . on internal and territorial waters" were forbidden.

During the sixteen months of Poland's great experiment, more than two thousand clandestine books and newspapers had been published, with help from the West. As many as 100,000 Polish citizens had been involved in their preparation, working as printers, writers, or distributors. Now the Military Council of National Salvation forbade the purchase of typewriter ribbons and typing paper without official permission.

The military would henceforth be responsible for running railroads, highways, mail service, broadcasting, distribution of petroleum products, firefighting, importing and exporting, and the manufacture of strategic goods. Polish borders were sealed and the country's airspace, closed. The newscasters on television now wore military uniforms.

Between twenty and thirty people had been killed in the early days of martial law, most of them murdered by security forces. Hundreds of others were injured and arrested at the shipyard at Gdansk, the birthplace of Solidarity, where thousands of workers had rushed when they first heard of the "state of war."

The most serious violence occurred at a coal mine near Katowice, where miners called a sit-down strike.

The violence at Katowice, which was reported by Polish state radio on the next day, Thursday, prompted John Paul II to begin writing a letter that afternoon to Jaruzelski.

Recent events in Poland since the declaration of martial law on December 13 [wrote the pope] have resulted in death and injury to our fellow countrymen, and I am moved to address this urgent and heartfelt appeal to you, a prayer for an end to the shedding of Polish blood.

During the last two centuries, the Polish nation has endured great wrongs, and much blood has been spilled in the struggle for power over our Fatherland. Our history cries out against any more bloodshed, and we must not allow this tragedy to continue to weigh so heavily on the conscience of the nation. I therefore appeal to you, General, to return to the methods of peaceful dialogue that have characterized efforts at social renewal since August 1980. Even though this may be a difficult step, it is not an impossible one.

The welfare of the entire nation depends upon it. People throughout the world, all those who rightly see the cause of peace furthered by respect for the rights of Man, are waiting for this return to nonviolent means. All humanity's desire for peace argues for an end to the state of martial law in Poland.

The Church speaks out for this desire. Soon it will be Christmas, when generation after generation of Poland's sons and daughters have been drawn together by Holy Communion. Every effort must be made so that our compatriots will not be forced to spend this Christmas under the shadow of repression and death.

I appeal to your conscience, General, and to the conscience of all those who must decide this question.

The Vatican 18 December 1981

John Paul II

This letter, like all of the pope's responses to martial law, stemmed in part from a central premise. However repugnant, martial law, in the pope's phrase, was a "lesser evil" than civil war or Soviet intervention. The pope correctly assumed that Jaruzelski would eventually need the Church's cooperation to find a way out of the terrible situation in which he and the nation now found themselves. Since Jaruzelski had only two choices—to turn toward the Church or toward Moscow—the pope believed that Jaruzelski would ultimately seek the protection of the Church.

~

No moment of his young papacy was as delicate, no problem as vexing, as the situation that faced Wojtyla in 1983 on his second trip to Poland. That winter had been an especially depressing one for Poles. Martial law seemed unrelenting. Dismissals, secret accusations, and acts of repression had poisoned the air.

As he arrived on June 16, 1983, John Paul II did not hide his sadness at the condition of his country. It was evident in his first words at Warsaw's airport, after he had kissed the ground: "I ask those who suffer to be particularly close to me. I ask this in the words of Christ: I was sick, and you visited me, I was in prison and you came to me. I myself cannot visit all those in prison [the crowd gasped], all those who are suffering. But I ask them to be close to me in spirit to help me, just as they always do."

Later that same morning he held the first of two private meetings at Belweder Palace with Prime Minister Jaruzelski, sessions in which real negotiations finally began. The man who had crushed Solidarity looked stiff, correct, and expressionless as he greeted the pope. His pale face wasn't shielded by his usual dark glasses. His uniform gave him a certain patriotic elegance, but John Paul II noticed that when the general spoke, his right hand, which held his prepared remarks, trembled, and his left was clenched in a fist. Jaruzelski has since admitted that he felt extremely nervous and excited. When the time came for official speeches, the pope placed a microphone between himself and Jaruzelski, as if to distance himself as much as possible from the man in charge of martial law. Then the pope publicly addressed Jaruzelski and Jablonski in a televised speech, asserting Poland's right to independence, "her proper place among the nations of Europe, between East and West." The path to true sovereignty and reform, he said, must take into account "social agreements stipulated by representatives of state authorities with representatives of the workers," that is, the Gdansk accords.

His idea, which he now passed on to a whole nation, was a variation of his own experience as a youth during the war: Victory was within. Spiritual victory forged from the suffering of their nation, the path of martyrdom, was possible. "Man is called to victory over himself," he declared. "It is the saints and the beatified who show us the path to victory that God achieves in human history." To achieve that victory requires "living in truth. . . . It means love of neighbor; it means fundamental solidarity between human beings." In a theme he repeated over and over in the following days, to the chagrin of the regime, he said that victory means "making an effort to be a person with a conscience, calling good and evil by name and not blurring them . . . developing in myself what is good, and seeking to correct what is evil by overcoming it in myself."

"You come to the Mother of Czestochowa with a wound in the heart, with sorrow, perhaps also with rage," he preached. "Your presence shows the force of a testimony, a witnessing which has stupefied the whole world: when the Polish worker made his own person the object of a demand, with the Gospel in his hand and a prayer on his lips. The images transmitted to the world in 1980 have touched hearts and consciences."

In his homily to another crowd of one million people in the steel town of Katowice (and to the Communist regime), he reiterated the basic rights of workers: "to a just salary," "to security," "to a day of rest." "Connected with the area of workers' rights is the question of trade unions," he said, "the right of free association," the right of all workers to form unions as "a mouthpiece for the struggle for social justice." Quoting the late Cardinal Wyszynski, he continued, "The state does not give us this right, it has only the obligation to protect and guard it. This right is given us by the Creator who made man as a social being." Each day his speeches alluded to these elements of the Gdansk agreements.

He met privately with Lech Walesa on the last day of his visit, as well as with intellectuals who were secretly in contact with the Solidarity underground. He received from them copies of underground newspapers.

After eighteen months of martial law, Solidarity was no longer a mass organization of labor, with membership cards and a list of workplace demands. The state had destroyed that body, and its resurrection seemed almost inconceivable. But with the pope's second visit, Solidarity became an idea, a consciousness, a set of values, even a way of life "in solidarity."

At the close of his visit, the pope and Jaruzelski met again, this time alone face to face for more than an hour and a half at the Wawel, "a place of great symbolic importance," as Jaruzelski noted. The meeting, unscheduled, had been requested the night before by the pope.

The pope stunned Jaruzelski with his directness: "I understand that socialism as a political system is a reality," he said, "but the point is that it ought to have a human face."

The pope always spoke "in terms of human rights or civil rights," the general noted. "And when we discussed rights we naturally mean[t] democracy. If there is democracy, then you have elections; if you have elections, then you have power. But he never put it that way. It showed his great culture and diplomacy, because in substance he used words and phrases that you couldn't argue with. Because if he had said, 'You have to share power with Solidarity,' we would have argued about it, naturally. But when one simply mentions human rights, it's such a general term, such a general notion, that you can have a constructive discussion, which eventually brought us [the regime] closer to that goal without losing face."

$\approx$

The pope's first real sign of "socialism with a human face"—three years and three months after the declaration of martial law in Poland—came in the unlikely form of a visit to the Vatican on February 27, 1985, by Soviet foreign minister Andrei Gromyko. In Moscow, unbeknownst to the pope, Konstantin Chernenko was near death. Twelve days later Gromyko, who had served every Soviet leader since Stalin, would play a crucial role in the selection of Mikhail Gorbachev to succeed Chernenko as general secretary of the Communist Party of the USSR.

Gromyko now let the pope know that the USSR might be interested in establishing diplomatic relations with the Holy See. When John Paul II voiced his concerns about world peace, particularly the need for progress at the stalled Geneva talks on arms control, and the plight of Catholics in the Soviet Union, Gromyko seemed unusually responsive. He suggested further explorations of such matters by representatives of the USSR and the Vatican. This overture took Wojtyla completely by surprise.

That spring, in May, he began receiving reports from Poland that Gorbachev might indeed be a different kind of Communist and that the Brezhnev era might finally be ending, two and a half years after his death. Gorbachev had traveled to Poland in late April to attend a meeting of the Consultative Political Committee of the Warsaw Pact. More consequentially, when the meeting adjourned, Gorbachev remained behind to speak with Jaruzelski. He had only an hour, the new general secretary said, but then the hour stretched into five as the two men conducted an exhaustive review of the situation in Poland and the USSR and a long discussion about the pope and the Vatican.

From this discussion, Jaruzelski concluded that Gorbachev was a different kind of Communist and took steps, through the primate, to inform the pope of their meeting. "It was a critical moment," Jaruzelski disclosed almost a decade later (and Gorbachev too confirmed the portentous nature of their encounter): "Five hours of conversation face to face without an interpreter. Much of it centered on the Church and Wojtyla, but first "we spoke about the past, about the origins of the system, about the necessity for change." Gorbachev had been general secretary for only a few weeks and he wanted to learn firsthand as much as possible about the internal situation in Poland and about the Holy See. Jaruzelski got the impression that, "though he was broad-minded" and had been a member of the Politburo for several years, "his knowledge of the Church and religion was superficial."

Jaruzelski clung to Gorbachev like a drowning man to a life preserver: Finally someone in the Kremlin was giving him a sympathetic ear—and not just anyone, but the general secretary himself.

"First of all I tried to explain the difference, the uniqueness of the Church's role in Poland, compared with that of the Church in other countries," Jaruzelski recounted. As rigidly controlled as conditions were then in Poland, the country had engaged in a bold experiment with human rights before the imposition of martial law, and both men agreed that Communist societies had to evolve in the direction of that experiment.

Gorbachev had yet to use the term *perestroika*—meaning "restructuring"— but this talk with Jaruzelski turned on some of the concepts he was later to introduce, including a broad guarantee of religious rights for Communist citizens. He asked Jaruzelski many questions about the failures of Poland's planned economy and about the moribund state of the Polish Communist Party. But the conversation kept returning to the Church, and eventually to the pope himself.

"What kind of a man is he?" Gorbachev asked. "What is his intellectual training? Is he a fanatic? Or is he a man with his feet on the ground?"

Jaruzelski replied that the pope was "an outstanding personality, a great humanist, a great patriot," above all a man committed to peace.

Gorbachev now began talking enthusiastically about peaceful coexistence between East and West, arms reductions, even the radical elimination of armaments. Jaruzelski knew how important this was because he had heard the pope take a similar tack on such issues. When he did, Jaruzelski told Gorbachev, "it was not only as the leader of a great religion, a great Church, but also as the son of a nation whose lot had been particularly hard. When this particular pope spoke about peace, it sounded different than when, say, Pius XII talked about it."

It now occurred to Jaruzelski that he could become the intermediary between the pope and Gorbachev, that he could explain one to the other. Later, Gorbachev, like the pope, credited him with playing just such a role.

～

The advent of Gorbachev brought rapid changes to Church-state relations in Poland and created an atmosphere in which Jaruzelski felt safe to begin relaxing many of the restrictions that had accompanied martial law.

Then, on June 2, 1985, the pope issued one of his most important encyclicals, *Slavorum Apostoli* (Apostles to the Slavs), charged with both religious and secular significance. It was an invitation to ecumenical dialogue with the Eastern churches in the USSR.

With the coming of Gorbachev, the Kremlin would no longer automatically interpret such offers as insidious attempts to undermine the foundation of Communist legitimacy. Twice in the next year, at Jaruzelski's urging, Primate Glemp was permitted to visit Minsk and Moscow, where he met with Catholic and Russian Orthodox leaders and clergy, along with secular officials and scholars. Never before had a Polish cardinal visited the Soviet Union.

The "Slavic encyclical" commemorated the eleven hundredth anniversary of the evangelism of Sts. Cyril and Methodius, who brought Christianity to most of the Slavic peoples of Eastern Europe. In this document, the pope invoked the metaphor of Europe as one "body that breathes with two lungs." In 1980 he had made Sts. Cyril and Methodius co-patrons (with St. Benedict) of Europe.

Gorbachev, a Slav and a Communist, and Wojtyla, a Slav and a Christian, were moving toward each other, each increasingly aware of the other's power and potential for doing good. Later that June, the new general secretary propounded the economic changes that would come to be known as *perestroika:* He spoke of a humanism that united the aspirations of Europe for economic and political peace and security. Similarly, the pope's *Ostpolitik* was grounded in the belief that the Church must speak not just for Western Europe, but for a single undivided entity and culture, from the Urals to the Atlantic, "with a pan-European tradition of humanism that encompassed Erasmus, Copernicus, and Dostoevsky," in a historian's phrasing.

The pope was excited and hopeful about the changes Gorbachev was initiating. There was no doubt that Poland, the Communist nations of the East, and even the USSR were on the verge of a great transformation.

That spring of 1985, to the immense satisfaction of the pope, the USSR Council for Religious Affairs recommended Soviet participation in the interreligious convocation that John Paul had called for in Assisi. But Wojtyla was also a realist; he had long years of experience dealing with Communist ideologues. Early in Gorbachev's tenure, the pope had a lengthy discussion about the new general secretary with Rocco Buttiglione, an Italian intellectual who frequently visited the Vatican. "Well, he's a good man, but he'll fail," the pope declared, "because he wants to do something that's impossible. Communism can't be reformed." The pope was never to change this judgment, though he hoped and prayed for Gorbachev's success. Gorbachev was already meeting resistance in the Soviet party and Politburo. *"Perestroika* is an avalanche that we have unleashed and it's going to roll on," the pope said to Father Mieczyslaw Maliliski, his fellow underground seminarian. *"Perestroika* is a continuation of Solidarity. Without Solidarity there would be no *Perestroika."*

The avalanche was rumbling through Czechoslovakia. In the spring of 1985, in commemoration of the eleven hundredth anniversary of the death of St. Methodius, eleven hundred priests—one-third of the Catholic clergy in Czechoslovakia—concelebrated mass at the Moravian shrine of Velehrad. Cardinal Frantisek Tomasek, eighty-six years old, who had been imprisoned by the Communists, read a letter from the pope urging the priests "to continue intrepidly in the spirit of St. Methodius on the path of evangelization and witness, even if the present situation makes it arduous, difficult, and even bitter."

"We felt how strong we were," said Bishop Frantisek Lobkowicz, who was a thirty-six-year-old pastor at the time. Until then the Church had not figured conspicuously in the Czech opposition, though some prominent Catholic intellectuals were affiliated with Charter 77, the umbrella organization of Czech resistance groups. Three months later, in "normalized" Czechoslovakia, 150,000 to 200,000 Catholic pilgrims marched to Velehrad for another observance in honor of St. Methodius. For months the government had tried to transform the event into a "peace festival." But when the Communist leaders took to the microphones, the pilgrims shouted back, "This is a pilgrimage! We want the pope! We want mass!" It was the largest independent gathering in Czechoslovakia since the Prague Spring of 1968.

～

The definitive sign that the era of martial law in Poland was finally ending came on September 11, 1986, when the regime announced a general amnesty and released the 225 prisoners who had been considered most dangerous to the state. The release of political prisoners had been the number one demand made by the underground since 1981.

For the first time in almost five years, all of Solidarity's leaders could meet freely. Polish jails were once more reserved for criminals, not political prisoners.

～

On January 13, 1987, for the first time since their conversation in the Wawel in 1981, John Paul II and General Jaruzelski met, in the pope's study in the Vatican. Jaruzelski would later describe the visit as "historic," because of what he saw as a crucial meeting of minds. For different reasons the pope's closest aides have used the term "historic" for the session. The discussion lasted eighty minutes, during which Jaruzelski delivered a firsthand report on his conversations with Gorbachev and what the general secretary called his new thinking.

By now, the regime was easing more of the restrictions on civil rights imposed during martial law: Travel in and out of the country was relatively easy, censorship had become less pervasive, the police less conspicuous, and some independent organizations were reinstated.

"I found that [the pope] had a complete understanding of the processes through which we were living," Jaruzelski said of their meeting. "I concluded that the pope saw in the trends and changes occurring in Poland a significance well beyond the Polish framework . . . that they [were], to a great extent, an impulse for the changes occurring in the other countries, especially in the Soviet Union."

By this time, Jaruzelski was openly courting the pope—and the forces of history. As usual, he sought the approval of those he admired, whether in the Kremlin or in the Vatican. In his (dubious) version of events, he claimed that, after imposing the brutal restrictions of martial law, he suddenly reversed direction out of a long-standing democratic impulse.

The pope's view of Jaruzelski, according to the people closest to John Paul II, was somewhat cooler than the general's perception of it, though there is no doubt that Wojtyla regarded Jaruzelski as above all a patriot. But in his dealings with Jaruzelski, the pope always tried to offer the general a vision preferable to Moscow's. This was one of his great accomplishments.

"The pope was aware," says Cardinal Deskur, "that Jaruzelski had a very strong religious background . . . Catholic school, Marian Fathers, etcetera. 'I think he is a man deeply *credente*—believing,' the pope said. 'He hasn't lost his faith.'" And Wojtyla intended to make the most of it.

∾

When Jaruzelski briefly visited Moscow in late April 1987 to sign a declaration of Soviet-Polish cooperation—in "ideology, science, and culture"—he was told by Gorbachev that *perestroika* was encountering fierce resistance.

John Paul II arrived triumphantly in Warsaw two months later, on June 8, 1987, for his third pontifical pilgrimage to his homeland, this time to reclaim Solidarity. Though his visit came against the backdrop of profoundly disturbing privation and suffering, the expectant spirit of his first pilgrimage—the hope, the excitement, the defiance—was in the air.

Solidarity was now operating in the open, though tentatively, and its adherents understandably held the authorities in great suspicion. During the week of his visit, the pope had met privately with Walesa near the Gdansk shipyard (after he finished his shift as an electrician) then served communion to him at a mass attended by hundreds of thousands. The pope made an unrelentingly emotional appeal to "the special heritage of Polish Solidarity," and each day his challenge to the regime became more overt.

At one of the most extraordinary masses of his pontificate, celebrated in Gdansk before a crowd of 750,000 workers and their families, the pope invoked the 1980 accords, tracing their roots to the bloody events at the shipyard in 1970. The Gdansk accords, he declared, "will go down in the history of Poland as an expression of the growing consciousness of the working people concerning the entire social-moral order on Polish soil." Looking out over a sea of Solidarity banners, the pope put aside his prepared text.

"I pray for you every day in Rome, I pray for my motherland and for you workers. I pray for the special heritage of Polish Solidarity." His audience was beside itself: weeping, applauding, praying, raising clenched fists.

John Paul II stood on a structure shaped like a gigantic ship, whose prow was in the form of St. Peter raising the keys to the kingdom and the Gospel in his hands. From his "ship," the pope told the crowd, "I'm glad to be here, because you have made me captain. . . . There is no struggle more effective than Solidarity!" He then asserted the workers' absolute right to "self-government." After the pope's speech in Gdansk, Walesa said, "I'm very happy. Now even a fool can understand that finding a passage in this labyrinth . . . requires Solidarity. This is the only road."

John Paul II used almost every stop of his journey to widen the perceived gulf between his vision and that of the regime—to the increasing chagrin of Jaruzelski. The pope called for a rethinking of the "very premises" of Poland's Communist order. "In the name of the future of mankind and of humanity the word 'solidarity' must be said out loud," he told hundreds of thousands of seamen at the port of Gdynia, near Gdansk, speaking from a towering altar set up near the harbor's gray waters. "This word was spoken right here, in a new way and in a new context. And the world cannot forget it. This word is your pride, Polish seamen."

The regime responded to the visit with television censorship, the deployment of tens of thousands of riot police, hundreds of detentions, and, finally, a bitter outburst by Jaruzelski at the farewell ceremonies for the pope at the Warsaw airport.

Following the pope's visit, events in Poland moved with methodical swiftness: At each important turn, the regime responded with half-measures to the pressures from Solidarity, the people, and the pope, and became overwhelmed. Recognizing that the economic reforms of the past five years had failed, it scheduled a referendum that asked Poles to vote for or against a program of radical economic change, dramatic austerity, and limited steps toward political pluralism. Solidarity urged a boycott of the referendum on the grounds that the government would use it as a vote of confidence. The boycott succeeded. When it failed to attract a majority of eligible voters to the polls, the government announced that it had lost the referendum, the first time in postwar history that a Communist government admitted that it had failed to win an election.

Trying to avoid direct negotiations with Walesa or other Solidarity leaders, Jaruzelski reached out to the Consultative Committee, whose members included Jerzy Turowicz and other Catholic intellectuals close to the pope. More than anything, Jaruzelski did not want to be the first Communist leader in the Warsaw Pact to be replaced by a non-Communist. There would be scores to settle. But his gesture was too little too late.

A series of spontaneous strikes in 1988 proved the turning point. Walesa had always warned that the workers would take matters into their own hands. The strikes, in April and May, turned into a tidal wave. But they weren't called by Solidarity. The strikers were almost all young, impoverished factory workers for whom the events of 1980 were the stuff of myth. They struck in anger because they were disgusted with their constantly eroding standard of living. Their raw emotions threatened chaos. The government flinched and turned to Walesa himself to coax the strikers back to work. But they refused—hundreds of thousands of them—until Jaruzelski and the regime promised that the government would begin talks about the country's future with an opposition that included Walesa.

On January 18, 1989, Jaruzelski announced that Solidarity would once again be legally recognized as a trade union. He had resigned as prime minister to become the president of Poland, with full executive powers. His successor as prime minister, Mieczyslaw Rakowski, formerly his deputy, made an official visit to Primate Glemp, as protocol dictated. Their conversation turned on the political situation, and Glemp now told the Communist Rakowski how essential it was to support Gorbachev's policies in the Soviet Union; he added that the pope was committed to those policies both in the USSR and in Poland.

On February 6, even as demonstrators around the country were protesting price increases, representatives of the government and the opposition sat down at what became known as the Round Table negotiations on the future of Poland. The end of an epoch was at hand.

The talks, quietly conducted under the aegis of the Church, lasted eight weeks and covered subjects ranging from economic policy to health care, from political reforms to the inalienable rights of Polish citizens. Walesa, General Czeslaw Kiszczak (the interior minister who had placed him under arrest in 1980), Politburo member Stanislaw Ciosek, and a gaggle of party advisers carried out the most sensitive part of the negotiations themselves, with Cardinal Macharski of Kraków or his representatives in attendance. "If neither side gave in," said Ciosek, "we always knew we could go to the Vatican for help."

The crucial agreement reached by the Round Table mandated free and open elections in June for seats to a new body to be called the Senate. The full legalization of Solidarity was also agreed upon.

When elections were held on June 4, Solidarity won all but one of the 262 seats it was allowed to contest. Parish priests had called on the faithful at mass that Sunday to back Solidarity candidates against the Communists. "This is a terrible result," said Jaruzelski. "It's the Church's fault."

Jaruzelski, with unofficial support from the union, narrowly won the presidency. But such a shaky coalition of two old foes was bound to fail. On August 19, Jaruzelski asked Tadeusz Mazowiecki, a Catholic intellectual who had advised Walesa during the Gdansk strikes of 1980, to form a cabinet, and on August 24 Mazowiecki became prime minister and Solidarity officially came to power.

Meanwhile, Walesa's first act after the Round Table accords were signed was to fly to Rome with five associates to thank John Paul II on behalf of Solidarity and the Polish people.

≈

The reverberations from the fall of Poland shook the Eastern bloc for the rest of the winter of 1989, until there was no bloc left.

And then there was the USSR.

≈

On December 1, 1989, the sidewalks of the great avenue leading to the Vatican were thronged with tens of thousands of people in a state of anticipation and excitement. The general secretary of the Communist Party of the USSR and the supreme pontiff of the Roman Catholic Church were about to meet for the first time.

Virtually every monsignor and archbishop of the Curia had stopped work to witness, either from an office window or on television, the arrival of Mikhail Gorbachev in his limousine (bearing the red flag with its hammer and sickle). For more than sixty years the Catholic Church and the Kremlin had struggled fiercely, and these men in black attire, trained in their seminaries to despise and fight the "enemies of God" throughout the world, had been in the front lines.

Yet the day before, in a speech in the Italian Capitol, the general secretary had spoken of the need for spirituality in the world. He had called for a "revolution in men's souls" while exalting "the eternal laws of humanity and morality of which Marx spoke."

"Religion helps *perestroika*," he declared. "We have given up pretending to have a monopoly on truth. . . . We no longer think that those who don't agree with us are enemies." This was truly a "new world order."

The first meeting between a general secretary of the USSR and a pontiff of the Roman Catholic Church was rich in symbolism for a new era.

Wojtyla, wearing his white robes, greeted Gorbachev and his wife, Raisa, enthusiastically in the reception room of the papal apartments. Then the two men adjourned to the pope's study.

"Generally speaking," the pope declared, "there are quite a few spots on this earth where peace is having a hard time. Perhaps we could act together in concert here." He was thinking particularly of regions with large Christian populations and historic Soviet influence.

Then John Paul offered the general secretary a homily on the subject of human rights:

> We have been waiting with great anxieties and hopes for the adoption, in your country, of a law on the freedom of conscience. We hope that the adoption of such a law will lead to a broadening of the possibilities of religious life for all Soviet citizens. A person becomes a believer by his own free will; it's impossible to force somebody to believe.

With such a law, the pope said, diplomatic relations between the Holy See and Moscow could move forward—something Gorbachev now desired more than the Vatican, owing to the need to strengthen his position at home and the pope's great international prestige. Gorbachev readily pledged that a law on freedom of conscience would soon be adopted by the Supreme Soviet.

∼

In August 1991, the Red Empire went into its death throes. At dawn on the 19th, in a coup d'etat, conservative members of the Politburo seized power in Moscow and put Gorbachev under house arrest in his Crimean dacha, announcing that he had been taken ill. Boris Yeltsin, president of the Russian Federal Republic, rebelled against the coup and transformed the Russian parliament building (called the White House for its marble facing) into the headquarters of the resistance.

Thanks to a radio transmitter belonging to Father van Straaten, which was intended to broadcast Catholic-Orthodox religious programs and was smuggled into the parliament's kitchens in a vegetable truck, Yeltsin was able to maintain contact with the outside world. His resistance prompted the West to support him.

A sincere cry of joy can be heard in the telegram that John Paul II sent to Gorbachev on August 23, the day the coup leaders surrendered: "I thank God for the happy outcome of the dramatic trial which involved your person, your family, and your country. I express my wish that you may continue your tremendous work for the material and spiritual renewal of the peoples of the Soviet Union, upon whom I implore the Lord's blessing."

John Paul II's hopes, like those of many other world leaders, were shortlived. Yeltsin's victorious resistance became a sign of the people's will to wipe out the Communist regime once and for all. On December 25, the man who invented *perestroika* left office, and in the afternoon the red flag was lowered over the green cupola of the Kremlin.

≈

Years later, much of the world came to hail Wojtyla as the conqueror of a war he had begun in 1978. The pope himself took a sober view. He expressly avoided parading as a kind of superman who had floored the Soviet bear. He urged his audience not to oversimplify things, not even to ascribe the fall of the USSR to the finger of God. When the Italian writer Vittorio Messori asked him about this, John Paul II replied: "It would be simplistic to say that Divine Providence caused the fall of communism. It fell by itself as a consequence of its own mistakes and abuses. It fell by itself because of its own inherent weakness."

John Paul II had experienced the crisis of communism from within, and above all he had meditated as a philosopher on the essence of communism's contradictions. Better than many Western politicians he understood that the Soviet system had collapsed through implosion. The external pressures had revealed the cracks in the system, but in the end the collapse had come from deep internal flaws.

In this collapse, economic and moral factors were interwoven. The economic resources of the USSR simply couldn't guarantee every citizen a secure existence, at however poor a level, while maintaining all the military apparatus of a superpower fighting a cold war. This was even clearer in the case of Communist East Germany, which, though far better organized than the USSR, was still facing economic bankruptcy on the eve of its collapse.

But it was above all ethical contradictions that had undermined the system. With Khrushchev the need for truth had stimulated an attempt to reform the system. With Brezhnev the denial of truth had produced stagnation and massive cynicism. With Gorbachev the thirst for truth, for *glasnost,* had become so intense as to overturn the system itself.

This theme of the truth and of the unsustainability of lies has always fascinated John Paul II in his thinking on totalitarianism. He read the works of both Andrei Sakharov and Aleksandr Solzhenitsyn and was moved by their moral conviction. Above all, Solzhenitsyn's booklet *Don't Lie* made a great impression on him, because he was convinced that the refusal to lie was the most powerful means of provoking a crisis in any totalitarian state. John Paul II spoke at length about ethics when Solzhenitsyn came to visit him in the Vatican in 1994. Communism, the pope had said in his first visit to post-Communist Prague in 1990, had "revealed itself to be an unattainable utopia because some essential aspects of the human person were neglected and negated: man's irrepressible longing for freedom and truth and his incapacity to feel happy when the transcendent relationship with God is excluded."

ERNEST EVANS

Observations: The Vatican and Castro's Cuba

Pope John Paul II is the best-traveled pope in history, and on his foreign travels he has shown no hesitation about speaking his mind, even when so speaking may upset his local hosts. As a consequence, his overseas visits often have resulted in friction with the local authorities. For example, when the pope visited Mexico in 1979 for a conference of the bishops of Latin America, the Mexican government went out of its way to emphasize the strict separation of church and state that exists in that country: At the airport, there were no papal flags, no banners proclaiming welcome, and no honor guard; the only official presence was Mexican President Jose Lopez Portillo and his wife Carmela, who were dressed as private citizens and who, after shaking the pope's hand and briefly greeting him, vanished into the crowd of well-wishers.[1] Similarly, when the pope visited Poland in 1983, two years after the repression of Solidarity, the Polish government allowed him to meet only briefly with Solidarity leader Lech Walesa; the government arranged the meeting in a secluded location and refused to allow the press to be present.[2] And, perhaps most famous, during his 1983 trip to Nicaragua the friction between the pope and his Sandinista hosts was so serious that the pope's outdoor mass was disrupted by pro-Sandinista protesters.[3]

The pope's visits to Mexico, Poland, and Nicaragua were all cases in which there was active hostility between the government in power and the local Catholic Church. As plans proceeded for the pope's January 1998 visit to Cuba there were fears of another such tense visit, in light of ongoing church-state conflicts in Cuba. But the visit was marked instead by mutual cordiality between the pope's party and the Castro government. In retrospect, such cordiality should not have been surprising because, while there are serious church-state disputes in Cuba, relations between the Castro regime and the Cuban church had never been as bad as they had been in most of the formerly Communist countries of the Soviet bloc.

There are other goals of Vatican foreign policy that also dictate accommodation and détente with Castro. However, it would be a mistake to assume that the warm and friendly atmosphere that marked the pope's visit to Cuba indicated a problem-free future for Vatican-Cuba relations; there remains great potential for conflict between these two parties. In this article I will discuss first the reasons for the Vatican's current policy of détente and accommodation with the Castro government, and then the reasons for possible serious conflicts.

The Castro government has never been as repressive of the Catholic Church as other Communist governments have been. The Cuban church did not make the mistake that the Mexican church made when it strongly opposed the uprising against the dictatorship of Porfirio Diaz.[4] Instead, although the Cuban hierarchy did not endorse Castro's struggle against Batista, it made clear its view that Batista should step down. Equally important, despite the fact that by 1961 Castro's revolution had become explicitly Communist, the Cuban church, while it strongly denounced the closing of church schools, universities, and newspapers, did not endorse armed counter-revolutionary efforts such as the 1961 Bay of Pigs invasion.[5] The importance of the church's not endorsing armed struggle against Castro is indicated by the fate of other churches that did call for the armed overthrow of Communist governments. In the Russian Civil War the Russian Orthodox Church endorsed the Whites' campaign against the Bolsheviks, and in the Spanish Civil War the Spanish Catholic Church endorsed the Nationalists. In both countries, thousands of clergy and dozens of bishops were killed.

However, Castro's relative benevolence toward the Cuban church is not based only on the church's not having called for armed resistance to his regime during its struggles to seize and consolidate power. Castro is well aware that despite the low levels of mass attendance by Catholics in Cuba and elsewhere in Latin America, there is a broad and deep respect for the church among the population—a respect and a reverence that can be awakened in the right circumstances, including the government repression of the church.[6] For example, in response to the growing radicalization of the Cuban revolution, including its increasingly anti-religion orientation, some one million Cubans attended the National Catholic Congress in Havana in November 1959; the previous year only 10,000 had attended this event.[7] And, in case Castro had any delusions that his decades in power had eradicated the popular Catholicism of the Cuban people, the pope's 1979 visit to Mexico—where he was greeted by huge and enthusiastic crowds—should have served to dispel any such notions. Several decades of strongly anticlerical government in Mexico had not eradicated that country's popular Catholicism.[8]

In brief, Castro had recognized with respect to Cuba what the Communist governments of Poland between 1945 and 1989 had also recognized: namely, their national Catholic Church had a deep enough hold on the loyalties of the populace that the sort of brutal repression of religion that took place in most Communist countries would have been most unwise. Joseph Stalin himself recognized that special accommodations had to be made with respect to the Polish church when he made his famous statement that fitting communism to Poland was like putting a saddle on a cow.[9]

The Vatican's policy toward Cuba is also influenced by the continuing (though diminished in recent years) appeal of the Castro regime to much of the Third World. In assessing this factor, one must understand that as the twentieth century has progressed the church has become, from its highest to its lowest levels, less and less a European church and more and more a Third World church. Whereas in 1900 there were 392 million Christians (Catholics, Protestants, Orthodox) in the developed world and 67 million in the rest of the world, in 1965 there were 637 million Christians in the developed countries and 370 million in the rest of the world. In 1960 there were 297 million Catholic Christians in the developed world and 251 million in the rest of the world; it is estimated that in the year 2000 there will be 380 million Catholics in the developed countries and 854 million in the rest of the world.[10] The steady growth in the Third World's proportion of church communicants has led to changes in the church hierarchy. Whereas in 1946 an absolute majority of the College of Cardinals was Italian and there was not a single cardinal from Asia or Africa, by the 1990s there were several dozen African and Asian cardinals.[11]

The Castro government's failure to significantly raise the living standards of the Cuban people—a failure made obvious to all after the end of the billions of dollars of annual foreign aid to Cuba following the 1991 collapse of the Soviet Union—has considerably reduced the appeal of the Cuban revolution in the Third World. Nevertheless, the Castro regime still evokes much sympathy in the developing world for the following reasons:

- Castro is seen as a hero by much of Latin America because he has defied "the colossus of the North" since 1959. The Cuban revolution's continuing appeal appeared in the explosion of Che Guevara memorabilia all over Latin America, especially among the young people, on the thirtieth anniversary of Guevara's death in 1997.

- Throughout the Third World, Castro has attracted support for his call for renunciation of the huge debts that most of those countries have incurred to banks in the developed world in the past twenty-five years. Many, if not most Third World leaders recognize that such a repudiation of their debts would be unwise in the long run, but even those who reject debt renunciation resent the banks of the developed countries. Therefore, Castro's call for debt renunciation (or at least a debt repayment moratorium) finds many sympathetic listeners in the Third World.

- In the aftermath of the collapse of the Soviet Union and the emergence of a world political system in which the United States is the sole superpower, there has been considerable resentment of what is seen as an overbearing and insensitive U.S. foreign policy. For example, the reluctance of most UN members to support U.S. military action against Iraq is rooted in large part in a sense that the United States is "bullying" Iraq. The continuation of tough U.S. sanctions against Cuba despite the collapse of the Soviet Union is also viewed by many in the Third World as "superpower bullying" of a poor country.

Yet the cordiality with which the Castro government received Pope John Paul II does not mean that there is no danger of future conflict. As has been widely reported, the pope and much of the leadership of the church are dismayed by what they see as the spread of the American "consumerist culture" throughout the formerly Communist countries of the Soviet bloc.[12] There can be little doubt that the overthrow of Cuban communism would also lead to a Cuban version of the same rampant consumerism. However, despite concerns that the dialectical materialism of communism has been replaced by a new consumer materialism, the church continues to strongly defend the basic human rights of freedom of speech, of conscience, of the press, and of assembly.

It is the Vatican's defense of these basic human rights that potentially puts it on a collision course with Castro's regime. A totalitarian government such as Castro's cannot allow its citizens such basic human rights without signing its own death warrant. This is the clear lesson of Mikhail Gorbachev's failed effort, through the reforms he called *glasnost* and *perestroika,* to reform the Soviet system without destroying the Communist Party's monopoly on political power.

Castro is no one's fool, as even his worst detractors will admit. He is well aware that the pope's visit to Cuba, in conjunction with his own efforts to make some reforms in the Cuban economy, could be the same sort of catalytic steps that set in motion the unraveling of the Communist governments of the Soviet bloc. Were the pope's visit and Castro's own reform efforts to lead, as in Poland after the 1979 papal visit, to efforts to organize independent trade unions and political groups, Castro would have to choose between the unpalatable options of reversing his own reforms and of watching his regime's power base fall apart.

Were Castro to respond to any stirrings of independent political organization with massive repression on the lines of the Polish government's repression of Solidarity in 1981, there can be little doubt that the Vatican would, as it did in Poland, support economic sanctions against Cuba. The Vatican learned some valuable lessons about the link between economic sanctions and democratization from its experience with Solidarity in Poland. The Vatican knew that the Communist government in Poland was mindful of the dangers of popular uprisings over economic conditions, such as those in Gdansk in 1970. Thus, the Polish government was frantic to lift the crippling economic sanctions imposed on Poland after the 1981 suppression of Solidarity. In the end, those sanctions caused enough pain that the Polish government had to choose between legalizing Solidarity, which it knew would soon result in its legally stepping down from power, and allowing popular discontent to build to violent revolution, as occurred in Romania in 1989.[13]

The Vatican believes that lifting the current U.S. sanctions against Cuba would give momentum to Castro's limited economic and political reforms. Moreover, the Vatican is aware of, and concerned about, the suffering of many ordinary people in Cuba because of U.S. sanctions. However, the Cuban government would be mistaken were it to assume that the Vatican's humanitarian concerns would cause it to oppose a return to sanctions in the event of a crackdown in Cuba. If the Vatican was willing to tolerate similar popular suffering in the pope's home country in the 1980s as a necessary sacrifice for the defense of basic human rights, there is no reason to believe that it would act any differently toward Cuba.

In sum, Fidel Castro would be making what could be the greatest mistake of his political career were he to believe that the warmth that marked Pope John Paul II's recent visit somehow represents a Vatican "stamp of approval" for his regime. True, the Vatican appreciates his policy of relative toleration for the Cuban Catholic Church and, conscious of its own growing Third World orientation, does not want to offend the many Catholics in the developing countries who admire Castro. But in the twentieth century the Vatican has learned through hard experience with both the Communist regimes of the Left and the Latin American national security states of the Right that it also has a very real stake in the defense of basic human rights. Hence it will continue to strongly press the Castro regime on those issues. At bottom, the message from the Vatican to Castro is simply this: Mr. Castro, your days as Cuba's dictator are numbered. You can depart à la Wojciech Jaruzelski, or à la Nicolae Ceausescu, which is to say, you can walk out or be carried out.

NOTES

1. Carl Bernstein and Marco Politi, *His Holiness: John Paul II and the Hidden History of Our Time* (New York: Doubleday, 1996), 202–3.

2. Ibid., 384–85.

3. Eric O. Hanson, *The Catholic Church in World Politics* (Princeton, NJ: Princeton University Press, 1987), 243–45.

4. J. Lloyd Mecham, *Church and State in Latin America* (Chapel Hill, NC: University of North Carolina Press, 1966), 380–82.

5. Ibid., 304–7.

6. Margaret Crahan, "Salvation Through Christ or Marx: Religion in Revolutionary Cuba." In *Churches and Politics in Latin America,* ed. Daniel H. Levine (Beverly Hills, CA: Sage Publications, 1980), 240–41.

7. Ibid.

8. Bernstein and Politi, *His Holiness,* 205–13.

9. Ibid., 75.

10. Andrej Kruetz, *Vatican Policy on the Palestinian-Israeli Conflict* (Westport, CT: Greenwood Press, 1990), 29.

11. Ibid., 4.

12. For a discussion of Pope John Paul II's concerns about what he sees as rampant consumerism in the late twentieth century see Bernstein and Politi, *His Holiness,* part 8, "The Angry Pope," 485–539.

13. Bernstein and Politi, *His Holiness,* 469–71.

$\sim$

JOSEPH RATZINGER
War Service and Imprisonment

Because of the increasingly worn-down condition of the men in the armed forces, our rulers came up with something new in 1943. They observed that boarding-school students already had to live in community away from their homes and that, therefore, nothing stood in the way of changing the place where they boarded—

namely, to the batteries of the anti-aircraft defense (Flak). And since in any event they could not be studying the whole day, it appeared quite normal to engage them in their free time for the service of defense against enemy planes. Even though I had not for quite a while now been in boarding school, still, juridically, I belonged to the minor seminary in Traunstein. So it was that the small group of seminarians from my class (those born in 1926 and 1927) were now drafted, and we had to go to the Flak in Munich. Being all of sixteen years of age, I now had to undertake a very peculiar kind of "boarding-school" existence. We lived in barracks like the regular soldiers, who were of course in the minority, wore uniforms similar to theirs, and basically had to perform the same services as they, with the only difference being that on the side we had in addition a reduced load of courses, given by the teachers of the renowned Maximilians-Gymnasium in Munich. In many respects this was an interesting experience. We now formed one class with the actual students of this *gymnasium,* who had likewise been drafted into the Flak, and so we entered a world that was new to us. Those of us from Traunstein were better in Latin and Greek, but we became aware that we had lived in the provinces and that the big city, with its multitude of cultural offerings, had opened other horizons to our new schoolmates. At first there was a lot of friction, but with time we all grew together to form a good community.

Our first location was Ludwigsfeld, to the north of Munich, where we had to protect a branch of the Bavarian Motor Works (BMW) that produced motors for airplanes. Then we went to Unterföhring, to the northwest of Munich, and for a brief time to Innsbruck, where the railroad station had been destroyed and protection seemed necessary. When no more attacks took place there, we were finally transferred to Gilching, just north of Lake Ammer, with a double commission: we had to defend the nearby Dornier-Werke, from which the first jets soared into the air, and, more generally, we had to stop the Allied flyers who gathered in this area for attacks on Munich.

I need not belabor the fact that my time with the Flak brought many an unpleasantness, particularly for so nonmilitary a person as myself. And yet I remember Gilching very fondly. There I belonged to telephone communications, and the noncommissioned officer in charge of us defended the autonomy of our group with tooth and nail. We were exempt from all military exercises, and no one dared to intrude into our little world. Autonomy reached its high point when I was assigned living quarters in the neighboring battery and, for inscrutable reasons, even got a room all to myself—primitive, but a real single room. Outside my hours of service, I could now do whatever I wanted and cultivate my interests without any hindrance. Besides, there was a surprisingly large group of active Catholics here who organized religious instruction and occasionally led visits to churches. And so, paradoxically, this summer is inscribed in my memory as a wonderful time of largely independent living.

To be sure, the overall climate of contemporary history was anything but encouraging. Early in the year our battery had been directly attacked, with one dead and many wounded as a result. In the summer, systematic large-scale attacks on

Munich began. Three times a week we were still allowed to travel into the city to attend classes at the Max-Gymnasium; but every time it was frightening to see new destruction and to experience how the city was falling into ruins bit by bit. The air was more and more filled with smoke and the smell of fire. In the end, regular train service was no longer possible. In this situation, most of us came to look on the Western allies' invasion of France, which finally began in July, as a sign of hope. Basically there was great trust in the Western powers and a hope that their sense of justice would also help Germany to begin a new and peaceful existence. However, which of us would live to experience it? None of us could be sure that he would live to return home from this inferno.

On September 10, 1944, having reached military age, we were released from the Flak, in which we had actually served as students. When I arrived home, the draft notice of the *Reichsarbeitsdienst* already lay on the table. On September 20 an endless trip took us to Burgenland, where we (including many friends from the *gymnasium* at Traunstein) were assigned to a camp in a spot where three countries— Austria, Czechoslovakia, and Hungary—meet. The weeks spent in the labor detail have left me with oppressive memories. Most of our superiors were former members of the so-called Austrian Legion and thus old Nazis who had done time in prison under Chancellor Dollfuss. They were fanatical ideologues who tyrannized us without respite. One night we were pulled out of bed and gathered together, half asleep in our exercise uniforms. An SS officer had each individual come forward and, by taking advantage of our exhaustion and exposing each of us before the gathered group, attempted to make "voluntary" recruits for the weapons branch of the SS. A whole series of good-natured friends were in this way forced into this criminal group. With a few others I had the good fortune of being able to say that I intended to become a Catholic priest. We were sent out with mockery and verbal abuse. But these insults tasted wonderful because they freed us from the threat of that deceitful "voluntary service" and all its consequences.

To begin with, we were trained according to a ritual invented in the 1930s, which was adapted from a kind of "cult of the spade," that is, a cult of work as redemptive power. An intricate military drill taught us how to lay down the spade solemnly, how to pick it up and swing it over the shoulder. The cleaning of the spade, which was not to show a single speck of dust, was among the essential elements of this pseudo-liturgy. This world of appearances suddenly collapsed overnight when neighboring Hungary, at whose border we were stationed, surrendered in October to the Russians, who in the meantime had penetrated deep into the center of the country. We thought we could hear the din of artillery at a distance; the front was drawing closer. Now the rituals with the spade came to an end, and every day we had to ride out to erect a so-called southwestern rampart: tank blockades and trenches, which we, along with an enormous army of allegedly volunteer workers from every country in Europe, had to dig directly across the fertile clay soil of Burgenland's vineyards. When we went home exhausted in the evening, the spades, which previously could not have a single speck of dust, now hung from the wall full of big clods of clay; but no one cared. Precisely this fall of the spade from cultic object to banal tool for everyday use allowed us to perceive the deeper collapse taking place there. A full-scale liturgy and the world behind it were being unmasked as a lie.

It was common practice, as the front drew closer, for those engaged in the work detail simply to be taken into the military. This is what we expected. But, to our grateful astonishment, something different happened. In the end, all work on the southwest rampart was stopped, and we lived in our camp without further orders. No cries of command were now heard, and an eerie, hollow silence reigned. On November 20 our suitcases with our civilian clothes were given back to us, and we were loaded onto railway cars. We thus undertook a journey home that was continually interrupted by air-raid alarms. Vienna, which only in September had still remained untouched by the events of the war, now showed the scars of bombs. I was even more strongly affected by the fact that in my beloved Salzburg not only did the train station lie in ruins, but it was evident from far off that the city's splendid centerpiece—the huge Renaissance cathedral—had been heavily damaged. If I remember correctly, the dome had caved in. Since, because of danger from the air, the train had to pass through Traunstein without stopping, the only thing to do was to jump off. It was an idyllically beautiful fall day. There was a bit of hoarfrost on the trees, and the mountains glowed in the afternoon sun. Seldom have I ever experienced the beauty of my homeland as on this return from a world disfigured by ideology and hatred.

Much to my amazement there was still no notice on the table drafting me into military service, as I might have expected. I had been granted almost three weeks for both interior and exterior renewal. Then we were called to Munich, where we were informed of our different destinations. The officer in charge was quite openly critical of the war and Hitler's system. He showed much understanding for us and tried to find the best possible assignment for each of us, the thing that would be most bearable. Thus, he assigned me to the infantry barracks in Traunstein, and with fatherly kindness he encouraged me to take a few more free days at home without rushing to report to my new post. The atmosphere I found in the barracks was a pleasant change from what I had known in the labor service. It is true that the head of the company liked to shout and that he apparently was still a faithful devotee of Nazism. But those in charge of our formation were experienced men who had tasted the horrors of war at the front and who did not want to make things more difficult for us than they already were. We celebrated Christmas in our living quarters with a heavy mood. Serving in the same unit with us young men there were several heads of families, nearly forty years of age, who, despite health problems, had now been called to arms in the last year of the war. My heart was deeply moved by their homesickness for wives and children. It was already difficult enough for them to be subjected to military drills like schoolboys along with us, who were twenty years their junior. After basic training, beginning in mid-January, we were continually relocated to different posts all around Traunstein, but, on account of an illness, I was largely exempt from military duty. Very strangely, we were not called to the front, which was drawing ever nearer. But we were given new uniforms and had to march through Traunstein singing war songs, perhaps in order to show the civilian population that the Führer still had young and freshly trained soldiers at his disposal. Hitler's death finally strengthened our hope that things would soon end. The unhurried manner of the American advance, however, deferred more and more the day of liberation.

At the end of April or the beginning of May—I do not remember precisely—I decided to go home. I knew that the city was surrounded by soldiers who had orders to shoot deserters on the spot. For this reason I used a little-known back road out of town, hoping to get through unmolested. But, as I walked out of a railroad underpass, two soldiers were standing at their posts, and for a moment the situation was extremely critical for me. Thank God that they, too, had had their fill of war and did not want to become murderers. Still, they had to find an excuse to let me go. Because of an injury I had my arm in a sling, and so they said: "Comrade, you are wounded. Move on!" In this way I came home unhurt. Sitting at the table were some of the English Sisters whom my sister knew well. They were poring over a map and trying to determine when we could finally count on the Americans' arrival. When I walked in, they thought that the presence of a soldier would be a sure protection for the house, but of course the opposite was the case. In the course of the next few days there lodged with us, first, a sergeant major of the air force, an agreeable Catholic from Berlin, who, following a strange logic we could not understand, still believed in the victory of the "German Reich." My father, who argued extensively with him on this matter, was finally able to win him over to the other side. Then two SS men were given shelter in our house, which made the situation doubly dangerous. They could not fail to see that I was of military age, and so they began to make inquiries about my status. It was a known fact that a number of soldiers who had left their units had already been hanged from trees by SS men. Besides, my father could not help voicing all his ire against Hitler to their faces, which as a rule should have had deadly consequences for him. But a special angel seemed to be guarding us, and the two disappeared the next day without having caused any mischief.

The Americans finally arrived in our village. Even though our house lacked all comfort, they chose it as their headquarters. I was identified as a soldier, had to put back on the uniform I had already abandoned, had to raise my hands and join the steadily growing throng of war prisoners whom they were lining up on our meadow. It especially cut my good mother's heart to the quick to see her boy and the rest of the defeated army standing there, exposed to an uncertain fate, prisoners under the custody of heavily armed Americans. We had hopes of being released soon, but Father and Mother quickly put together a number of things that could be useful for the road ahead, and I myself slipped a big empty notebook and a pencil into my pocket—which seemed a most impractical choice, but this notebook became a wonderful companion to me, because day by day I could enter into it thoughts and reflections of all kinds. I even tried my hand at Greek hexameters. During three days of marching, we advanced on the empty expressway in a column moving toward Bad Aibling that was gradually becoming endless. The American soldiers liked especially to take pictures of us, the youngest ones, and also of the oldest, in order to take home with them souvenirs of the defeated army and the woeful condition of its personnel. Then for a few days we lay about in an open field at the military airport of Bad Aibling, until we were shipped off to an area of enormous farmlands near Ulm, where about fifty thousand prisoners had been brought. The magnitude of these numbers apparently taxed the abilities of the Americans themselves. Until the end of our captivity, we slept outdoors. Our rations consisted of one ladleful of soup and a little bread per day. A few fortunate individuals had brought a tent with them into the prisoner-of-war camp. When, after a period of good weather, the rains started, "tent clubs" began to be formed for primitive protection against the inclemency of the weather. In front of us, at the very horizon, rose the majestic contours of the Ulm cathedral. Day after day the sight of it was for me like a consoling proclamation of the indestructible humaneness of faith. In the camp itself, moreover, numerous initiatives were undertaken to lend help. There were a few priests present who now celebrated Holy Mass every day in the open air. Those who came were not exactly a huge crowd, but they were grateful indeed. Theological students in their final semesters, and also academicians of different backgrounds (jurists, art historians, philosophers), began to meet formally, so that a wide-ranging program of conferences developed that brought some structure to our empty days. Real knowledge was imparted, and slowly friendships began to grow across the different blocks of the camp. We lived without a clock, without a calendar, without newspapers; only through rumors—often strangely distorted and confused—did something of what was happening in the larger world penetrate through the barbed-wire fence into our own separate world. Then, around the beginning of June, if I remember correctly, the releases began, and every new gap in our ranks was a sign of hope. The different occupations determined the order of release: farmers first, and last of all—because the least needed in this situation—students. Quite a few academicians understandably declared themselves to be farmers, and very many suddenly remembered a distant relative or acquaintance in Bavaria in order to be released into that region, because the American sector appeared to be the most secure and promising. Finally it was my turn, too. On June 19, 1945, I had to pass through the various inspections and interrogations, until, overjoyed, I held in my hand the certificate of release that made the end of the war a reality for me, too. We were brought by American trucks to the northern edge of Munich, and then each of us had to fend for himself in finding a way to get home. I teamed up with a young man from Trostberg, in the vicinity of Traunstein, to find our way home together. In three days we hoped to cover the 120 or so kilometers that separated us from our families. We planned to spend the night along the way with farming families, who would also give us a bite to eat. We had passed Ottobrunn when we were overtaken by a truck, powered by wood gas and loaded with milk. Both of us were too shy to signal to it, but the driver stopped on his own and asked us where we were headed. He laughed when we said that Traunstein was our destination, because he worked for a dairy in Traunstein and was now on his way home. So it was that, unexpectedly, I arrived in my home city even before sunset; the heavenly Jerusalem itself could not have appeared more beautiful to me at that moment. I heard praying and singing coming from the church: it was the evening of the Feast of the Sacred Heart of Jesus. I did not want to create a disturbance, so I did not go in. Rather, I rushed home as fast as I could. My father could hardly believe it as I suddenly stood there before him, alive and well. My mother and sister were in church. On the way home they learned from some girls that they had seen me rushing by. In my whole life I have never again had so magnificent a meal as the simple one that Mother then prepared for me from the vegetables of her own garden.

Yet something was still missing to make our joy complete. Since the beginning of April there had been no news from my brother. And so a quiet sorrow hung over our house. What an explosion of delight, then, when one hot July day we suddenly heard steps, and the one we had missed for so long suddenly stood there in our midst, with a brown tan from the Italian sun. Full of thanksgiving at his deliverance, he now sat down at the piano and intoned the hymn "Grosser Gott, wir loben dich" [Holy God, we praise thy Name]. The months that followed were full of a sense of newly won freedom, something we were only now learning really to treasure, and this period belongs to the most beautiful memories of my entire life. Little by little all of us who had been strewn so far apart began to gather again. We were continually searching each other out, exchanging recollections and comparing plans for our new life. My brother and I worked with other returnees to make the seminary buildings—so run-down after six years as a military hospital—again usable for their intended purpose. No books could be bought in a Germany that lay desolate and in a total economic shambles. But we could borrow some from the pastor and the seminary and so attempt to take our first steps into the unknown land of philosophy and theology. My brother devoted himself passionately to music, his particular gift. At Christmas we were able to organize a class reunion. Many had fallen in the war, and we who had returned home were all the more grateful for the gift of life and for the hope that again rose high above all destruction.

3. *On the World Stage*

JOHN PAUL II

Address to the Fiftieth General Assembly of the United Nations Organization

New York, October 5, 1995

Mr. President, Ladies and Gentlemen,

1. It is an honour for me to have the opportunity to address this international Assembly and to join the men and women of every country, race, language and culture in celebrating the fiftieth anniversary of the founding of the United Nations Organization. In coming before this distinguished Assembly, I am vividly aware that through you I am in some way addressing the whole family of peoples living on the face of the earth. My words are meant as a sign of the interest and esteem of the Apostolic See and of the Catholic Church for this Institution. They echo the voices of all those who see in the United Nations the hope of a better future for human society.

I wish to express my heartfelt gratitude in the first place to the Secretary General, Dr. Boutros Boutros-Ghali, for having warmly encouraged this visit. And I thank you, Mr. President, for your cordial welcome. I greet all of you, the members of this General Assembly: I am grateful for your presence and for your kind attention.

I come before you today with the desire to be able to contribute to that thoughtful meditation on the history and role of this Organization which should accompany and give substance to the anniversary celebrations. The Holy See, in virtue of its specifically spiritual mission, which makes it concerned for the integral good of every human being, has supported the ideals and goals of the United Nations Organization from the very beginning. Although their respective purposes and operative approaches are obviously different, the Church and the United Nations constantly find wide areas of cooperation on the basis of their common concern for the human family. It is this awareness which inspires my thoughts today; they will not dwell on any particular social, political, or economic question; rather, I would like to reflect with you on what the extraordinary changes of the last few years imply, not simply for the present, but for the future of the whole human family.

A COMMON HUMAN PATRIMONY

2. Ladies and Gentlemen! On the threshold of a new millennium we are witnessing an extraordinary global acceleration of that quest for freedom which is one of the great dynamics of human history. This phenomenon is not limited to any one part of the world; nor is it the expression of any single culture. Men and women throughout the world, even when threatened by violence, have taken the risk of freedom, asking to be given a place in social, political, and economic life which is commensurate with their dignity as free human beings. This universal longing for freedom is truly one of the distinguishing marks of our time.

During my previous Visit to the United Nations on 2 October 1979, I noted that the quest for freedom in our time has its basis in those universal rights which human beings enjoy by the very fact of their humanity. It was precisely outrages against human dignity which led the United Nations Organization to formulate, barely three years after its establishment, that Universal Declaration of Human Rights, which remains one of the highest expressions of the human conscience of our time. In Asia and Africa, in the Americas, in Oceania and Europe, men and women of conviction and courage have appealed to this Declaration in support of their claims for a fuller share in the life of society.

3. It is important for us to grasp what might be called the inner structure of this worldwide movement. It is precisely its global character which offers us its first and fundamental "key" and confirms that there are indeed universal human rights, rooted in the nature of the person, rights which reflect the objective and inviolable demands of a universal moral law. These are not abstract points; rather, these rights tell us something important about the actual life of every individual and of every social group. They also remind us that we do not live in an irrational or meaningless world. On the contrary, there is a moral logic which is built into human life and which makes possible dialogue between individuals and peoples. If we want a century of violent coercion to be succeeded by a century of persuasion, we must find a way to discuss the human future intelligibly. The universal moral law written on the human heart is precisely that kind of "grammar" which is needed if the world is to engage this discussion of its future.

In this sense, it is a matter for serious concern that some people today deny the universality of human rights, just as they deny that there is a human nature shared by everyone. To be sure, there is no single model for organizing the politics and economics of human freedom; different cultures and different historical experiences give rise to different institutional forms of public life in a free and responsible society. But it is one thing to affirm a legitimate pluralism of "forms of freedom," and another to deny any universality or intelligibility to the nature of man or to the human experience. The latter makes the international politics of persuasion extremely difficult, if not impossible.

TAKING THE RISK OF FREEDOM

4. The moral dynamics of this universal quest for freedom clearly appeared in Central and Eastern Europe during the nonviolent revolutions of 1989. Unfolding in specific times and places, those historical events nonetheless taught a lesson which goes far beyond a specific geographical location. For the nonviolent revolutions of 1989 demonstrated that the quest for freedom cannot be suppressed. It arises from a recognition of the inestimable dignity and value of the human person, and it cannot fail to be accompanied by a commitment on behalf of the human person. Modern totalitarianism has been, first and foremost, an assault on the dignity of the person, an assault which has gone even to the point of denying the inalienable value of the individual's life. The revolutions of 1989 were made possible by the commitment of brave men and women inspired by a different, and ultimately more profound and powerful, vision: the vision of man as a creature of intelligence and free will, immersed in a mystery which transcends his own being and endowed with the ability to reflect and the ability to choose—and thus capable of wisdom and virtue. A decisive factor in the success of those nonviolent revolutions was the experience of social solidarity: in the face of regimes backed by the power of propaganda and terror, that solidarity was the moral core of the "power of the powerless," a beacon of hope and an enduring reminder that it is possible for man's historical journey to follow a path which is true to the finest aspirations of the human spirit.

Viewing those events from this privileged international forum, one cannot fail to grasp the connection between the values which inspired those people's liberation movements and many of the moral commitments inscribed in the United Nations Charter: I am thinking, for example, of the commitment to "reaffirm faith in fundamental human rights (and) in the dignity and worth of the human person"; and also the commitment "to promote social progress and better standards of life in larger freedom" (Preamble). The fifty-one States which founded this Organization in 1945 truly lit a lamp whose light can scatter the darkness caused by tyranny—a light which can show the way to freedom, peace, and solidarity.

THE RIGHTS OF NATIONS

5. The quest for freedom in the second half of the twentieth century has engaged not only individuals but nations as well. Fifty years after the end of the Second World War, it is important to remember that that war was fought because of violations of the rights of nations. Many of those nations suffered grievously for no

other reason than that they were deemed "other." Terrible crimes were committed in the name of lethal doctrines which taught the "inferiority" of some nations and cultures. In a certain sense, the United Nations Organization was born from a conviction that such doctrines were antithetical to peace; and the Charter's commitment to "save future generations from the scourge of war" (Preamble) surely implied a moral commitment to defend every nation and culture from unjust and violent aggression.

Unfortunately, even after the end of the Second World War, the rights of nations continued to be violated. To take but one set of examples, the Baltic States and extensive territories in Ukraine and Belarus were absorbed into the Soviet Union, as had already happened to Armenia, Azerbaijan, and Georgia in the Caucasus. At the same time the so-called People's Democracies of Central and Eastern Europe effectively lost their sovereignty and were required to submit to the will dominating the entire bloc. The result of this artificial division of Europe was the Cold War, a situation of international tension in which the threat of a nuclear holocaust hung over humanity. It was only when freedom was restored to the nations of Central and Eastern Europe that the promise of the peace which should have come with the end of the war began to be realized for many of the victims of that conflict.

6. The Universal Declaration of Human Rights, adopted in 1948, spoke eloquently of the rights of persons; but no similar international agreement has yet adequately addressed the rights of nations. This situation must be carefully pondered, for it raises urgent questions about justice and freedom in the world today.

In reality the problem of the full recognition of the rights of peoples and nations has presented itself repeatedly to the conscience of humanity, and has also given rise to considerable ethical and juridical reflection. I am reminded of the debate which took place at the Council of Constance in the fifteenth century, when the representatives of the Academy of Krakow, headed by Pawel Wlodkowic, courageously defended the right of certain European peoples to existence and independence. Still better known is the discussion which went on in that same period at the University of Salamanca with regard to the peoples of the New World. And in our own century, how can I fail to mention the prophetic words of my predecessor, Pope Benedict XV, who in the midst of the First World War reminded everyone that "nations do not die," and invited them "to ponder with serene conscience the rights and the just aspirations of peoples" (*To the Peoples at War and Their Leaders*, 28 July 1915)?

7. Today the problem of nationalities forms part of a new world horizon marked by a great "mobility" which has blurred the ethnic and cultural frontiers of the different peoples, as a result of a variety of processes such as migrations, mass-media and the globalization of the economy. And yet, precisely against this horizon of universality we see the powerful reemergence of a certain ethnic and cultural consciousness, as it were an explosive need for identity and survival, a sort of counterweight to the tendency toward uniformity. This is a phenomenon which must not be underestimated or regarded as a simple left-over of the past. It demands seri-

ous interpretation, and a closer examination on the levels of anthropology, ethics, and law.

This tension between the particular and the universal can be considered immanent in human beings. By virtue of sharing in the same human nature, people automatically feel that they are members of one great family, as is in fact the case. But as a result of the concrete historical conditioning of this same nature, they are necessarily bound in a more intense way to particular human groups, beginning with the family and going on to the various groups to which they belong and up to the whole of their ethnic and cultural group, which is called, not by accident, a "nation," from the Latin word "nasci": "to be born." This term, enriched with another one, "patria" (fatherland/motherland), evokes the reality of the family. The human condition thus finds itself between these two poles—universality and particularity—with a vital tension between them; an inevitable tension, but singularly fruitful if they are lived in a calm and balanced way.

8. Upon this anthropological foundation there also rest the "rights of nations," which are nothing but "human rights" fostered at the specific level of community life. A study of these rights is certainly not easy, if we consider the difficulty of defining the very concept of "nation," which cannot be identified a priori and necessarily with the State. Such a study must nonetheless be made, if we wish to avoid the errors of the past and ensure a just world order.

A presupposition of a nation's rights is certainly its right to exist: therefore no one—neither a State nor another nation, nor an international organization—is ever justified in asserting that an individual nation is not worthy of existence. This fundamental right to existence does not necessarily call for sovereignty as a state, since various forms of juridical aggregation between different nations are possible, as for example occurs in Federal States, in Confederations, or in States characterized by broad regional autonomies. There can be historical circumstances in which aggregations different from single state sovereignty can even prove advisable, but only on condition that this takes place in a climate of true freedom, guaranteed by the exercise of the self-determination of the peoples concerned. Its right to exist naturally implies that every nation also enjoys the right to its own language and culture, through which a people expresses and promotes that which I would call its fundamental spiritual "sovereignty." History shows that in extreme circumstances (such as those which occurred in the land where I was born) it is precisely its culture that enables a nation to survive the loss of political and economic independence. Every nation therefore has also the right to shape its life according to its own traditions, excluding, of course, every abuse of basic human rights and in particular the oppression of minorities. Every nation has the right to build its future by providing an appropriate education for the younger generation.

But while the "rights of the nation" express the vital requirements of "particularity," it is no less important to emphasize the requirements of universality, expressed through a clear awareness of the duties which nations have vis-à-vis other nations and humanity as a whole. Foremost among these duties is certainly that of living in a spirit of peace, respect, and solidarity with other nations. Thus the exercise of the rights of nations, balanced by the acknowledgement and the practice of duties, promotes a fruitful "exchange of gifts," which strengthens the unity of all mankind.

RESPECT FOR DIFFERENCES

9. During my pastoral pilgrimages to the communities of the Catholic Church over the past seventeen years, I have been able to enter into dialogue with the rich diversity of nations and cultures in every part of the world. Unhappily, the world has yet to learn how to live with diversity, as recent events in the Balkans and Central Africa have painfully reminded us. The fact of "difference," and the reality of "the other," can sometimes be felt as a burden, or even as a threat. Amplified by historic grievances and exacerbated by the manipulations of the unscrupulous, the fear of "difference" can lead to a denial of the very humanity of "the other": with the result that people fall into a cycle of violence in which no one is spared, not even the children. We are all very familiar today with such situations; at this moment my heart and my prayers turn in a special way to the sufferings of the sorely tried peoples of Bosnia-Hercegovina.

From bitter experience, then, we know that the fear of "difference," especially when it expresses itself in a narrow and exclusive nationalism which denies any rights to "the other," can lead to a true nightmare of violence and terror. And yet if we make the effort to look at matters objectively, we can see that, transcending all the differences which distinguish individuals and peoples, there is a fundamental commonality. For different cultures are but different ways of facing the question of the meaning of personal existence. And it is precisely here that we find one source of the respect which is due to every culture and every nation: every culture is an effort to ponder the mystery of the world and in particular of the human person—it is a way of giving expression to the transcendent dimension of human life. The heart of every culture is its approach to the greatest of all mysteries: the mystery of God.

10. Our respect for the culture of others is therefore rooted in our respect for each community's attempt to answer the question of human life. And here we can see how important it is to safeguard the fundamental right to freedom of religion and freedom of conscience as the cornerstones of the structure of human rights and the foundation of every truly free society. No one is permitted to suppress those rights by using coercive power to impose an answer to the mystery of man.

To cut oneself off from the reality of difference—or, worse, to attempt to stamp out that difference—is to cut oneself off from the possibility of sounding the depths of the mystery of human life. The truth about man is the unchangeable standard by which all cultures are judged; but every culture has something to teach us about one or other dimension of that complex truth. Thus the "difference" which some find so threatening can, through respectful dialogue, become the source of a deeper understanding of the mystery of human existence.

11. In this context, we need to clarify the essential difference between an unhealthy form of nationalism, which teaches contempt for other nations or cultures, and patriotism, which is a proper love of one's country. True patriotism never seeks to advance the well-being of one's own nation at the expense of others. For in the end this would harm one's own nation as well: doing wrong damages both aggressor and victim. Nationalism, particularly in its most radical forms, is thus the antithesis of true patriotism, and today we must ensure that extreme nationalism does not continue to give rise to new forms of the aberrations of totalitarianism. This is a commitment which also holds true, obviously, in cases where religion itself is made the basis of nationalism, as unfortunately happens in certain manifestations of so-called fundamentalism.

FREEDOM AND MORAL TRUTH

12. Ladies and Gentlemen! Freedom is the measure of man's dignity and greatness. Living the freedom sought by individuals and peoples is a great challenge to man's spiritual growth and to the moral vitality of nations. The basic question which we must all face today is the responsible use of freedom, in both its personal and social dimensions. Our reflection must turn then to the question of the moral structure of freedom, which is the inner architecture of the culture of freedom.

Freedom is not simply the absence of tyranny or oppression. Nor is freedom a license to do whatever we like. Freedom has an inner "logic" which distinguishes it and ennobles it: freedom is ordered to the truth, and is fulfilled in man's quest for truth and in man's living in the truth. Detached from the truth about the human person, freedom deteriorates into license in the lives of individuals, and, in political life, it becomes the caprice of the most powerful and the arrogance of power. Far from being a limitation upon freedom or a threat to it, reference to the truth about the human person—a truth universally knowable through the moral law written on the hearts of all—is, in fact, the guarantor of freedom's future.

13. In the light of what has been said we understand how utilitarianism, the doctrine which defines morality not in terms of what is good but of what is advantageous, threatens the freedom of individuals and nations and obstructs the building of a true culture of freedom. Utilitarianism often has devastating political consequences, because it inspires an aggressive nationalism on the basis of which the subjugation, for example, of a smaller or weaker nation is claimed to be a good thing solely because it corresponds to the national interest. No less grave are the results of economic utilitarianism, which drives more powerful countries to manipulate and exploit weaker ones.

Nationalistic and economic utilitarianism are sometimes combined, a phenomenon which has too often characterized relations between the "North" and the "South." For the emerging countries, the achievement of political independence has too frequently been accompanied by a situation of de facto economic dependence on other countries; indeed, in some cases, the developing world has suffered a regression, such that some countries lack the means of satisfying the essential needs of their people. Such situations offend the conscience of humanity and pose a formidable moral challenge to the human family. Meeting this challenge will obviously require changes in both developing and developed countries. If developing countries are able to offer sure guarantees of the proper management of resources and of assistance received, as well as respect for human rights, by replacing where necessary unjust, corrupt, or authoritarian forms of government with participatory and democratic ones, will they not in this way unleash the best civil and economic energies of their people? And must not the developed countries, for their part, come to renounce strictly utilitarian approaches and develop new approaches inspired by greater justice and solidarity?

Yes, distinguished Ladies and Gentlemen! The international economic scene needs an ethic of solidarity, if participation, economic growth, and a just distribution of goods are to characterize the future of humanity. The international cooperation called for by the Charter of the United Nations for "solving international problems of an economic, social, cultural, or humanitarian character" (art. 1.3) cannot be conceived exclusively in terms of help and assistance, or even by considering the eventual returns on the resources provided. When millions of people are suffering from a poverty which means hunger, malnutrition, sickness, illiteracy, and degradation, we must not only remind ourselves that no one has a right to exploit another for his own advantage, but also and above all we must recommit ourselves to that solidarity which enables others to live out, in the actual circumstances of their economic and political lives, the creativity which is a distinguishing mark of the human person and the true source of the wealth of nations in today's world.

THE UNITED NATIONS AND THE FUTURE OF FREEDOM

14. As we face these enormous challenges, how can we fail to acknowledge the role of the United Nations Organization? Fifty years after its founding, the need for such an Organization is even more obvious, but we also have a better understanding, on the basis of experience, that the effectiveness of this great instrument for harmonizing and coordinating international life depends on the international culture and ethic which it supports and expresses. The United Nations Organization needs to rise more and more above the cold status of an administrative institution and to become a moral centre where all the nations of the world feel at home and develop a shared awareness of being, as it were, a "family of nations." The idea of "family" immediately evokes something more than simple functional relations or a mere convergence of interests. The family is by nature a community based on mutual trust, mutual support, and sincere respect. In an authentic family the strong do not dominate; instead, the weaker members, because of their very weakness, are all the more welcomed and served.

Raised to the level of the "family of nations," these sentiments ought to be, even before law itself, the very fabric of relations between peoples. The United

Nations has the historic, even momentous, task of promoting this qualitative leap in international life, not only by serving as a centre of effective mediation for the resolution of conflicts but also by fostering values, attitudes, and concrete initiatives of solidarity which prove capable of raising the level of relations between nations from the "organizational" to a more "organic" level, from simple "existence with" others to "existence for" others, in a fruitful exchange of gifts, primarily for the good of the weaker nations but even so, a clear harbinger of greater good for everyone.

15. Only on this condition shall we attain an end not only to "wars of combat" but also to "cold wars." It will ensure not only the legal equality of all peoples but also their active participation in the building of a better future, and not only respect for individual cultural identities, but full esteem for them as a common treasure belonging to the cultural patrimony of mankind. Is this not the ideal held up by the Charter of the United Nations when it sets as the basis of the Organization "the principle of the sovereign equality of all its Members" (art. 2.1), or when it commits it to "develop friendly relations between nations based on respect for the principle of equal rights and of self-determination" (art. 1.2)? This is the high road which must be followed to the end, even if this involves, when necessary, appropriate modifications in the operating model of the United Nations, so as to take into account everything that has happened in this half century, with so many new peoples experiencing freedom and legitimately aspiring to "be" and to "count for" more.

None of this should appear an unattainable utopia. Now is the time for new hope, which calls us to expel the paralyzing burden of cynicism from the future of politics and of human life. The anniversary which we are celebrating invites us to do this by reminding us of the idea of "united nations," an idea which bespeaks mutual trust, security, and solidarity. Inspired by the example of all those who have taken the risk of freedom, can we not recommit ourselves also to taking the risk of solidarity—and thus the risk of peace?

BEYOND FEAR: THE CIVILIZATION OF LOVE

16. It is one of the great paradoxes of our time that man, who began the period we call "modernity" with a self-confident assertion of his "coming of age" and "autonomy," approaches the end of the twentieth century fearful of himself, fearful of what he might be capable of, fearful for the future. Indeed, the second half of the twentieth century has seen the unprecedented phenomenon of a humanity uncertain about the very likelihood of a future, given the threat of nuclear war. That danger, mercifully, appears to have receded—and everything that might make it return needs to be rejected firmly and universally; all the same, fear for the future and of the future remains.

In order to ensure that the new millennium now approaching will witness a new flourishing of the human spirit, mediated through an authentic culture of freedom, men and women must learn to conquer fear. We must learn not to be afraid, we must rediscover a spirit of hope and a spirit of trust. Hope is not empty optimism springing from a naive confidence that the future will necessarily be better than the past. Hope and trust are the premise of responsible activity and are nurtured in that inner sanctuary of conscience where "man is alone with God" (*Gaudium et Spes,* 16) and he thus perceives that he is not alone amid the enigmas of existence, for he is surrounded by the love of the Creator!

Hope and trust: these may seem matters beyond the purview of the United Nations. But they are not. The politics of nations, with which your Organization is principally concerned, can never ignore the transcendent, spiritual dimension of the human experience, and could never ignore it without harming the cause of man and the cause of human freedom. Whatever diminishes man—whatever shortens the horizon of man's aspiration to goodness—harms the cause of freedom. In order to recover our hope and our trust at the end of this century of sorrows, we must regain sight of that transcendent horizon of possibility to which the soul of man aspires.

17. As a Christian, my hope and trust are centered on Jesus Christ, the two thousandth anniversary of whose birth will be celebrated at the coming of the new millennium. We Christians believe that in his Death and Resurrection were fully revealed God's love and his care for all creation. Jesus Christ is for us God made man, and made a part of the history of humanity. Precisely for this reason, Christian hope for the world and its future extends to every human person. Because of the radiant humanity of Christ, nothing genuinely human fails to touch the hearts of Christians. Faith in Christ does not impel us to intolerance. On the contrary, it obliges us to engage others in a respectful dialogue. Love of Christ does not distract us from interest in others, but rather invites us to responsibility for them, to the exclusion of no one and indeed, if anything, with a special concern for the weakest and the suffering. Thus, as we approach the two thousandth anniversary of the birth of Christ, the Church asks only to be able to propose respectfully this message of salvation, and to be able to promote, in charity and service, the solidarity of the entire human family.

Ladies and Gentlemen! I come before you, as did my predecessor Pope Paul VI exactly thirty years ago, not as one who exercises temporal power—these are his words—nor as a religious leader seeking special privileges for his community. I come before you as a witness: a witness to human dignity, a witness to hope, a witness to the conviction that the destiny of all nations lies in the hands of a merciful Providence.

18. We must overcome our fear of the future. But we will not be able to overcome it completely unless we do so together. The "answer" to that fear is neither coercion nor repression, nor the imposition of one social "model" on the entire world. The answer to the fear which darkens human existence at the end of the twentieth century is the common effort to build the civilization of love, founded on the universal values of peace, solidarity, justice, and liberty. And the "soul" of the civilization of love is the culture of freedom: the freedom of individuals and the freedom of nations lived in self-giving solidarity and responsibility.

We must not be afraid of the future. We must not be afraid of man. It is no accident that we are here. Each and every human person has been created in the "image and likeness" of the One who is the origin of all that is. We have within us the capacities for wisdom and virtue. With these gifts, and with the help of God's grace, we can build in the next century and the next millennium a civilization worthy of the human person, a true culture of freedom. We can and must do so! And in doing so, we shall see that the tears of this century have prepared the ground for a new springtime of the human spirit.

~

DEREK S. JEFFREYS

John Paul II and Participation in International Politics

The failure of the United Nations to prevent, and subsequently, to stop the genocide in Rwanda was a failure by the United Nations system as a whole. The fundamental failure was the lack of resources and political commitment devoted to developments in Rwanda and the United Nations presence there. There was a persistent lack of political will by Member States to act, or to act with enough assertiveness.[1]
—Report of the Independent Inquiry into the Actions of the United Nations during the 1994 Genocide in Rwanda

Hope and trust: these may seem matters beyond the purview of the United Nations. But they are not. The politics of nations, with which your Organization is principally concerned, can never ignore the transcendent, spiritual dimensions of the human experience, and could never ignore it without harming the cause of man and the cause of freedom.

—John Paul II[2]

When John Paul II appeared before the United Nations General Assembly in 1995, he confronted political realities drastically different from those he faced in 1979. At the United Nations in 1979, he spoke to a "bipolar" world divided between the United States and the Soviet Union. People referred to the "Third World," those political communities outside the orbit of the two superpowers. In 1995, this had all changed. The Soviet Union had collapsed, a host of new nation-states had emerged, and the United States became the sole superpower. In this new context, John Paul II urged the United Nations to promote international solidarity. In a compelling speech, he called upon nations to embrace a "civilization of love" that values the dignity of the human person. He insisted that the "United Nations organization needs to rise more and more above the cold status of an administrative institution and to become a moral centre where all the nations of the world feel at home and develop a shared awareness of being, as it were, a 'family of nations'" (1995UN, 14). Despite its moral and rhetorical power, however, there was something disturbing about John Paul II's speech. Coming on the heels of the United Nations' abject failure to prevent genocide in Rwanda, his comments about a family of nations had an air of unreality about them. The Member States of the UN showed little or no concern for members of their "family" on the African continent. Repeatedly, they stifled constructive responses to the Rwandan crisis, haggling over the definition of genocide while hundreds of thousands of people died. This terrible failure had little or no impact on John Paul II's speech to the United Nations. He mentions the Rwandan genocide, and clearly, some of his remarks about virulent nationalism apply to it. However, he never discusses why the so-called international community utterly failed to stop it. After so much post–World War II rhetoric about preventing genocide, this failure represented a moral stain on international relations. The contrasts between John Paul II's words about a family of nations and the realities of peacekeeping were stunning.

Undoubtedly, John Paul II understands the darker elements of politics, articulating a conception of sin that reduces utopian aspirations. He also undermines the ethical consequentialism so dominant in international politics. However, unlike many realists, John Paul II often ignores clashes between his ethical ideals. Realists emphasize the ambiguities of political choices, arguing that we often confront clashes of values that admit of no easy resolution. John Paul II develops rich conceptions of peace, human rights, democracy, and international relations, but often leaves the details of implementation to policy-makers. Unfortunately, this creates difficulties when he considers issues like humanitarian intervention. Humanitarian intervention presents the United Nations with seemingly intractable problems that drive many to despair. East Timor, Sierra Leone, Liberia, Somalia, the Congo, the former Yugoslavia, Kosovo, and Afghanistan have all seen humanitarian crises that seemed impossible to resolve. They brought responses from the international community, some successful but others utterly futile. These events provoked considerable ethical and political debate with important implications for a new century that has begun with terrorism and war.

In this chapter, I consider how John Paul II applies his ethic to humanitarian and military intervention. First, I outline the ethical issues in humanitarian intervention, describing realist and liberal approaches to it. On one hand, intervention may prevent genocide or mass starvation, embodying the virtue of solidarity. On the other hand, it may undermine state sovereignty, allowing intervening states to cavalierly override national self-determination. Second, I carefully outline John Paul II's understanding of participation, describing how it shapes his approach to international politics. Participation illustrates how he creatively uses the phenomenology of moral cognition to analyze international affairs. Third, applying the concept of participation to international politics, I explore John Paul II's account of the rights of nations, a civilization of love, and our duty to undertake humanitarian intervention. I suggest that prima facie, these elements of his political thought conflict, producing an acute clash between human rights and the right to national identity. Fourth, I discuss how some contemporary thinkers resolve such conflicts by invoking "moral blind alleys," the "lesser of two evils," and the just war principle of proportionality. I argue that these approaches succumb to the difficulties inherent in consequentialism. Fifth, I argue that John Paul II can address conflicts in his political thought by altering his concept of the rights of nations. As a personalist, he should attribute rights to nations only analogically, explicitly subordinating them to the value of the person. Finally, I maintain that John Paul II fails to apply his conception of sin to the United Nations. He urges it to cultivate deep knowledge of the person, but I argue that its response to the Rwandan genocide indicates that it can barely promote knowledge of our common humanity.

SHOULD WE INTERVENE?
THE DILEMMAS OF HUMANITARIAN INTERVENTION

In the 1990s, the tragedies in the former Yugoslavia, Rwanda, and Somalia led to a heated debate about morality and humanitarian intervention. It took place within the larger context of fundamental changes in international politics. In the place of the two superpowers, the United States emerged as the central military and economic power, with no serious rivals. Regional powers like China and the European Union also developed. Japan and other Asian countries confronted serious economic difficulties, generating great uncertainty about the global financial system. Finally, at the beginning of this century, terrorism emerged as a major threat to industrialized nations. J. Bryan Hehir argues that such changes have "eroded ideas once taken for granted in the discussion of world politics. At stake in the process are the two key principles of international order: the sovereignty of states and the norm of nonintervention" (Hehir 1995, 2). Often ignored practically, these ideas nevertheless played a central role in international politics in the last three hundred years.

In recent years, support for them has waned, challenged by human rights activists, international law, terrorism, preemptive military action, and economic interdependence. Ignatieff details how in the 1990s, a "humanitarian internationalism" emerged, a vision of international politics guided by "one set of minimum norms to which every regime in the world formally subscribed" (Ignatieff 1997, 89).[3] Numerous organizations created constituencies for international development, new human rights regimes appeared, along with "newly globalized media like CNN to create a popular demand for international humanitarian intervention" (ibid., 90). Ignatieff boldly claims that changes in media, information, and other technologies made it increasingly impossible to restrict moral concern to family, neighborhood, and province, thus changing "the modern moral imagination" (ibid.). Many in industrialized democracies extended their moral concern to people living far away from them. This concern, along with the normal self-interested behavior of nations, led to the large-scale humanitarian interventions of the 1990s. For humanitarian internationalists, these interventions proved to be a great disappointment. Unable to fundamentally change the international system, in despair, many retreated from activism. Some in the United States and Western Europe responded to perceived failures in Bosnia and Somalia by withdrawing from internationalism and embracing forms of isolationism. Harshly condemning these developments, Ignatieff nevertheless acknowledges that the "internationalism of the early 1990s resembles less the creative moment of 1945 than the failure of Wilsonian internationalism after World War I" (ibid., 91). Echoing these comments at the end of the 1990s, Michael J. Smith called humanitarian efforts "global evangelism" for a new international system, but noted that it "at best limps along, led by a motley if erudite array of philosophers and human-rights activists" (Smith 1999, 278).

Despite such developments, however, humanitarian internationalism embodied ideas that remain important for international politics. To illustrate this point, I employ Smith's helpful distinction between liberal and realist approaches to humanitarian intervention. Undoubtedly, the liberal tradition has often rigidly supported the nation-state system but also contains "a more universalist conception of human rights in which sovereignty is a subsidiary and conditional value" (Smith 1999, 278). On this view, according sovereignty an absolute value may support an unjust status quo, perpetuated by extremist demagogues who allegedly represent nations. To prevent this injustice, we ought to subordinate sovereignty to human rights and occasionally intervene in the affairs of other nations. The liberal conception of intervention assumes that the moral standing of a society "rests on its ability to respect and to protect the rights of its members and on their consent, explicit or implicit, to its rules and institutions" (ibid., 288). For example, Saddam Hussein's tyrannical regime in Iraq lacked moral legitimacy because it trampled on the rights of its citizens. From a moral point of view, "we look at social groupings formed by persons as derivative and constructed and as drawing their legitimacy from the will and consent of these persons" (ibid.). State sovereignty should never trump all other values, and it cannot immunize a state from outside intervention to stop ethnic cleansing, genocide, or other crimes. Humanitarian intervention, therefore, may be justified in order to override the sovereignty of an abusive state.

Smith also describes a realist approach to humanitarian intervention that emphasizes state sovereignty. Realists often maintain that humanitarian intervention represents little more than a fig leaf for the pursuit of national interest. Nation-states act entirely in their self-interest, and therefore, we ought to be wary of calls to help those suffering from famine or war. In international affairs, nations are well advised to pursue their national interests, rather than getting bogged down in overseas adventures that waste treasure and lives.[4] Henry Kissinger articulates this realist vision well, defending the Westphalian state system put in place by European powers in the seventeenth century (Kissinger 2001). This arrangement proscribed religious and political interference in the affairs of other states, producing the concept of noninterference in domestic politics. In Kissinger's view, this system maintained peace and order in international affairs for much of the nineteenth century. Although it did not prevent wars altogether, it limited them, preventing messianic interference in international relations.[5]

Kissinger sees the humanitarian interventions of the 1990s as disastrous departures from the Westphalian system that amount to "a revolution in the way the international system has operated for more than three hundred years" (Kissinger 2001, 235). Commenting on American interventions, he argues that "the new doctrine of humanitarian intervention asserts that humane convictions are so integral a part of the American tradition that both treasure and, in the extreme, lives must be risked to vindicate them around the world" (ibid., 253). For Kissinger, this doctrine embodies a moralism that ignores historical and political context. Moreover, it has an ad hoc character, driven by domestic politics and media attention. It is highly selective; American and European powers occupy Kosovo but disregard human rights violations in Chechnya, "intervene in Bosnia, but refuse to send military forces to Sierra Leone" (ibid., 257). Like many realists before him, Kissinger roundly condemns such selective moralism, accusing humanitarian internationalists of easing their consciences while ignoring widespread suffering.

With Kissinger, then, we see the elements of the realist approach to humanitarian intervention. For the realist, we should avoid making universal claims about a moral obligation to intervene, focusing instead on interventions serving a nation's national interest. We should pay careful attention to historical context, rejecting abstract principles that have little bearing on concrete political realities. Finally, we should be very attentive to how humanitarian interventions affect the nation-state system. The principle of nonintervention has served international politics well, preventing religious and political zealots from imposing their views on others. We should think hard before jettisoning it, particularly when confronting well-organized terrorist movements seeking to undermine world order.

This realist vision conflicts fundamentally with liberal approaches to humanitarian intervention. Liberals emphasize human rights before sovereignty, refusing to credit the Westphalian system with the benefits Kissinger ascribes to it. Instead of focusing on the national interest, they consider the rights of stateless populations and promote international human rights regimes. Instead of emphasizing the particulars of international politics, liberals embrace universal conceptions of human rights. Particular cases illustrate conflicts between liberal and realist principles. For example, early in the 1990s crisis in the former Yugoslavia, the Vatican and some European powers alienated Serbia by officially recognizing Croatia and Slovenia as nation-states.[6] On one hand, this seemed like a legitimate acknowledgment of the right to self-determination, an important element in the nation-state system. On the other hand, as both Serbia and later Croatia began committing terrible crimes within their new "nations," many Americans and Europeans called for NATO to stop them. National sovereignty and respect for human rights clashed, and few people at the time knew how to resolve this conflict.

PARTICIPATION: THE KEY TO UNDERSTANDING
INTERNATIONAL POLITICS

When approaching these kinds of problems, John Paul II draws heavily on the concept of participation, a product of his engagement with phenomenology. He develops this idea in order to capture the lived experience of communal action. By using it as opposed to the concept of intersubjectivity, he emphasizes how action reveals the person. *Intersubjectivity* is an important term for Husserl, describing the way in which multiple subjects shape consciousness by interacting. However, for John Paul II, it suggests primarily the "cognitive dimensions of intersubjectivity," rather than action as the "fundamental source for the cognition of man as person" (Wojtyla 1979, 315 n. 75).[7] Understanding cognition is indispensable for political life, but John Paul II thinks the acting person should be our focus. He also distinguishes his notion of participation from metaphysical understandings of the term, which Aquinas retrieved and developed from Neoplatonic sources.[8] Instead of developing a comprehensive participatory metaphysic, John Paul II analyzes how persons experience communal action.

Participation, John Paul II writes, is a "property of the person, a property that expresses itself in the ability of human beings to endow existence and action with a personal (personalistic) dimension when they exist and act together with others" (Wojtyla 1993, 237). Human beings often act and live together; however, this fact indicates "nothing about community, but speaks only of a multiplicity of beings, of acting subjects, who are people" (ibid., 238). A community, in contrast, denotes a "specific unity," a relation or sum of relations among individuals that is accidental to them (ibid.). Objectively, we can use the unity of persons to classify associations, but subjectively, we can also consider how a group affects its members' lived experience. In fact, the concept of participation involves a "positive relation to the humanity of others, understanding *humanity* here not as the abstract idea of the human being," but as "the personal self, in each instance unique and unrepeatable" (ibid., 237). Metaphysically, we define communities by focusing on beings and relations, and as a Thomist, John Paul II endorses this analysis. However, he also thinks that participation reveals elements of lived experience often absent in purely metaphysical analyses. As I noted in the last chapter, he presents a gradual movement from categorial knowledge of species-membership to knowledge of the person's particularity. Participation presupposes categorial knowledge of the person's value, an awareness that persons and things differ in value. Nevertheless, it is a preliminary step toward deeper knowledge of a person. John Paul II proposes that at the political level, we gradually come to know the irreducibility of persons.

To understand how such a radical change occurs, John Paul II describes dyadic structures of community. The first, the *I-thou* relationship, reflects the "interhuman, interpersonal dimension of community" (Wojtyla 1993, 241). I recognize another person as "one of many whom I could describe" (Wojtyla 1993, 243). I relate to her but am also potentially related to others. John Paul II emphasizes the *reflexivity* of this relationship, saying that when I relate to her, I acknowledge a "relation that somehow proceeds from me, but also returns to me" (ibid., 241). In this way, I partially constitute myself through my relations.[9]

In the I-thou relationship, two people "mutually become an *I* and a *thou* for each other and experience their relationship in this manner" (Wojtyla 1993, 243). By acting and reacting to each other, they constitute a unique form of human community. Factually, they come to know each other as personal subjects, but they also sense that they ought to "abide in mutual affirmation of the transcendent value of the persons (a value that may also be called *dignity)* and 'confirm' this in action" (ibid., 247). The "ought" thus enters into a factual relationship. In this analysis, I think we again see the limitations of the "is-ought" problem in twentieth-century ethics. What appears to be merely a fact, a relationship between persons, also contains a normative element that we uncover through lived experience. Summarizing the elements of the I-thou form of community, John Paul II says that it is "reducible to treating and really experiencing 'the other as oneself' (to use an expression taken directly from the Gospel)" (ibid., 244).

John Paul II contrasts the I-thou form of community with the *I-we* form, which he identifies with the traditional Roman Catholic concept of the common good. It differentiates social and interpersonal dimensions of community, highlighting how our relationships presuppose and form larger communities. The *we* in the dyad *I-we* refers "directly to multiplicity and indirectly to the persons belonging to this multiplicity" (Wojtyla 1993, 246). It originates when multiple persons become aware that they are united around a value, form a specific *we,* and partially constitute themselves by relating to it. The I-we link is also both a fact and a task because we *find* ourselves related to others in community, but must also *will* to foster this relationship. It takes on a normative character, because we feel the pull of an authentic community calling us to unite around a common value. Recasting a traditional teaching about the common good, John Paul II argues that it has a "greater fullness of value than the individual good of each separate *I* in a particular community" (ibid., 250). It is also "essentially free from utilitarianism," eliciting sacrifices that utilitarianism cannot explain (ibid., 251). Human persons grasp its great *spiritual* value, are often willing to sacrifice their lives for it, and eschew utilitarianism's myopic calculations of self-interest.

Importantly, John Paul II suggests that the common good can be "quantitatively diverse: two in the case of marriage (no longer just one + one, but a couple), several in the case of the family, millions in the case of a particular nation, billions in the case of all humankind" (Wojtyla 1993, 249). Subject to differentiation, it is an analogy of proportionality. An analogy of proportionality exists when "the intrinsic similarity between analogates is expressed by a term that is applied to all the analogates in its proper and literal meaning, but with a proportional difference as found in each" (Clarke 2001, 49). For example, we apply the concept of the common good "in accord with the specific communal nature" proper to a community (Wojtyla 1993, 251). In different associations, persons realize it differently, but each association must be a "clear reflection of the human *I,* of personal subjectivity, rather than something opposed to this subjectivity. And if it happens to be opposed, human beings as subjects must institute reforms" (ibid.).

In this presentation of participation, I again see John Paul II's differences with Scheler. As a task, participation is a potentiality we must will to actualize (Wojtyla 1993, 202–3). Referring specifically to Scheler, John Paul II asks if the impulse toward participation is emotional and spontaneous, suggesting that this is how Scheler understands it.[10] He notes that emotions are "enormous resources, variously distributed among people," and acknowledges that Scheler establishes a "basic, innate disposition to participate in humanity as a value, to spontaneously open up to others" (ibid., 203). Nevertheless, Scheler mistakenly thinks we can achieve participation by relying solely on emotion. This is erroneous, John Paul II argues, because we must choose to affirm one person among others. Emotional connections surely "facilitate this choice," but by themselves, they are insufficient to actualize it (ibid., 204). People may, for example, sympathize with those suffering from famine, but unless they will to develop solidarity with them, this emotion will pass, becoming just another crisis highlighted by media outlets. In contrast, as they enter into complex relations, they can realize that participation is a task they must undertake. Thus, when discussing participation, John Paul II accentuates the will, which he thinks is absent from Scheler's political thought. Both thinkers emphasize lived experience as a central element in political life and recognize how emotions shape our relations with others. However, John Paul II insists that we must will to love in community, an idea Scheler rejects vociferously.

THE PROBLEM OF ALIENATION
AND INAUTHENTIC ATTITUDES

The will is particularly important because we often confront social situations that create alienation. Deftly adopting this concept from Marxism, John Paul II removes it from the purely economic sphere, applying it instead to "the realm of specifically human and interpersonal relations" (Wojtyla 1993, 205).[11] Undoubtedly, cultural and economic structures produce alienation, but at its core it "means the negation of participation, for it renders participation difficult or even impossible" (ibid., 206). Alienation undermines the community of persons by closing people in on themselves or subsuming them into collectives.[12] Like participation, it relates not merely to the person as a member of the human species, but also to the "human being as a personal subject" (ibid., 255). People continue to interact in alienating conditions, but the *we* in their relation is stifled and deformed. Alienation may, at times, even annihilate it, as in the case of totalitarianism. The family and other I-thou relationships can also promote an alienation that "subverts the lived, experience of truth of the humanity, the truth of the essential worth of the person, in the human *thou*" (ibid., 256). A loved one or neighbor becomes a stranger or an enemy, negating what is particularly valuable in his personhood.

In addition to alienation, inauthentic attitudes like conformism and avoidance undermine participation. Conformism "denotes a tendency to comply with the accepted custom and to resemble others" in a servile way (Wojtyla 1979, 345). Naturally, complying with custom is indispensable for developing any community, but it often develops into passiveness, a failure to share in constructing community. It also reveals an incapacity to choose, making us merely subjects of what happens, rather than actors shaping our persons. Conformism produces indifference toward the common good that in its "servile form then becomes a denial of participation in the proper sense of the term" (ibid.). Avoidance, on the other hand, is "nothing but a withdrawal," originating when people simply turn away from participation because they find it too difficult (ibid.). In extreme circumstances, people may legitimately withdraw from an unjust social order. However, mere avoidance amounts to abandoning responsibility, denying the rich experience of participation.[13]

To summarize what John Paul II says about alienation and participation, these are opposed concepts capturing lived experience. Alienation exists when social structures destroy participation. Conformism and avoidance are attitudes that negate our responsibilities toward others. In contrast, participation is a property of persons enabling them to endow their interaction with others with a personalistic character. It moves the person from a categorial knowledge of the value of persons to the intuition of a *particular* and irreducible person. Persons do not automatically arrive at this insight but must will to actualize it. Finally, participation captures the lived experience of the common good, revealing how we actualize a value absent from our individual personhoods.

JOHN PAUL II AT THE UNITED NATIONS: THE RIGHTS OF NATIONS

Turning to how John Paul II applies this idea of participation to international politics, we see him confounding those who want to easily classify him. Recognizing changes in international politics in the aftermath of the Cold War, he embraces elements of both realism and liberalism. I noted in chapter 3 that in his 1995 speech to the United Nations, he defends the rights of nations, a traditional element of realism. Recall that he describes how the twentieth century saw terrible crimes in which nations and cultures were eliminated because they were considered inferior. In particular, he describes how the former Soviet Union annexed the Baltic States and Eastern Europe, eliminating their sovereignty under the guise of sham democracies (1995UN, 5). He also notes that the 1948 Universal Declaration of Human Rights says little about the rights of nations. The rights of nations raise "urgent questions about justice and freedom in the world today" (ibid.). John Paul II discusses these rights in terms of the universal and particular elements of human nature. Human beings find themselves between the universal "pole" of human nature and the particular "pole" of nation and ethnicity. We can never disregard the universal elements in human nature, for doing so plunges us into ethical and cultural relativism. Nevertheless, we also cannot forget the particular pole expressed by nations and ethnic groups. The word *nation,* with its Latin roots in the word *nasci,* "to be born," highlights how culture powerfully conditions our universal human nature. We are usually more intensely bound to particularity than to universality. As a fact, we find ourselves participating in the humanity of those sharing our language and culture. Usually, we must will to participate in a common humanity extending beyond this context.

This anthropological framework establishes the rights of nations, which John Paul II thinks are "nothing but 'human rights' fostered at the level of community life" (1995UN, 8). Naturally, we may have difficulty defining a particular nation's boundaries, because the nation and state are not isomorphic, and often the nation exists within a state arbitrarily created by external powers. This was particularly true during the Cold War, and when it ended, the bipolar political order disintegrated, spawning many new nations. With this context in mind, John Paul II cautiously attributes rights to nations. A nation has a right to exist, which "entails that no one—neither a State nor another nation, nor an international organization—is ever justified in asserting that an individual nation is not worthy of existence" (ibid.). This right differs from the modern concept of sovereignty, because various forms of political organization are compatible with nationhood. John Paul II also maintains that every nation enjoys a right to "its own language and culture," which it exercises through its educational system (ibid.). In an intriguing phrase, he says that it involves "spiritual sovereignty" that may even exist within the borders of a hostile state. Endorsing spiritual sovereignty is dangerous in a world that has seen ethnic cleansing, and John Paul II qualifies his claims by saying that a nation should shape its culture "according to its own traditions, excluding, of course, every abuse of human rights and in particular the oppression of minorities" (ibid.). Our common humanity should restrain how we express cultural or national identity. Here, John Paul II marshals his conception of human value as a counterweight against those who elevate the particular over the universal.

In addition to this familiar theme, John Paul II uses his conception of love to support cultural diversity (1995UN, 8). Different cultures, he maintains, are "but different ways of facing the question of the meaning of personal existence" (ibid., 9). Speaking to artists and intellectuals in the Republic of Georgia in 1999, he discussed love and transcendence, saying:

> It is precisely in this movement of self-transcendence, of recognition of the other, of the need to communicate with the other, that culture is created. But this drive towards the other is possible only through love. Ultimately, it is love alone which succeeds in uprooting the tragic selfishness that lies deep within the human heart. It is love which helps us to place others and the Other at the centre of our lives. Christians have always sought to create a culture which is fundamentally open to the eternal and transcendent, while at the same time attentive to the temporal, the

concrete, the human. Generations of Christians have striven to build and to pass on a culture, the goal of which is an ever more profound and universal fraternal communion of persons. Yet this universality is not one of oppressive uniformity. Genuine culture respects the mystery of the human person, and must therefore involve a dynamic exchange between the particular and the universal. It must seek a synthesis of unity and diversity. Love alone is capable of holding this tension in a creative and fruitful balance. (1999 Culture, section 2)

Many of the elements of John Paul II's understanding of love appear in this speech, shaping how he approaches the rights of nations. Love is a movement toward others enabling us to move beyond our selfish orbits. It is a creative force drawing us toward higher values and undermining perverse ones. It enables us to embrace persons, forming a community in which persons commit themselves fully to others. Most importantly, it locates God at the center of our *ordo amoris.* Love, then, becomes a way to celebrate cultural diversity.

This subtle position is likely to engender misunderstanding, because it navigates between universality and particularity in a political context in which forces are moving in both directions. It celebrates difference, rejecting a homogenized global culture, while disciplining the accent on diversity by appealing to a universal human nature. Some might easily confuse it with cultural relativism, which accepts even the most appalling cultural practices in the name of diversity. However, John Paul II carefully rules relativism out by insisting that the "truth about man is the unchangeable standard by which all cultures are judged; but every culture has something to teach us about one or other dimension of that complex truth" (1995UN, 10). Rather than endorsing an ill-defined pluralism, he articulates a conception of human nature allowing for diverse cultural expressions.

Critics may also question why John Paul II thinks all cultures manifest some answer to transcendent questions. I think we see a deeper treatment of this idea in "Fides et Ratio," where he identifies fundamental questions that all cultures address, including "Who am I? Where have I come from and where am I going? Why is there evil? What is there after life?" (FR, 1).[14] In a controversial passage, he goes further, describing substantive metaphysical ideas that constitute "a core of philosophical insight within the history of thought as a whole" (FR, 4). This core includes not only logical principles like the principle of noncontradiction, but also the concept of a free person who can know God, beauty, truth and moral norms. This passage supports the value of cultural diversity.[15] Different cultures express diverse answers to fundamental metaphysical questions. To cut ourselves off from one of them robs us of important insight into the meaning of human life. John Paul II recognizes that participation occurs within a particular social and linguistic context that we should respect and enhance. The rights of nations protect nations from those seeking to destroy their particularity in the name of a universal culture. These rights, however, must never be used to violate human dignity. Participation obliges us to both acknowledge the irreducibility of persons and recognize cultural uniqueness.

THE CIVILIZATION OF LOVE

By defending the rights of nations, John Paul II bolsters the realist approach to humanitarian intervention. However, when he discusses the family of nations, he moves toward the liberal approach. The United Nations, he argues, must be more than simply a bureaucracy performing important functions in the international system. Instead, it must serve as a

> moral center where all the nations of the world feel at home and develop a shared awareness of being, as it were, a "family of nations." The idea of a "family" immediately evokes something more than simple functional relations or mere convergence of interests. The family is by nature a community based on mutual trust, mutual support and sincere respect. In an authentic family the strong do not dominate; instead, the weaker members, because of their weakness, are all the more welcomed and served. (1995UN, 14)

The international system should be neither a Hobbesian war of all against all, nor simply a society tenuously held together by regimes or contracts. Instead, it should be a family-like community that views cultural identities "as a common treasure belonging to the cultural patrimony of mankind" (1995UN, 15). This requires nations not only to live with others, but also to live for them by exchanging gifts. Rejecting the idea that this vision is an "unattainable utopia," John Paul II urges the United Nations to promote a family of nations (1995UN, 15). The dramatic end of the Cold War illustrates how a vision that appears utopian can be quite realistic, shaping international relations in profound ways.

To support a family of nations, John Paul II retrieves from Pope Paul VI and others the concept of a "civilization of love." The United Nations, he insists, should undertake a "common effort to build the civilization of love, founded on the universal values of peace, solidarity, justice and liberty" (1995UN, 18). The heart of this civilization should be "freedom of individuals and the freedom of nations, lived in self-giving solidarity and responsibility" (1995UN, 18). Invoking a familiar theme in his writings, John Paul II emphasizes that freedom is neither mere license, nor simply the absence of tyranny. Instead, it is anchored in the truth about the human person, a "creature of intelligence and free will, immersed in the mystery which transcends his own being and endowed with the ability to reflect and the ability to choose—and thus capable of wisdom and virtue" (1995UN, 4). The civilization of love, then, requires nations and persons to exercise freedom using this truth as a guide.

What are some of the other characteristics of the civilization of love? A year before speaking to the United Nations, John Paul II described them in his "Letter to Families," arguing that the word "civilization" refers to human culture, which "answers man's spiritual and moral needs" ("Letter to Families," 13).[16] Approaching the concept of the civilization of love negatively and positively, John Paul II describes "two civilizations," one marked by utilitarianism, the other characterized by self-giving love. The utilitarian civilization suffers from a "crisis of concepts" because it has lost any sense of what love, freedom, and the person mean. It reduces these ideas to use and production, developing them in a "one-sided way." It also violates the personalistic norm by using persons merely as instruments, and debases humanity by fastening on lower values, falsely identifying the truth with the "pleasant and useful." In fact, utilitarian happiness is "immediate gratification for the exclusive benefit of the individual, apart from or opposed to the objective demands of the true good." In sum, the utilitarian civilization promotes excessive individualism, ethical subjectivism, and a dehumanizing ethos of use. In contrast, the civilization of love creates and shares "the good of persons and of communities." It recognizes that love is demanding, requiring patience, endurance, and constant cultivation. In it, persons exert themselves to give to others selflessly. The civilization of love embodies the "radical acceptance of the understanding of man as a person who 'finds himself' by making a sincere gift of self."

I want to suggest that in this discussion of the civilization of love, John Paul II describes participation in theological language. Like participation, the civilization of love requires acknowledging the personhood of another in all its particularity. At its highest level, it manifests the reciprocal recognition of personhood. Finally, like participation, it requires effort and is demanding. By contrasting the two civilizations, John Paul II links his account of participation, his attack on utilitarianism, and his understanding of love. In the violent world of nations, he urges leaders to abandon narrow conceptions of the national interest in order to cultivate self-giving love. In doing so, he rejects the realist emphasis on national interest, urging nations to move beyond it to cultivate self-giving love in international affairs.

A DUTY TO INTERVENE

Such selflessness may require the strong to help the weak, lending support for humanitarian intervention. In fact, responding to the horrors of the 1990s, John Paul II adopted strong language about our obligation to intervene to prevent profound suffering. For example, addressing the United Nations Food and Agricultural Organization in 1993, he stated that

> the idea is maturing within the international community that humanitarian action, far from being the right of the strongest, must be inspired by the conviction that intervention, or even interference when objective situations require it, is a response to a moral obligation to come to the aid of individuals, peoples or ethnic groups whose fundamental right to nutrition has been denied to the point of threatening their existence. (1993 Food and Agriculture)

Speaking to those charged with alleviating starvation and malnutrition, he rejected simplistic understandings of famine, focusing instead on its root causes. Perhaps he had in mind cases like Somalia in 1992, where armed thugs interfered with food shipments, threatening thousands of people with starvation. In such circumstances, John Paul II suggests that we have a duty to intervene to help those in need.

In the first year of this century, John Paul II again affirmed humanitarian intervention as a duty, insisting that "an offense against human rights is an offense against the conscience of humanity as such, an offense against humanity itself" (2000Peace, sec. 7). Rejecting sovereignty as a buffer against external interference, he argued that crimes against humanity are never merely internal affairs within sovereign nations. They not only affect regional peace, but also invariably harm the innocent. With these words, John Paul II positions himself with liberal thinkers who reject sovereignty as an absolute value. He goes further, asserting that in the fluid and dangerous world of international politics, "there is a need to affirm the preeminent value of humanitarian law and the consequent duty to guarantee the right to humanitarian aid to suffering civilians and refugees. The duty to protect these rights extends beyond the geographical and political borders within which they are violated" (ibid.). Here, John Paul II asserts a right that seems to exceed what international law recognizes. As some contemporary thinkers note, international law restricts intervention severely, primarily because it originated within the nation-state system as an attempt to limit conflict. John Paul II proposes that we move away from this restrictive framework and embrace an obligation to help those suffering from famine or human rights abuses. The duty to intervene rests on the priority of the person to the collective. The "moral and political legitimacy" of the right to intervene is "in fact based on the principle that the good of the human person comes before all else and stands above all human institutions" (2000Peace, sec. 9). We ought to reject any proposal to subsume the person into an international collective.

To summarize how John Paul II approaches international politics, he adopts elements from both realist and liberal understandings of the international arena. To counter dangerous nationalism and value cultural diversity, he affirms the rights of nations. He also presents the civilization of love as a normative ideal for international politics. Finally, he articulates a duty to intervene to prevent humanitarian disasters. In all three of these areas, John Paul II's pre-papal understanding of participation plays an important role. Although he rarely mentions it, he presents it both theologically and philosophically in many of his speeches.

THE RIGHTS OF NATIONS OR HUMAN RIGHTS?

Commenting on one of John Paul II's early calls for humanitarian intervention, Weigel correctly notes that it "raised more questions than it answered" (Weigel 1999, 666). John Paul II rarely specifies to whom the obligation to intervene applies. The "international community," as Weigel notes, is a vague locution, more of a rhetorical device than a conceptual tool. Often, nations use it knowing full well that large powers do most of the work of the "international community." Without knowing which parties constitute it, we can make little sense of the idea of a duty to intervene to prevent humanitarian disasters. More importantly, by defending this duty, the rights of nations, and the civilization of love, John Paul II creates a conflict between ethical ideals. For example, in the 1990s, Serbia claimed the right to self-determination and nationhood. Yet, it pursued this goal through ethnic cleansing, a profoundly immoral policy. In such a case, should we endorse its right to nationhood? Or, do the rights of persons trump it? If so, what are the precise grounds for making this judgment? What does it mean to say that the right of nation is "trumped" or overridden by the concern for individual dignity? Are we allowed to simply deny self-determination in the name of humanitarian intervention, or must we give some credence to even the most unappealing forms of nationalism? These questions suggest some significant conflicts within John Paul II's approach to international politics.

These conflicts are particularly acute because John Paul II affirms a hierarchy of value ranking spiritual over material values. When analyzing globalization, he condemns untrammeled economic growth, arguing that it reflects a distorted hierarchy of value. He identifies a conflict between material and spiritual values, and then resolves it by making spiritual values preeminent. He confronts a different problem when the rights of nations and the dignity of the person conflict. In his words, nations have "spiritual sovereignty"; they not only protect a populace from external harm, and provide for material needs, but also embody answers to spiritual questions. However, we now have a conflict between spiritual values that we cannot resolve by affirming the preeminence of spiritual values. We seem to be at an impasse, confronting a conflict between spiritual values that all demand our respect.

At times, John Paul II seems to recognize these difficulties. For example, discussing peace, he notes that

> There is also the difficulty of combining principles and values which, however reconcilable in the abstract, can prove on the practical level to be resistant to any easy synthesis. In addition, at a deeper level, there are always the demands which ethical commitment makes upon individuals, who are not free of self-interest and human limitations. (2000Peace, sec. 3)

Because of its complexity, humanitarian intervention presents seemingly intractable conflicts. Unfortunately, John Paul II says little about how to resolve them. This is frustrating for those struggling to respond to humanitarian disasters. As pontiff, John Paul II often rightfully refuses to present detailed policy blueprints, arguing that the Church must avoid making precise policy recommendations. Nevertheless, when he offers guidance at the level of moral principles, we find diverse concepts that apparently clash. It is reasonable, therefore, to ask if we can resolve this conflict.

CONSEQUENTIALISM AS A GUIDE?

Like realists in the past, some contemporary thinkers maintain that we cannot resolve it. For example, although they are not realists, Robert McNamara and James Blight argue that we cannot avoid doing evil when intervening to help others. They use philosopher Thomas Nagel's work in the 1970s to argue that humanitarian intervention presents us with "moral blind-alleys" (McNamara and Blight 2001, 122).[17] A moral blind alley is a situation in which "one cannot find a way to refrain from doing (or not doing) that which one believes is morally wrong" (ibid., 123). Any course of action we choose will be morally unacceptable. The post–Cold War international arena, McNamara and Blight argue, presents us with such inescapable moral blind alleys. Communal violence is driven by the "incompatible claims of self-determination and nationalist extremism," and in this climate, no one can retain clean hands (ibid.). In Liberia, Sierra Leone, Kosovo, Bosnia, and other places, the United Nations has confronted moral blind alleys in which doing evil was inevitable. Similarly, in the aftermath of the September 11 terrorist attacks on the United States, the United States attacked both the Taliban and al-Qaeda in Afghanistan. Using technologically sophisticated bombs that penetrated caves, American forces expelled the Taliban and al-Qaeda forces from numerous locations in Afghanistan. These bombs allowed Americans to avoid becoming mired in a vicious ground war that would have cost many lives. However, they also led to civilian casualties, and for some, this put the United States in a moral blind alley from which it could not exit.

Interestingly, McNamara and Blight criticize John Paul II and the United States Catholic bishops for suggesting that we might extricate ourselves from such moral blind alleys. Both, they suggest, mistakenly think we can intervene to prevent genocide and ethnic cleansing without doing evil. Discussing how the United Nations failed to prevent genocide in Rwanda, McNamara and Blight suggest that even if it had intervened, it would have confronted the possibility of hostage taking, and might have killed innocent civilians. They note that John Paul II

> states that it is our *duty* to intervene in such cases. Yet in the case of Rwanda, it is not at all clear that an attempt to carry out this "duty" would have led to a morally satisfactory conclusion. Yet the inverse is also true; not intervening was clearly not morally satisfactory. (Ibid., 129)

With John Paul II in mind, McNamara and Blight warn "those who would embark on an intervention to correct an egregious evil" that "the morality of the outcome will be determined by far more than the intention to do good" (ibid., 131). Before pronouncing an intervention morally legitimate, we must weigh its probable consequences, knowing full well that we will commit evil acts.

The moral blind alley approach captures the horrors peacekeepers often face when intervening to prevent humanitarian disasters. Sometimes, it appears, they can only do evil. McNamara and Blight also legitimately criticize John Paul II for failing to carefully consider the quagmires of humanitarian intervention. Peacekeepers in Bosnia and Rwanda have confronted terrible situations. For example, in Rwanda in 1994, ten Belgian peacekeepers were brutally tortured and murdered while trying to prevent genocide. Their bodies were "so badly cut up that they had become impossible to count" (Power 2002, 332). Such events seemed to trap peacekeepers in impossible situations. Philosophically, McNamara and Blight capture this sense that peacekeeping involves moral blind alleys.

Despite its attractiveness, however, the moral blind alley approach suffers from conceptual confusions and creates political apathy. First, it offers us little guidance about how to act in the international arena. What do McNamara, Blight, and others propose we do when confronting a moral blind alley? They assume we have reason to intervene to prevent genocide, but if intervention and nonintervention both involve doing evil acts, I see no reason to intervene. Inaction and action both become legitimate choices. If we do have reason to intervene, as McNamara and Blight clearly think we do, then one choice is clearly preferable to another, and we are not in a moral blind alley. McNamara and Blight explicitly distinguish their position from the "lesser of two evils" approach, but as far as I can tell, it quickly becomes indistinguishable from it. Humanitarian intervention implies that it is in some way better than inaction and therefore suggests that we have chosen a lesser evil.[18] Additionally, this view undermines any motivation to intervene. American and European publics are notoriously reluctant to commit troops and treasure to goals only remotely connected to their nations' immediate national interest. Telling them that they confront a moral blind alley only bolsters this reluctance, undermining attempts to build international coalitions to prevent genocide, famine, or terrorism. In sum, there is little political or conceptual reason to endorse the "moral blind alley" approach to humanitarian intervention.

If the moral blind alley position amounts to choosing the lesser evil, why not embrace the idea of a "lesser evil"? Kaplan proposes that this is exactly what we should do. As I noted in the last chapter, he says that when dealing with "failed states," the best policy involves "doing or accepting a certain amount of 'evil' to make possible a proportionately greater amount of good" (Kaplan 2000, 121–22). Reviving the realist conception of national interest, Kaplan argues that when a large power confronts genocide or chaos, it must carefully decide if intervening will promote more good than evil. He declares that "dealing with bad people will always be necessary to prevent even greater evil" (ibid., 103). Leaders may have difficulty ascertaining which policies promote good over evil, but they must try to achieve some good in terrible circumstances.

Although it appears to offer more guidance than the "moral blind-alley approach," the "lesser evil" approach suffers from all of the arbitrariness endemic to consequentialism. Generally, those advocating it tell us that we must "balance" or "weigh" various goods and evils. However, this vague language offers no assistance to those responding to a humanitarian crisis. Which values should we "balance" or "weigh" when deciding whether to use force to feed the starving in Somalia? How can we measure how air attacks against Serbia affect the personhood of Belgrade's inhabitants? How do we ascertain how intervening in Bosnia affects the spiritual lives of Muslims and Orthodox Christians? How do we "balance" the risk of civilian casualties in Afghanistan over against the great benefits of freedom from the intolerant and oppressive Taliban regime? Usually, discussions about humanitarian interventions ignore these questions, arbitrarily focusing on tangible values. We are again back to what Scheler and John Paul II repeatedly say, that consequentialism is an unworkable ethical project. It provides us with no guidance about how to help those in need.

Some Roman Catholic thinkers reject the lesser-evil idea, proposing instead to resolve conflicts over humanitarian intervention by adopting the just war tradition's principle of proportionality. For example, Hehir carefully outlines criteria for humanitarian intervention (Hehir 1995). Insisting on multilateral authorization, he expands the idea of a just cause beyond genocide, and urges intervening forces to use just means. Like Weigel, he endorses the criterion of proportionality, proposing that it helps us intervene justly. For example, writing about NATO's 1999 air war in Kosovo, Hehir states that combatants must use the principle of proportionality before acting, continuously review it during a war, and consider it when assessing their conduct after a war (Hehir 1999). Writing about how the United States should respond to the September 11 attacks, he emphasizes that any response must adhere to the just war tradition's criterion of proportionality. Against how many states can the United States declare war, Hehir asks, "without being itself defined as a threat to international order?" (Hehir 2001).

Hehir rejects consequentialism as a way of developing ethical principles but employs it selectively when discussing proportionality. Unfortunately, in doing so, he also succumbs to arbitrariness. For example, putting on a tactician's hat, Hehir makes complex judgments about how to wage war in Kosovo, at one point stating that he would "drop some bridges (those carrying military supplies) at night and not turn off the lights" (Hehir 1999). Yet, in this analysis, it is entirely unclear what he is doing. Military planners and soldiers have a moral obligation to consider proportionality in order to avoid embarking on disastrous military adventures. They make proportionate judgments using a limited set of values involving lives and equipment lost. This is the kind of proportionate reason Finnis, Boyle, and Grisez identify as important and legitimate. In contrast, Hehir purports to provide a *moral* evaluation of the humanitarian intervention in Kosovo, and he cannot consider only one set of values. He says virtually nothing about spiritual values, focusing conveniently on military matters. For a religious and moral analysis, this simply will not do. Hehir arbitrarily ignores the spiritual values related to the person, failing to discuss how the war in Kosovo affected them. This is understandable, because if he were to consider them, his analysis would devolve into an incoherent attempt to calculate spiritual values. Like Weigel, Hehir employs a selective consequentialist reasoning that has little philosophical merit. We cannot, therefore, use it to resolve dilemmas in humanitarian intervention.

THE PRIORITY OF PERSON OVER COLLECTIVE: HOW JOHN PAUL II CAN ADDRESS THE DILEMMAS OF HUMANITARIAN INTERVENTION

Without adopting one of the positions I have discussed, can John Paul II resolve the ethical dilemmas of humanitarian intervention? Do the rights of nations take precedence over those suffering from famine or genocide? Or do the needs of persons supersede these rights, permitting us to override national sovereignty to help the needy? In my view, John Paul II cannot address these questions without altering his understanding of the rights of nations, which confuses the person and the collective. He creates this confusion by moving too easily from individual rights to the rights of nations. We cannot say, as he does in his 1995 United Nations speech, that the rights of nations are "nothing but 'human rights' fostered at the specific level of community life" (1995UN, 8). This quick conceptual move ignores John Paul II's own numerous warnings about attributing moral agency to collectives. We have already seen that when discussing structures of sin, he insists that we attribute sin to collectives only analogically. Institutions lack the inner life necessary to be sinful, and therefore, a "situation—or likewise an institution, society itself—is not in itself the subject of moral acts. Hence a situation cannot be good or bad" (RP, 16). Analogically, social structures can be sinful, but we should avoid attributing sin literally to "some vague entity or anonymous collectivity such as the situation, the system, society, structures or institutions" (RP, 16).

This argument applies not only to sin, but also to rights. In defending human rights, John Paul II grounds them in persons who possess an inner life, a capacity for self-determination, and the freedom to relate to truth. Things and collectives lack these characteristics and therefore cannot have rights. John Paul II tells us that when considering communities, we should speak

> of a "quasi-subjectiveness," rather than of a proper subject of acting. All the people existing and acting together are obviously exercising a role in a common action, but in a different way than when each of them performs an action in its entirety. The new subjectiveness is the share of all the members of a community, or, in a broader sense, of a social group. In fact, it is but a quasi-subjectiveness, because even when the being and acting is realized together with others it is the *man-person who is always its proper subject.* (Wojtyla 1979, 277)[19]

The acting person is always our guide in thinking about community, and when analyzing social units, we must avoid thinking about them as subjects. I think this warning applies particularly to nations. Undoubtedly, they express unique cultures and understandings of the metaphysical mysteries confronting human beings. However, they have no inner life in any meaningful sense of this term and therefore cannot have the rights a subject possesses. As a personalist, John Paul II cannot attribute rights to them in anything more than an analogical or legal sense.[20]

Unfortunately, when speaking to the United Nations, John Paul II conflates univocal and analogical uses of the term *right*. Unless he avoids univocal language about the rights of nations, he cannot resolve the dilemmas of humanitarian intervention. In a study of the language of rights in the United States, Mary Ann Glendon warns that the "occasions for conflict among rights multiply as catalogs of rights grow longer" (Glendon 1991, 16), and this is a danger that John Paul II ought to consider. He affirms a host of individual rights, taking the 1948 Universal Declaration of Human Rights as his guide.[21] In recent years, critics of human rights language have argued that it ignores our social responsibilities and presupposes an atomistic conception devoid of a social nature. Needless to say, such criticisms hardly apply to John Paul II, who locates human rights within his conception of participation. Nevertheless, by expanding the scope of rights to nations in 1995, he created significant conflicts between the rights of persons and the rights of nations. I cannot see how he can retain them both as equally important.

John Paul II can resolve this conflict by emphasizing the univocal character of language about the human person, as well as the analogical character of language about collectives. The common good, as he tells us when writing about participation, involves an analogy of proportion. By emphasizing this analogy, he could avoid attributing rights to collectives, in keeping with his work on structures of sin. Furthermore, he could still indicate how vitally important culture is in forming the human person. Finally, when nationalism and the value of the person conflict, he could argue that the rights of the person take precedence over those of nations. The nation always serves the person, and promoting it by harming her is inherently contradictory. In fact, when discussing humanitarian intervention, John Paul II suggests, but does not develop, this approach. For example, five years after his 1995 United Nations speech, he stated, "the good of the human person comes before all else and stands above all human institutions" (2000Peace, sec. 9). We ought to institutionalize this idea by seeking "a *renewal of international law and international institutions,* a renewal whose starting-point and basic organizing principle should be the primacy of the good of humanity and of the human person over every other consideration" (ibid., sec. 12.32). Such strong language provides ample ground for ranking the person's dignity above the rights of nations. Participation serves the person, and it should never be subordinated to the nation. When national and individual rights clash, we order our ethical principles by affirming the primacy of the person over the group. I think John Paul II's theory of value and his critique of consequentialism leave him no other option but to adopt this conclusion.

HOW SHOULD WE INTERVENE?
CRITERIA FOR HUMANITARIAN INTERVENTION

Concretely, what does it mean to prioritize the person over the nation? Realists and nonrealists understandably worry that setting this priority may undermine the nation-state system, authorizing interventions that create disorder in international politics. For example, Hehir argues that we ought to be very careful before overriding national sovereignty. The international system, he correctly notes, contains "enormous differences of power and potential" between states, and large states often use humanitarian intervention "for reasons of power politics" (Hehir 1995, 8). Consequently, the "wisdom of Westphalia should be heeded. Intervention may be necessary, but it should not be made easy. Hence the need to sustain the presumption against it" (ibid.). Hehir's remarks reflect a genuine worry about how recent attacks on nonintervention may legitimize new forms of imperialism and coercion.[22]

In the wake of the September 11 terrorist attacks, many nations have become particularly worried about this problem, for they perceive in U.S. foreign policy a new unilateralism. Some maintain that it is a form of imperialism, while others worry that the United States often tragically overreaches when trying to help other countries.[23] In an eloquent essay entitled "The Seductiveness of Moral Disgust" (written before the September 11 attacks), Ignatieff articulates these worries, describing the negative consequences and hypocrisy of humanitarian interventions in the 1990s. Purporting to be postimperial, interventions in Bosnia and other places were often instead haunted by "ambitions, follies, and ironies of an imperial kind" (Ignatieff 1998, 92–93). As Ignatieff puts it, we "intervened not only to save others, but to save ourselves, or rather an image of ourselves as defenders of universal decencies" (ibid., 95). Intervening powers illegitimately assumed that they "had the power to do anything. This assumption of omnipotence often stood between indignation and insight, between feeling strongly and knowing what it was possible to do" (ibid., 96). Such excessive ambitions and aspirations produced great disillusion, creating an unwillingness to intervene to prevent future humanitarian disasters.

Ignatieff overstates his case, sometimes ignoring the dedicated activists and aid workers who struggled to respond to humanitarian disasters. Nevertheless, he reveals the dangers of uncritically pursuing policies that value the person over the nation. John Paul II recognizes these dangers, and offers criteria for when and how to intervene.[24] He identifies those to whom the obligation applies, mentioning international agencies, regional bodies, religious institutions, and humanitarian organizations (2000Peace, sec. 10). He discusses the *means* they should use, insisting that they initially include nonviolent mediation and negotiations. Additionally, he legitimizes armed intervention, noting that "when a civilian population risks being overcome by the attacks of an unjust aggressor and political efforts and nonviolent defence prove to be of no avail, it is legitimate and even obligatory to take concrete measures to disarm the aggressor" (ibid., sec. 11). Violence is not only morally legitimate to defend the innocent, but at times it may be *obligatory*. Despite his deep sympathies for nonviolence, therefore, John Paul II rejects a pacifist position proscribing violence in humanitarian interventions. He also carefully sets conditions for using violence, insisting that interventions "must be limited in time and precise in their aims. They must be carried out in full respect for international law, guaranteed by an authority that is internationally recognized and, in any event, never left to the outcome of armed intervention alone" (ibid.). Peacekeepers may use violence, but only under strict conditions that limit it.[25]

In his understanding of humanitarian intervention, John Paul II joins others who develop criteria for humanitarian intervention. For example, Hehir calls for a multinational approach to humanitarian intervention guided by the principles of the just war tradition (Hehir 1995). McNamara and Blight argue that state sovereignty is not an absolute value and insist on multinational action for humanitarian interventions (McNamara and Blight 2001, ch. 3). Finally, Smith calls for carefully restraining humanitarian intervention, insisting that it be measured and careful (Smith 1999). Therefore, John Paul II is part of a growing trend to rethink humanitarian intervention on multinational and ethical grounds. Because he understands the value of a nation, he retrieves elements of a realist approach to humanitarian intervention. However, he also shares with liberals a commitment to the priority of the human person. What he adds to the discussion is a sophisticated account of participation that values collective life without denigrating the person. He shares with many the language of human rights, but at the end of the day, he always returns to the acting person.

At this point, those committed to consequentialism might rightfully ask how John Paul II arrives at his criteria for humanitarian intervention. Does he calculate the consequences of various policies, thus falling prey to his own criticisms of consequentialism? Some in the contemporary debate defend their views this way. For example, Kissinger maintains that the "ultimate dilemma of the statesman is to strike a balance between values and interests, and, occasionally, between peace and justice" (Kissinger 2001, 286). Scathingly, he argues that the United States failed to achieve this balance in its humanitarian interventions in the 1990s. The language of "balance" here clearly indicates Kissinger's commitment to consequentialism. Among contemporary scholars, it is not difficult to find similar consequentialist defenses of principles of humanitarian intervention.

John Paul II rarely defends his criteria for humanitarian intervention, but I think he can without appealing to consequentialism. For example, he might agree with McNamara and Blight, who defend multilateralism by arguing that it has cognitive and perceptual advantages over unilateralism (McNamara and Blight 2001, 132–50). Humanitarian intervention presents enormously complex problems that few leaders can understand without assistance from others. Similarly, intelligence-gathering is a vital part of battling terrorism, and no nation can rely solely on its own intelligence agencies. Acting multilaterally, therefore, provides indispensable information. For example, the United States military won a quick victory over Iraq in the Second Gulf War in 2003. However, it encountered significant difficulties after the war, incurring casualties and criticism for its failure to account for various contingencies. Many countries maintained that a multilateral approach would have enabled the United States to construct a more effective post-war policy in Iraq. When a great power consults others, it also reduces the perception that it is bullying or initiating some kind of neocolonialism. In the intense debates at the United Nations prior to the Second Gulf War, many diplomats opposed an invasion of Iraq by appealing to the perceptual and informational benefits of multilateralism. Such justifications for multilateralism avoid balancing spiritual goods in an incoherent fashion. They involve fallible judgments and cannot establish absolute rules about when to intervene. Sometimes, nations may have to intervene unilaterally. Nevertheless, the cognitive and perceptual advantages of multilateralism give us good reason to generally prefer it to unilateralism. Similarly, John Paul II can use the person's value to justify his strictures on violence in humanitarian intervention. It provides ample warrant for saying that we ought to seek nonviolent solutions before resorting to violence. Violence destroys the person and should only be a last resort. Reaching this conclusion requires no computation of spiritual values. Finally, John Paul II can also support his appeal to a public authority by maintaining that we need an agent to promote the common good. He might maintain that the very idea of the common good requires an agent to promote it.

In such reflections, I have provided a very sketchy nonconsequentialist defense of criteria for humanitarian intervention, and going further would require a separate essay on this issue. I simply want to indicate that it is mistaken to think that without consequentialism we are ethically lost when intervening in troubled parts of the world. Statespeople often adopt consequentialism when intervening but are not required to do so. Undoubtedly, by prioritizing the value of the person over the nation, John Paul II creates great potential for disorder and abuse of power in international relations. However, he is attentive to this danger, cautiously endorsing armed, multilateral intervention, guided by international law and clear military and political objectives.

THE SINFULNESS OF THE UNITED NATIONS

With this ethical vision clear, however, I want to close this chapter by arguing that in his writings on international politics, John Paul II confuses the aims of associations and fails to apply his conception of sin to the United Nations. To address the first point, I think John Paul II confounds the aims of transnational institutions with those of the family, mistakenly asserting that international relations should be a "family of nations." He tells us that in an objective sense, we classify communities by identifying the common value their members pursue. Persons form a "community of acting," defined by the "aim that brings men to act together" (Wojtyla 1979, 279). Subjectively, we classify communities by considering how they help persons fulfill themselves. Using these ways of classifying social entities, I think it is obvious that nation-states and families differ substantially in subjective and objective ways. The family, in John Paul II's writings, forms a community of persons, serves life, participates in developing society, and shares in the life and mission of the church.[26] It cultivates deep emotional bonds between persons, providing them with unique opportunities to develop their personhood. We need not endorse a Hobbesian conception of international politics to see that these features are simply absent from the world of nation-states. Size is the obvious dissimilarity between families and nations. Moreover, we have to institutionalize political life in a nation-state, producing impersonal bureaucracies unlike anything we find in the family. Operated by these bureaucracies, nation-states lack a moral center. When we apply concepts like self-gift, trust, and solidarity to them, who exactly is the moral agent?

In his 1995 speech to the United Nations, John Paul II recognizes this problem when urging the United Nations to rise above the "cold status" of a bureaucracy and move toward "mutual trust, mutual support, and sincere respect" (1995UN, 14). However, he overlooks the possibility that an association may reach a size that renders it incapable of performing particular functions. Ideally, family members know each other very well and address problems in an intimate and effective way. This is not true in the world of nations. Reinhold Niebuhr makes this point convincingly, arguing that nations "do not have direct contact with other national communities, with which they must form some kind of international community. They know the problems of other peoples only indirectly and at second hand" (Niebuhr 1983, 85). Famously, Niebuhr distinguishes between interpersonal and political ethics, a distinction I reject. Nevertheless, he highlights important differences between nations and other associations that too many people today have forgotten. Niebuhr reminds us of the unpleasant truth that we rarely treat those living far from us with familial empathy. The transition from the interpersonal to the international realm is extremely difficult to make.

Niebuhr wrote his famous work on the immorality of nations years before the United Nations came on the international scene, and John Paul II is correct in saying that today it serves as an important forum for promoting contact between nations. However, he also underestimates sin's power over it. For example, I believe its failure to prevent genocide in Rwanda exemplified a sinful indifference to the fate of those living in countries with little power or influence in international politics. Analysts disagree about whether the United Nations could have prevented the genocide, but it never seriously tried to do so. A damning 1999 Independent Inquiry into the United Nations action concluded that Member States showed an appalling unwillingness to commit resources and displayed terrible paralyses of will that stifled attempts to prevent genocide.[27] General Romeo A. Dallaire, commander of the United Nations Observer Mission (UNAMIR) before and during the genocide, writes despairingly about how the United Nations ignored his pleas for assistance in preventing it. It failed to provide his troops with adequate equipment and support, created inefficient command and control systems, and disregarded repeated requests for further assistance.[28] The Report of the Independent Inquiry agrees with this assessment, concluding that the "fundamental capacity problems of UNAMIR led to the terrible and humiliating situation of the UN peacekeeping force almost paralyzed in the face of a wave of some of the worst brutality humankind has seen in this century" (United Nations 1999, "Conclusions," sec. 1). General Dallaire concludes that those who could effectively stop the genocide refused, while contingents from poor nations valiantly battled it. Poor nations "shamed the world by doing the right thing," while others procrastinated, obfuscating the truth of what was happening in Rwanda (Dallaire 1998, 85).

This shameful episode illustrates perfectly the inauthentic attitudes of avoidance and conformism. United Nations representatives evaded their responsibilities to their own forces, never mind the people of Rwanda. Avoiding a deeper involvement in Rwanda became "a kind of substitute or compensatory attitude for those who find solidarity or opposition too difficult" (Wojtyla 1979, 347). Member States in the United Nations refused to admit that genocide was occurring. To again quote the Independent Inquiry, "the lack of will to act in response to the crisis in Rwanda becomes all the more deplorable in light of the reluctance of key members of the International Community to acknowledge that the mass murder being pursued in front of global media was a genocide" (United Nations 1999, "Conclusions," sec. 5). Linda Melvern notes that in Rwanda, the "incitement to genocide was broadcast via a radio station and the people were psychologically prepared for months, and were ordered and coerced to carry out the extermination" (Melvern 2000, 4).[29] Despite the transparency of the genocide, members of the international community exhibited willful ignorance about what was happening before their eyes. To admit that genocide was occurring would have required them to take action under the 1948 Convention on the Prevention and Punishment of the Crime of Genocide, so they played semantic games to avoid their responsibilities.[30] Additionally, many in America and Europe ignored what was happening in Rwanda, conforming to prevailing attitudes about the United Nations. Ill-informed politicians denigrated it, adopting popular and mistaken conceptions of its failures in Somalia and elsewhere. The sins of conformism and avoidance produced structures of sin that impeded a constructive response to genocide.

In writing about structures of sin, John Paul II mentions other sins that are relevant here, the "very personal sins of those who cause or support evil or who exploit it; of those who are in a position to avoid, eliminate or at least limit certain social evils but who fail to do so out of laziness, fear or the conspiracy of silence, through secret complicity or indifference; of those who take refuge in the supposed impossibility of changing the world and also of those who sidestep the effort and sacrifice required, producing specious reasons of higher order" (RP, 16). This catalog of sins of omissions and commissions goes beyond bureaucratic inefficiency. It includes failures of the will, an important element in the Rwandan tragedy. To again quote Melvern, what happened in Rwanda "showed that despite the creation of an organization set up to prevent a repetition of genocide—for the UN is central to this task—it failed to do so, even when the evidence was indisputable" (Melvern 2000, 5). Nation-states took refuge in "specious reasons of higher order" to evade their moral responsibilities. Philip Gourevitch, a journalist who witnessed the terrible aftermath of the Rwandan genocide, captures the significance of these sins, noting bitterly that

> Rwanda had presented the world with the most unambiguous case of genocide since Hitler's war against the Jews, and the world sent blankets, beans, and bandages to camps controlled by the killers, apparently hoping that everybody would behave nicely in the future. The West's post-Holocaust pledge that genocide would never again be tolerated proved to be hollow, and for all the fine sentiments inspired by the memory of Auschwitz, the problem remains that denouncing evil is a far cry from doing good. (Gourevitch 1998, 170)

Sadly, John Paul II rarely discusses this terrible failure of will and what it suggests about the United Nations and the civilization of love.

CAN THE UNITED NATIONS RESPOND TO DISTORTIONS IN GLOBALIZATION AND NATIONALISM?

Despite such failures in the area of humanitarian intervention, however, perhaps the United Nations can address the spiritual distortions in globalization and nationalism. Often, John Paul II suggests that it is the proper vehicle for this kind of work. For example, considering globalization, he notes that the United Nations has the opportunity to

> contribute to the globalization of solidarity by serving as a meeting place for States and civil society and as a convergence of the varied interests and needs— regional and particular—of the world at large. Cooperation between international agencies and non-governmental organizations will help to ensure that the interests of States—legitimate though they may be—and of the different groups within them, will not be invoked or defended at the expense of the interests or rights of other peoples, especially the less fortunate. Political and economic activity conducted in a spirit of international solidarity can and ought to lead to the voluntary limitation of unilateral advantages so that other countries and peoples may share in the same benefits. In this way the social and economic well-being of everyone is served. (2000UN, sec. 3)

In this passage, John Paul II provides a detailed account of how the United Nations can respond to globalization's distortions. In his view, it can serve as an umbrella organization under which nongovernmental organizations can meet. It can provide indispensable checks on nation-state power and foster cooperation between states and nongovernmental agencies, leading nations to voluntarily limit their pursuit of narrow national interest.

Undoubtedly, dialogue among nations and nongovernmental organizations can prevent terrible disasters. However, why does John Paul II think that by itself, it can alter value distortions in international affairs? If we recall the central elements of his understanding of sin, such scenarios seem unlikely. Sin is an intentionality toward using others, grounded in a distorted *ordo amoris*. It is an *axiological reduction*, diminishing our relationship to values. It reflects our alienation from God, which is particularly acute today because of modernity's "ways of denial." Those promoting the narrow interests of a nation-state often reflect these dynamics. They relate only to a narrow set of values, ignoring the needs of persons in other countries. They receive emotional and other support for this willful ignorance from domestic constituencies. Dialogue and cooperation seem unlikely to alter such fundamental distortions. For example, in 2002–2003, the United States, France, Russia, and other countries failed to reach any agreement about how to respond to Iraq.

Extensive dialogue yielded only recriminations and anger that many observers of the United Nations believe significantly damaged its credibility. Michael J. Glennon goes so far as to declare that the United Nations' "grand attempt to subject the use of force to the rule of law had failed" (Glennon 2003). Even if we do not share his dour assessment of what happened before the Second Gulf War, it should be clear that dialogue failed utterly to change anyone's mind about this war. Similarly, we have little reason to believe that the United Nations can counter the powerful economic and social forces promoting a homogenized global culture. Undoubtedly, it can make important structural changes in areas like international finance and debt relief that can reduce the negative elements of globalization. In some countries like Cambodia and Namibia, the United Nations has also exerted important cultural influences on the populace. However, in others, it has little or no influence, particularly in those countries where people have access only to state-controlled media. In these settings, it is hard to see how the United Nations can fulfill the cultural mandates John Paul II accords to it.

John Paul II's own experiences with the international conferences in Cairo and Beijing in the 1990s suggest that the United Nations may, in fact, impede positive responses to globalization.[31] These conferences focused on population growth, poverty, and women's rights in the developing world. Both witnessed sharp, public conflicts between the Vatican, the United Nations, and various nongovernmental organizations over issues like contraception, the family, and limiting population growth. John Paul II harshly criticized draft documents for these conferences, accusing them of undermining the value of human life and the family. Immediately before the Cairo conference in 1994, he penned a strongly worded letter to U.S. President Clinton. Discussing the draft document, he stated that

> the idea of sexuality underlying this text is totally individualistic, to such an extent that marriage now appears as something outmoded. An institution as natural, fundamental and universal as the family cannot be manipulated by anyone. Who could give such a mandate to individuals or institutions? The family is part of the heritage of humanity! Moreover, the Universal Declaration of Human Rights clearly states that the family is "the natural and fundamental group unit of society" (Art. 16.3). The International Year of the Family should therefore be a special occasion for society and the state to grant the family the protection which the universal declaration recognizes it should have. Anything less would be a betrayal of the noblest ideals of the United Nations. (1994Clinton)

In writing about these developments, John Paul II maintains that a minority of activists and United Nations officials wrested control of the population conferences in order to impose an ideological agenda on them. These attempts represented more than simply the incapacity to rise above a cold bureaucracy. They also went beyond forms of conformism and avoidance. Some who advocated for abortion rights and different models of the family rejected John Paul II's conception of a proper *ordo amoris*. Their disagreement was not simply intellectual, but revealed deep-seated affective orientations. In "Evangelium Vitae," John Paul II analyzes these orientations with great eloquence, famously describing them as a "culture of death." He details the institutional support for the culture of death, uncovering its deep roots in a culture that rejects the dignity of the human person. He recognizes that changing the culture of death requires not only deep institutional changes, but also a profound change in our orientation toward values. Unfortunately, when he writes about the United Nations, John Paul II departs from this powerful message, maintaining that dialogue alone will alter axiological distortions. I see a glaring and inexplicable contrast between his speeches before the United Nations and his writings on the culture of death.

Much to the dismay of some participants at the Cairo and Beijing conferences, the Vatican successfully opposed key elements of conference agendas. However, as Weigel shows, it did so by shrewd political maneuvers that failed to alter the ideological commitments of others.[32] In fact, many activists went away from these experiences embittered and entrenched in their ideological positions. Weigel describes John Paul II's interventions during these conferences as moral victories that stifled attempts to internationalize a right to abortion and coercive population policies. I agree with this assessment but think that there is a substantial difference between prevailing politically and cultivating a civilization of love. The battles over the Cairo and Beijing conferences illustrate how forces within the United Nations can embrace and cling to value-distortions. Sadly, they leave us little reason to believe that the United Nations can overcome ideological differences, promote international solidarity, and correct globalization's distortions.

These dynamics should also generate skepticism about the idea that the United Nations can successfully combat virulent nationalism. John Paul II's own careful analysis of virulent nationalism suggests just how difficult a challenge it presents. Virulent nationalism reflects a distorted *ordo amoris* that embraces the nation as the highest value. It is a form of deep-seated idolatry that perverts the proper order of values. Finally, it is often impervious to change, solidifying distortions even under severe pressure to change. Ignatieff gives us some sense of how difficult it is to alter these dynamics. Reflecting on the war in the former Yugoslavia, he describes how such conflicts originate when a state holding various nationalities together disintegrates, terrible Hobbesian fear takes hold, and nationalist paranoia emerges (Ignatieff 1997, 45). Often, these dynamics lead people to dehumanize those outside of their group. For example, Ignatieff tells us that in the former Yugoslavia, media outlets "were readying their populations to think of the other side as vermin, insects, dogs, and other noisome creatures" (ibid., 56).[33] A deep intolerance emerged, a "willed refusal to focus on individual difference, and a perverse insistence that individual identity can be subsumed in the group" (ibid., 63). Cognitive illusions shaped perverse willing, leading people to see the world entirely in terms of group membership. What is wrong with this form of nationalism, Ignatieff writes, is "not the desire to be master in your own house, but the conviction that only people like yourself deserve to be in the house" (ibid., 59).

The United Nations can also do very little when virulent nationalists deliberately undermine the emotional bonds conducive to participation. They actively oppose recognizing the irreducible in others, choosing instead to classify them according to group membership. They employ epistemological devices to deny the uniqueness of the individual. They place excessive importance on minor differences that allegedly locate persons in fixed groups.[34] Despite its power, the United Nations cannot easily counter these destructive forces, because it plays little role in cultivating emotional bonds between persons. Member States like the United States repeatedly refuse to allow it to act in their stead, creating hostility toward it among some segments of their populations. The United Nations' well-known failures and incompetence further diminish its credibility as an effective cultural force. Nationalist and terrorist movements demonize it, disdaining it as invader and occupier. In the face of such powerful resistance, the emotional prerequisites for participation are simply absent. Perhaps, however, we need not develop emotional bonds in order to respond to virulent nationalism. I cannot ascertain if John Paul II thinks emotional resources are a necessary condition for participation.[35] Perhaps he believes that even absent emotional bonds, persons can will to acknowledge the personhood of others.

I think the United Nations is an unlikely vehicle for realizing such a project, and John Paul II should lower his aspirations for it.[36] In recent years, large nation-states like the former Soviet Union have collapsed, and similar developments may occur in other parts of the world. The war on terrorism may aggravate existing ethnic or regional conflicts, producing further disorder. The divisive debates over the Second Gulf War have also substantially weakened the United Nations. Nevertheless, if it is wise, it may be able to serve as a crucial third party that alleviates the Hobbesian fear fueling nationalist movements. Given the forces arrayed against it, perhaps all we can hope for is that it cultivates knowledge of a common human nature. This would be a major accomplishment, because claims about the universality of human nature are under siege in many parts of the globe. Philosophically, a host of contemporary thinkers deny that we share a common nature, derisively dismissing this idea as "essentialism." Politically, demagogues of all political persuasions are only too happy to valorize ethnic difference and demonize those outside of their groups. In light of such philosophical and political developments, it is a major achievement simply to retain knowledge of a common human nature.

The United Nations can cultivate this knowledge by promoting policies fostering the person's development and by refraining from endorsing those that promote the culture of death. These important steps, however, differ from those enhancing the *eidetic intuition* of the irreducibility of the other. Most people in the world have little or no contact with the United Nations. The little contact they have bears no resemblance to the intense interaction they experience in families or churches. To again bring Niebuhr into this discussion, "what lies beyond the nation, the community of mankind, is too vague to inspire devotion" (Niebuhr 1983, 85). Local forces are much more likely to develop participation than is an enormous international organization. Events like the Rwandan genocide support this conclusion. In 1994, most of the populations of the industrialized world completely ignored the Rwandan genocide. Members of the human species were systematically slaughtered and dismembered; yet many people simply disregarded this horror as something happening far away on a continent with unsolvable problems. They not only lacked any insight into the uniqueness of persons in Rwanda, but also ignored their species membership and value. Similarly, those who murdered several thousand innocent people in New York and Washington, D.C., in 2001 effaced their knowledge of our common humanity, deliberately using innocent human beings merely as tools for their projects. They appeared to lack any sense of our common humanity. Naturally, we should never exclude the possibility that we can actualize the ideal of participation for all persons in a global community. To do so ignores the power to change that John Paul II has embodied in his public life. He is right to point to the events in Poland during the Cold War as illustrating the capacity to develop participation.[37] Nevertheless, on this matter, the political realists have wisdom that John Paul II ignores. The world of nation-states is not a family, and its political apathy, disorder, and nationalism produce profound alienation. Entities like the family and church must promote participation, and we should be grateful if the United Nations manages to retain awareness of our common humanity.

NOTES

1. United Nations 1999, introduction.

2. "Address of His Holiness Pope John Paul II to the Fiftieth General Assembly of the United Nations Organization," section 16.

3. For a discussion of the optimism about international politics that was so powerful after the Cold War's end, see Melvern 2000, chapter 8.

4. For Smith's discussion of realism, see Smith 1999, 280–83.

5. Kissinger's arguments about the merits of the Westphalian system are deeply controversial, and I will not assess them. My own view is that they ignore how the Westphalian system had detrimental consequences for political communities outside of Europe. For one critical discussion of Kissinger, see Smith 1987.

6. For a discussion of the Vatican, see Weigel 1999, 652–53.

7. For a good introduction to the concept of intersubjectivity, see Sokolowski 2000, chapter 10. Edith Stein was deeply interested in this concept. In her dissertation written under Husserl, she focused on empathy and intersubjectivity; see Stein 1989.

8. For these understandings of participation, see Cornelio Fabro's famous work on Thomas Aquinas and participation (Fabro 1950).

9. John Paul II notes that metaphysically, this relationship is an accident, because relating to a particular person is an accidental property. However, as a lived experience it occurs between "fully constituted, separate, personal subjects, along

with all that comprises the personal subjectivity of each of them" (Wojtyla 1993, 242).

10. I will not evaluate the accuracy of this interpretation, but I think Scheler's position is more complex than John Paul II describes.

11. 1 agree with Buttiglione and others who argue that Marxism has little influence on how John Paul II uses this concept; see Buttiglione 1997, chapter 8.

12. These are the two forms of alienation John Paul II identifies at the end of *The Acting Person,* which he calls individualism and totalism. See Wojtyla 1979, 328–22.

13. John Paul II's reflections on alienation and participation are clearly shaped by his experiences living in Communist Poland and his historic work with Solidarity. For background on these experiences, see Weigel 1999, chapters 10–12.

14. For an excellent collection of essays devoted to this encyclical, see Smith and McInerny 2001.

15. With others, I believe that some of the substantive concepts in this core are not, in fact, universal, but are culturally particular. I have learned a great deal about this issue from conversations with Paul J. Griffiths.

16. All references in this paragraph will be to "Letter to Families," sections 13–14.

17. For Nagel's work, see Nagel 1974.

18. Here, I pass over some questions about ethical conflicts that figure prominently in contemporary ethics. In the last several decades, Martha Nussbaum (Nussbaum 1988), Bernard Williams (Williams 1985), and others have explored situations of moral conflict. A key question in this debate is whether moral agents can find themselves in a situation where they must do evil, out of no fault of their own. For an excellent but neglected treatment of these issues, see Santurri 1987.

19. See also "The Person: Subject and Community," in Wojtyla 1993, 238.

20. I recognize that to say more about this topic, I would have to develop the idea of analogy, applying it to political thought. I am grateful to Paul J. Griffiths for his comments about analogy and collectives.

21. For example, see 1979UN, section 13.

22. For one discussion of imperialism, see Ignatieff 2002.

23. For excellent discussions of what the United States action in the Second Gulf War means for the international system and international law, see Rubenfield 2003; Slaughter 2003; Glennon 2003; and Hathaway 2003.

24. I do not want to criticize Weigel for missing these speeches, because he published his work in 1999.

25. John Paul II made similar arguments when opposing the U.S. action in the Second Gulf War. See the "Address of His Holiness John Paul II to the Diplomatic Corps," section 4, January 13, 2003.

26. See "Familiaris Consortio," section 17.

27. See the *Report of the Independent Inquiry into the Actions of the United Nations during the 1994 Genocide in Rwanda.* For a riveting account of what hap-

pened in Rwanda, see Gourevitch 1999, 40. For a good discussion of General Dallaire's actions; see Power 2002, 335–45.

28. In her book on the Rwandan genocide, Melvern offers considerable evidence showing that international aid agencies, the United Nations, and individual nation-states like the United States all willfully ignored or even contributed to the genocide. I find her arguments not only persuasive but profoundly depressing.

29. Samantha Power describes how the Clinton administration opposed using the term *genocide* to describe what was happening in Rwanda, see Power 2002, 358–64.

30. For the text of this convention, see Melvern 2000, appendix 2.

31. For a good account of these conferences, see Weigel 1999, 715–19, 766–71.

32. See Weigel 1999, 715–27, 766–71.

33. This is a well-documented phenomenon in studies of genocide. For example, in Rwanda, the state-run radio repeatedly broadcasted hate messages that portrayed the Tutsi in dehumanizing ways. Melvern does an excellent job of discussing this vile institution; see Melvern 2000, chapter 7.

34. See Ignatieff's essay "The Narcissism of Minor Differences" in Ignatieff 1997.

35. Scheler undoubtedly believed this to be the case; see Scheler 1973a, 526–61.

36. Power carefully discusses why the "international community" has so often failed to adequately respond to genocide; see Power 2002, chapter 14. As I do, she hopes that it will not reproduce its failures in Rwanda and the former Yugoslavia.

37. For a beautiful discussion of the role of spiritual forces in bringing the Cold War to an end, see "Centesimus Annus," 24–25.

REFERENCES

Clarke, W. Norris, S.J. 2001. *The One and the Many: A Contemporary Thomistic Metaphysic.* Notre Dame, IN: University of Notre Dame Press.

Dalliare, Romeo A. 1999. The End of Innocence: Rwanda 1994. In *Hard Choices: Moral Dilemmas in Humanitarian Intervention,* edited by Jonathan Moore. Lanham, MD: Rowman and Littlefield.

Fabro, Cornelio. 1950. *La nozione metafisica di partecipazione secondo S. Tomasso d'Aquino.* Torino: Società editrice internazionale.

Glendon, Mary Ann. 1991. *Rights Talk: The Impoverishment of Political Discourse.* New York: Free Press.

Glennon, Michael J. 2003. "Why the Security Council Failed." *Foreign Affairs* 82 (May/June): 16–36.

Gourevitch, Philip. 1998. *We Wish to Inform You That Tomorrow We Will Be Killed with Our Families: Stories from Rwanda.* New York: Farrar, Straus, and Giroux.

Hehir, J. Bryan, S.J. 1995. "Intervention: From Theories to Cases." *Ethics and International Affairs* 9: 1–13.

———. 1999. "Kosovo: The War of Values and the Values of War." *America* 180 (May 15): 7–12.

———. 2001. "What Can Be Done? What Should Be Done?" *America* 185, no. 10 (October 8): 9–12.

Ignatieff, Michael. 1998. *The Warrior's Honor: Ethnic War and the Modern Conscience.* New York: Metropolitan Books.

Kaplan, Robert D. 2000. *The Coming Anarchy: Shattering the Dreams of the Post–Cold War.* New York: Random House.

Kissinger, Henry. 2001. *Does America Need a Foreign Policy? Toward a Diplomacy for the 21st Century.* New York: Simon and Schuster.

McNamara, Robert S., and James G. Blight. 2001. *Wilson's Ghost: Reducing the Risk of Conflict, Killing, and Catastrophe in the 21st Century.* New York: Public Affairs.

Melvern, Linda. 2000. *A People Betrayed: The Role of the West in Rwanda's Genocide.* London: Zed Books.

Niebuhr, Reinhold. 1983. *Moral Man and Immoral Society.* New York: Macmillan.

Nussbaum, Martha C. 1986. *The Fragility of Goodness: Luck and Ethics in Greek Tragedy.* Cambridge, UK: Cambridge University Press.

Power, Samantha. 2002. *"A Problem from Hell": America and the Age of Genocide.* New York: Basic Books.

Smith, Michael Joseph. 1999. "Humanitarian Intervention: An Overview of the Issues." In *Ethics and International Affairs: A Reader.* 2nd ed. Edited by Joel H. Rosenthal. Washington, D.C.: Georgetown University Press.

United Nations. 1995. *Report of the Independent Inquiry into the Actions of the United Nations during the 1994 Genocide in Rwanda.* Available online at http://www.un.org/News/db/latest/rwanda.htm.

Weigel, George. 1999. *Witness to Hope: The Biography of Pope John Paul II.* New York: Cliff Street Books.

Williams, Bernard. 1982. *Moral Luck.* Cambridge, UK: Cambridge University Press.

Wojtyla, Karol. 1979. *The Acting Person.* Translated by Andrezej Potocki. Dordrecht: D. Reidel.

———. 1993. Person *and Community: Selected Essays.* Translated by Teresa Sandock. New York: Peter Lang.

RENÉ COSTE AND ROSEMARY A. PETERS

View from the Vatican

THE MORAL DIMENSION OF INTERVENTION

Humanitarian intervention has only recently gained international recognition; it was not until December 8, 1988, that it was formally established among the proceedings of the United Nations. Bearing this in mind, we cannot avoid some surprise at the Holy See's rapid and frank acknowledgment of this phenomenon, which serves as proof that the Holy See views it as an issue of great ethical significance. Despite the habitual prudence with which he takes diplomatic action—prudence that bears witness to his wisdom regarding a diversity of situations both moving and controversial—the Pope is not afraid to take a prophetic stance when he believes it necessary. We will look, first of all, at his declarations and the stands he has taken concerning humanitarian intervention. (Readers may examine such declarations within the framework of considerable current Papal contributions to the promotion of peace. See, for example, *Paths to Peace: A Contribution,* Documents of the Holy See to the International Community and The Holy See in International Relations.) Next, we will sketch out a doctrinal synthesis; and finally, we will pose the problem of his extension.

DECLARATIONS AND STANCES

John Paul II's vigorous stance on humanitarian intervention shocked his audience at the International Conference of Nutrition in Rome on December 5, 1992. His view comprised part of a touching plea in favor of effective recognition of the fundamental right to adequate nutrition: "It is imperative that wars between nations and internal conflicts not be allowed to condemn defenseless citizens to starvation because of egotistical or partisan motives." The allusion to still developing tragic conflicts is evident in such places as Bosnia-Herzegovina, various territories of the former USSR, Iraq, Somalia, Liberia and Cambodia. All are tainted with the stigmata of egotistical or partisan choices. "In these cases," affirmed John Paul II, "we must by all means ensure aid, whether alimentary or sanitary, and lift all obstacles, including those which arise from arbitrary recourse to the principle of non-interference in a country's domestic affairs."

We notice that the Pope does not contest the principle of non-intervention (or non-interference) stated in Article 2, paragraph 7 of the Charter of the United

Nations, which stipulates, moreover, that this principle does not undermine the application of coercive measures anticipated in Chapter VII. He simply challenges the "arbitrary recourse" to this principle on the part of the nations involved. The idea is, in effect, sound, since each nation has the right to settle its own domestic problems without outside intervention—with the condition, however, that the government, even with regard to its own citizens, respects the fundamental ethical juridical rights of human life as established by key international texts (the Charter of the United Nations, the 1976 Statement of the International Human Rights, etc.). Fortunately, in conformity with the constant teachings of the Catholic Church, the human ethical conscience no longer permits making the concept of sovereignty absolute, as has too often been the case in international relations.

Then comes the decisive stance in the speech: "The conscience of humankind, sustained henceforth by its liability to international human rights, asks that humanitarian interference be rendered mandatory in situations which gravely compromise the survival of entire peoples and ethnic groups: this is an obligation for both individual nations and the international community as a whole." The principal components of this statement deserve to be emphasized. First, the appeal to the human conscience: incontestably, new instances of ethical awareness (which would normally lead to new juridical measures) come to light concerning the respect and promotion of human rights. Behavior previously considered normal—or at least tolerable—now appears unacceptable.

Second, we notice that the range of the application of obligatory humanitarian intervention is limited to situations of extreme gravity (alas, too frequent in these times), because it concerns only the survival of entire peoples and ethnic groups. This, in itself, does not exclude the possibility that other scenarios can be envisioned.

Third, how can we ignore the strong formulation of an ethical imperative for such situations, by means of the demand that humanitarian interference be rendered mandatory and the assertion that it is an obligation for both individual nations and the international community as a whole? It is a duty, not merely a right, and one which involves nations individually, not just the international community all together. One must talk of an ethical imperative, as we have done.

John Paul II took up the problem of humanitarian intervention thematically near the end of his remarkable speech of January 16, 1993, to an accredited diplomatic corps of the Holy See. He provided important specifics about his conditions of legitimacy (one might think of deontology) and about the responsibility that they can imply. He presumes the worst (all too often verified): that populations "[are] in the process of succumbing to the pressures of an unjust aggressor." By this hypothesis, from the ethical point of view, intervention is imposed as a necessity: "nations no longer have the right to be indifferent"; "the principles of nations' sovereignty and of non-intervention in their domestic affairs—which remain valid—nonetheless cannot be construed as a screen behind which one can torture and assassinate." In sum, governing powers cannot be permitted to play the role of Pontius Pilate.

Let us not forget the intercalary sentence: "It certainly seems that their responsibility is to disarm this aggressor, if all means have proven effective." Note the discretion of the wording ("it certainly seems") and also its projecting the possible duty of coercion. We will end up at politico-military interference, at the initiative of the Security Council, to which Chapter VII of the Charter of the United Nations gives the right "to undertake, by means of aerial, naval, or ground forces, any action it deems necessary to maintain or to reestablish international peace and security" (Article 42). We are the ones who contribute these details, in order to give shape to a thought evidently inscribed in the channels of international law. John Paul II—who intends to remain on the level of ethics—does not wish to formulate himself the points he considers to be outside his jurisdiction: "The lawyers ought to look into this new reality and refine its contours."

The basic role of the Holy See in international proceedings is to insist that "societal organization has no meaning unless it makes the human dimension the central preoccupation in a world made by and for people." As he wrote in his encyclical *Redemptor Hominis,* "man . . . is the primary and fundamental path of the Church, a path demarcated by Christ himself." He has the firm intention of placing himself at this level with regard to humanitarian interference and all other social issues.

On the same subject, we must take into account equally the declarations of its supporters in the Secretariat of State, who contribute greatly to the formulation of the Pope's thought and to the development of his actions in the international domain. The statements of Cardinal Angelo Sodano (Secretary of State) to the press, printed on August 6, 1992, held the public's attention at the time. Sodano intended to make public a conversation he had just held with John Paul II. Not content merely to affirm the principle of humanitarian interference, he applied it immediately to the crisis in Bosnia-Herzegovina, with the assertion that "the European states and the United Nations have the duty and the right of intervention to disarm one who has just killed." In his view, the happenings in that region were the "most sobering contemporary scandal before all of humanity." He accused Europe of setting "a bad example" with its seriously insufficient actions to end the violent conflicts.

These disclosures provoked quite a stir: it was believed that the Holy See was directly advocating political and military intervention in Bosnia-Herzegovina. Forgotten was the fact that the Holy See had long encouraged, to the greatest degree, peacefully solving conflicts through nonviolent means and that John Paul II in particular had taken a critical attitude toward the Gulf War.

From Monsignor Jean-Louis Tauran, Secretary of Relations with States, we document two especially significant statements of opinion: the first, in an interview he accorded to *Le Monde;* the second, at the World Conference on Human Rights, held in Vienna in June 1993. In the first case, he estimates that a sufficiently dissuasive military escort for humanitarian convoys would be a complex as well as dangerous enterprise to enact. Remaining resigned and passive, however, is not an option. In the second, he states bluntly that all human rights have been systematically violated in a permanent manner in Bosnia-Herzegovina. He adds the chilling remark that "the procrastination of everyone with a political and moral obligation in these fratricidal struggles will be severely judged by history."

We remember also two stances of Monsignor Lebeaupin of the Secretariat of State, both of which were heard under the auspices of meetings of high-ranking civil servants during the Conference on Security and Cooperation in Europe (CSCE) in Prague, September 1992 and February 1993. In the first of these, Lebeaupin stated categorically that the community of states should recognize not only the right but also the requirement to intervene, and that a firm political determination on the part of all the States in the CSCE was absolutely necessary in Bosnia-Herzegovina. In the second case, after speaking of "the courage of peace," Lebeaupin synthesized in the following terms the doctrine of the Holy See on the theme we are exploring here: "The Holy See does not cease to assert that humanitarian assistance is the first obligation of the global community. To be sufficient and effective, this must proceed from a decisive political will, fixing clear objectives for interventive maneuvers capable of saving entire populations taken hostage. To this end, intervention may need the support of force, in measures that are meticulous, regulated and definitively executed. For this reason it is inadmissible for the forces of peace in the international community to be, themselves, taken hostage or objects of attack."

DOCTRINAL SYNTHESIS

The ensemble of highly significant texts cited above demonstrates with ample evidence that the Holy See is quite favorable to this new institution established in international practice and sanctioned by the United Nations—humanitarian intervention, considered as not merely a privilege but also a duty. One is asked to resort to this duty each time it is at once ethically necessary and possible. With regard to the conditions of legitimacy of this specific right or responsibility, such as they arise from the statements of the Holy See, we will accept as our own the criteria formulated by Father Joblin: the observation of a serious violation, intolerable and repeated, of the fundamental rights of a human being; an intervention which does not drag along consequences worse than the evils it is meant to remedy; a permanent international control; and recourse as the last resort, after having attempted by every means a peaceable resolution to the situation.

The ethical argument of the Holy See in favor of humanitarian interference appeals both to the principle of universal interpersonal solidarity and to that of the indispensable recognition of the fundamental rights of human beings. These are two essential accents of Catholic social teaching as it has evolved under John Paul II. With regard to the first, we find the most vigorous constructions of it in his Message for the World Day of Peace (January 1, 1987) and in his encyclical *Sollicitudo Rei Socialis*. In these two documents, the principle of universal interpersonal solidarity is presented as a basic principle of social life (in an intrinsic link with that of social justice, which conserves all its validity) and is explained in very expressive terms, both philosophically and theologically. It is thus that, in the second document, while adapting the motto of Pius XII—*Opus Iustitiae Pax,* peace is the fruit of justice—he adds Opus Solidaritatis Pax, peace is the fruit of solidarity.

As for human rights, we know, from *Redemptor Hominis* and the Pope's speech to the United Nations on October 2, 1979, the decisive importance he accords them, which has never declined in the intervening years. Let us remember this unfaltering statement of the encyclical: "By definition, peace amounts to respect for inviolable human rights—opus iustitiae pax—while war is conceived in the violation of these rights and entails even more heinous abuses of them." Can we find a more explosive confirmation of the truth of that assertion than the tragic events in Bosnia-Herzegovina, Somalia, or Cambodia? Introducing these human rights into the concept of "the shared patrimony of humanity" (which should have become an essential ethical and juridical concept in international life) should be amply orchestrated. We will be satisfied with the reminder that this ethical and anthropological argument, which could—and should—be recognized by all, accompanies, in Catholic social teaching, convictions that are fundamental to Christian faith: the eminent dignity of every human being, created "in the image" of God; the unity of the great human family, making brothers and sisters of all human beings; our common responsibility before Him, the Creator who bestowed upon humanity the management of His creation; and Charity (the essential global principle in the ethics of the New Testament), the word that acts as the Christian name for solidarity. This supermotivation of faith is of great existential importance.

The duty of humanitarian intervention may come to be thought of as a "duty of assistance." Just as Bishop Rozier of Poitiers said in a statement in the early part of 1993, "we must consider that there is an obligation to assist anyone in danger. Should we not, then, transpose to the international scheme this principle which commands a duty of intervention on behalf of anyone in danger and which establishes that abstention from that duty is a moral sin and a crime?" The evangelical parable of the Good Samaritan (to which Archbishop Tauran alludes) is the most evocative biblical symbol of this view. Nothing would exempt us from offering aid to a severely wounded person we meet by the side of the road. One could evoke also both the sad figure of Pontius Pilate (who lacked the courage to prevent what he knew to be a politico-religious assassination) and God's ominous question to Cain, who murdered his own brother: "Where is your brother Abel?" (Gen 4:9).

EXPANDING HUMANITARIAN INTERVENTION

However necessary it may be, humanitarian intervention falls under the vocabulary of emergency. As D. Hedin has remarked, intervention can bring only a belated solution to crisis situations that often call for other measures. Is it not conceivable, Hedin asks, that interference of this kind could be made an instrument of prevention and maintenance, not only in political and military crises, but also in the realms of terrorism and the environment? He concludes with the observation that "recourse to intervention outside the field of humanitarian interests helps to evolve, and will continue to do so, the political foundings of widespread interests, from the defense of human rights to the protection of higher interests of humanity."

We must further this evolution of international life with all our might. The biggest problems in society shall, henceforth, be global problems that cannot be resolved except through dialogue and cooperation. Although states still have a role of capital importance to play, they should no longer be considered as the primary actors, but rather as members—by the populations they represent—of the vast and unique human family. It is humanity itself which should be considered as the central figure in the order of creation (given that, for Christians, this must be in the perspective of faith in He who is the Creator and the author of history, who entrusted Earth to the responsible management of humanity as a whole). Every human being should be viewed in the framework of his or her own inalienable dignity and his or her own personal, interdependent responsibility. The contemporary world desperately needs a surge of planetary humanism.

That is the type of humanism that Catholic social teaching has endeavored ardently to promote, especially since John XXIII and Vatican II. As John Paul II said in his October 20, 1979, speech to the United Nations, "it is essential that we come together in the name of humanity, seen in the plenitude and many-faceted richness of its spiritual and material existence." Planetary interdependence calls for the rhetoric of solidarity: as the encyclical *Sollicitudo Rei Socialis* explains it, "an unshaking and persevering determination to work for the common good: that is to say, for the good of all and of each because we are each truly responsible for all." The work *Centesimus Annus* also asserts that "we must take definitive steps in order to create or to consolidate international structures capable of intervention, for appropriate arbitration in conflicts that surface between nations, of such design that each among them may validate its proper rights and come to a just agreement and a peaceful compromise with the rights of others."

JOHN PAUL II

Solidarity Is Essential in the Fight on World Hunger

Message to the World Food Summit Sponsored by the Food and Agriculture Organization (June 10, 2002)

Since I am unable to be among you personally on this solemn occasion, I have asked Cardinal Angelo Sodano, secretary of state, to convey all my esteem and regard for the arduous work that you have to undertake in order to ensure that everyone has their daily bread.

I offer a special greeting to the president of the Italian republic, and to all the heads of state and government who have come to Rome for this summit. During my pastoral visits to various parts of the world, as well as at the Vatican, I have already had an opportunity to meet many of them personally: To all go my deferential best wishes for themselves and the nations they represent.

I extend this greeting to the secretary-general of the United Nations, as well as to the director-general of the Food and Agriculture Organization and to the heads of other international organizations present at this meeting. The Holy See expects much from their efforts on behalf of humanity's material and spiritual progress.

I express the hope that the present World Food Summit will be crowned with success: This is what millions of men and women throughout the world expect.

The last summit in 1996 had already established that hunger and malnutrition are not phenomena of a merely natural or structural nature, affecting only certain geographic areas, but are to be seen as the consequence of a more complex situation of underdevelopment resulting from human inertia and self-centeredness.

If the goals of the 1996 summit have not been met, that can be attributed also to the absence of a culture of solidarity, and to international relations often shaped by a pragmatism devoid of ethical and moral foundations. Moreover, a cause for concern is to be found in the statistics according to which assistance given to poor countries in recent years appears to have decreased rather than increased.

Today more than ever, there is an urgent need in international relationships for solidarity to become the criterion underlying all forms of cooperation, with the acknowledgment that the resources which God the Creator has entrusted to us are destined for all.

Of course, much is expected from the experts, whose task it is to point out when and how to increase agricultural resources, how to achieve better distribution of products, how to set up food-security programs and how to devise new techniques to boost harvests and increase herds.

The preamble to the FAO constitution itself proclaimed the commitment of each country to raise its level of nutrition and improve the conditions of its agriculture, and of its rural population, in such a way as to increase production and secure an effective distribution of food supplies in all parts of the world.

These goals, however, involve a constant reconsideration of the relationship between the right to be freed from poverty and the duty of the whole human family to provide practical help to the needy.

For my part, I am pleased that the present World Food Summit is once more urging the various sectors of the international community, governments and intergovernmental institutions to make a commitment to somehow guaranteeing the right to nutrition in cases where an individual state is unable to do so because of its own underdevelopment and poverty. Such a commitment can be seen as entirely necessary and legitimate, given the fact that poverty and hunger risk compromising even the ordered coexistence of peoples and nations and constitute a real threat to peace and international security.

Hence the importance of the present World Food Summit, with its reaffirmation of the concept of food security and its call for a mobilization of solidarity aimed at reducing by half, by the year 2015, the number of people in the world who are undernourished and deprived of the bare necessities of life. This is an enormous challenge, and one to which the Church, too, is fully committed.

The Catholic Church is ever concerned for the promotion of human rights and the integral development of peoples, and will therefore continue to support all who work to ensure that every member of the human family receives adequate daily food. Her intimate vocation is to be close to the world's poor, and she hopes that everyone will become practically involved in speedily resolving this problem, one of the gravest facing the human family.

May the Almighty, who is rich in mercy, send His blessing upon each one of you, upon the work you do under the aegis of FAO, and upon all those who strive for the authentic progress of the human family.

∾

John Paul II

Private Property and the Universal Destination of Moral Goods

The modern business economy has positive aspects. Its basis is human freedom exercised in the economic field, just as it is exercised in many other fields. Economic activity is indeed but one sector in a great variety of human activities, and like every other sector, it includes the right to freedom, as well as the duty of making responsible use of freedom. But it is important to note that there are specific differences between the trends of modern society and those of the past, even the recent past. Whereas at one time the decisive factor of production was the land, and later capital—understood as a total complex of the instruments of production—today the decisive factor is increasingly man himself, that is, his knowledge, especially his scientific knowledge, his capacity for interrelated and compact organization, as well as his ability to perceive the needs of others and to satisfy them.

However, the risks and problems connected with this kind of process should be pointed out. The fact is that many people, perhaps the majority today, do not have the means which would enable them to take their place in an effective and humanly dignified way within a productive system in which work is truly central. They have no possibility of acquiring the basic knowledge which would enable them to express their creativity and develop their potential. They have no way of entering the network of knowledge and intercommunication which would enable them to see their qualities appreciated and utilized. Thus, if not actually exploited, they are to a great extent marginalized; economic development takes place over their heads, so to speak, when it does not actually reduce the already narrow scope of their old subsistence economies. They are unable to compete against the goods which are produced in ways which are new and which properly respond to needs, needs which they had previously been accustomed to meeting through traditional forms of organization. Allured by the dazzle of an opulence which is beyond their reach, and at the same time driven by necessity, these people crowd the cities of the Third World where they are often without cultural roots, and where they are exposed to situations of violent uncertainty, without the possibility of becoming integrated. Their dignity is not acknowledged in any real way, and sometimes there are even attempts to eliminate them from history through coercive forms of demographic control which are contrary to human dignity.

Many other people, while not completely marginalized, live in situations in which the struggle for a bare minimum is uppermost. These are situations in which the rules of the earliest period of capitalism still flourish in conditions of "ruthlessness" in no way inferior to the darkest moments of the first phase of industrialization. In other cases the land is still the central element in the economic process, but those who cultivate it are excluded from ownership and are reduced to a state of quasi-servitude. In these cases, it is still possible today, as in the days of *Rerum Novarum,* to speak of inhuman exploitation. In spite of the great changes which have taken place in the more advanced societies, the human inadequacies of capitalism and the resulting domination of things over people are far from disappearing. In fact, for the poor, to the lack of material goods has been added a lack of knowledge and training, which prevents them from escaping their state of humiliating subjection.

Unfortunately, the great majority of people in the Third World still live in such conditions. It would be a mistake, however, to understand this "world" in purely geographic terms. In some regions and in some social sectors of that world, development programs have been set up which are centered on the use not so much of the material resources available but of the "human resources."

Even in recent years it was thought that the poorest countries would develop by isolating themselves from the world market and by depending only on their own resources. Recent experience has shown that countries which did this have suffered stagnation and recession, while the countries which experienced development were those which succeeded in taking part in the general interrelated economic activities at the international level. It seems therefore that the chief problem is that of gaining fair access to the international market, based not on the unilateral principle of the exploitation of the natural resources of these countries but on the proper use of human resources.

However, aspects typical of the Third World also appear in developed countries, where the constant transformation of the methods of production and consumption devalues certain acquired skills and professional expertise, and thus requires a continual effort of retraining and updating. Those who fail to keep up with the times can easily be marginalized, as can the elderly, the young people who are incapable of finding their place in the life of society and, in general, those who are weakest or part of the so-called Fourth World. The situation of women too is far from easy in these conditions.

The church acknowledges the legitimate role of profit as an indication that a business is functioning well. When a firm makes a profit, this means that productive factors have been properly employed and corresponding human needs have been duly satisfied. But profitability is not the only indicator of a firm's condition. It is possible for the financial accounts to be in order, and yet for the people—who make up the firm's most valuable asset—to be humiliated and their dignity offended. Besides being morally inadmissible, this will eventually have negative repercussions on the firm's economic efficiency. In fact, the purpose of a business firm is not simply to make a profit, but is to be found in its very existence as a community of persons who in various ways are endeavoring to satisfy their basic needs, and who form a particular group at the service of the whole of society. Profit is a regulator of the life of a business, but it is not the only one; other human and moral factors must also be considered which, in the long term, are at least equally important for the life of a business.

We have seen that it is unacceptable to say that the defeat of so-called real socialism leaves capitalism as the only model of economic organization. It is necessary to break down the barriers and monopolies which leave so many countries on the margins of development, and to provide all individuals and nations with the basic conditions which will enable them to share in development. This goal calls for programmed and responsible efforts on the part of the entire international community. Stronger nations must offer weaker ones opportunities for taking their place in international life, and the latter must learn how to use these opportunities by making the necessary efforts and sacrifices and by ensuring political and economic stability, the certainty of better prospects for the future, the improvement of workers' skills, and the training of competent business leaders who are conscious of their responsibilities.

These general observations also apply to the role of the state in the economic sector. Economic activity, especially the activity of a market economy, cannot be conducted in an institutional, juridical or political vacuum. On the contrary, it presupposes sure guarantees of individual freedom and private property, as well as a stable currency and efficient public services. Hence the principal task of the state is to guarantee this security, so that those who work and produce can enjoy the fruits of their labors and thus feel encouraged to work efficiently and honestly. The absence of stability, together with the corruption of public officials and the spread of improper sources of growing rich and of easy profits deriving from illegal or purely speculative activities, constitutes one of the chief obstacles to development and to the economic order.

Another task of the state is that of overseeing and directing the exercise of human rights in the economic sector. However, primary responsibility in this area belongs not to the state but to individuals and to the various groups and associations which make up society. The state could not directly ensure the right to work for all its citizens unless it controlled every aspect of economic life and restricted the free initiative of individuals. This does not mean, however, that the state has no competence in this domain, as was claimed by those who argued against any rules in the economic sphere. Rather, the state has a duty to sustain business activities by creating conditions which will ensure job opportunities, by stimulating those activities where they are lacking or by supporting them in moments of crisis.

The state has the further right to intervene when particular monopolies create delays or obstacles to development. In addition to the tasks of harmonizing and guiding development, in exceptional circumstances the state can also exercise a substitute function, when social sectors or business systems are too weak or are just getting under way, and are not equal to the task at hand. Such supplementary interventions, which are justified by urgent reasons touching the common good, must be as brief as possible, so as to avoid removing permanently from society and business systems the functions which are properly theirs, and so as to avoid enlarging excessively the sphere of state intervention to the detriment of both economic and civil freedom.

In recent years the range of such intervention has vastly expanded, to the point of creating a new type of state, the so-called welfare state. This has happened in some countries in order to respond better to many needs and demands, by remedying forms of poverty and deprivation unworthy of the human person. However, excesses and abuses, especially in recent years, have provoked very harsh criticisms of the welfare state, dubbed the "social assistance state." Malfunctions and defects in the social assistance state are the result of an inadequate understanding of the tasks proper to the state. Here again the principle of subsidiarity must be respected: a community of a higher order should not interfere in the internal life of a community of a lower order, depriving the latter of its functions, but rather should support it in case of need and help to coordinate its activity with the activities of the rest of society, always with a view to the common good.

By intervening directly and depriving society of its responsibility, the social assistance state leads to a loss of human energies and an inordinate increase of public agencies, which are dominated more by bureaucratic ways of thinking than by concern for serving their clients, and which are accompanied by an enormous increase in spending. In fact, it would appear that needs are best understood and satisfied by people who are closest to them and who act as neighbors to those in need. It should be added that certain kinds of demands often call for a response which is not simply material but which is capable of perceiving the deeper human need. One thinks of the condition of refugees, immigrants, the elderly, the sick, and all those in circumstances which call for assistance, such as drug abusers: All these people can be helped effectively only by those who offer them genuine fraternal support, in addition to the necessary care.

≈

JOHN PAUL II

The Role of Religion
in a Uniting of Europe

Message to the European Study Congress on the theme "Toward a European Constitution?" (June 20, 2002)

1. I am pleased to send cordial greetings on the occasion of the European Study Congress, which the Vicariate of Rome's Office for the Pastoral Care of the University has sponsored in conjunction with the Commission of the Episcopates of the European Union and the Federation of the Catholic Universities of Europe.

The question that is the theme of the Congress—"Toward a European Constitution?"—stresses the importance of the current phase in the process of building the "common European house." Indeed, it seems that the time has come to begin the important institutional reforms hoped for and prepared in recent years, which have become more urgently needed with the scheduled admission of new member states.

The expansion of the European Union or, rather, for the process of "Europeanization" of the whole continental area, that I have fostered, is a priority to be pursued courageously and quickly in order to respond effectively to the expectations of millions of men and women who know that they are bound together by a common history and who hope for a destiny of unity and solidarity. It requires a rethinking of the European Union's institutional structures to adapt them to the greater needs. At the same time, there is an urgency to establish a new order to identify clearly what are the objectives of the European construction, the responsibilities of the union and the values on which it must be based.

2. As she contemplates the various possible solutions to this important European "process" in a way that is faithful to her identity and her evangelizing mission, the Church applies what she has already said about individual states: that she "is not entitled to express preferences for this or that institutional or constitutional solution" and respects the legitimate autonomy of the democratic order (cf. *Centesimus Annus,* no. 47). At the same time, by virtue of her identity and mission, she cannot

be indifferent to the values that inspire the various institutional decisions. Doubtless, the various decisions in this regard involve moral dimensions since the deliberations that result from them in a particular historical context inevitably lead directly to conceptions of the person, society and the common good from which they sprang and which are inherent in them. On this precise consciousness are founded the Church's right and duty to intervene by making her own contribution, which reflects the vision of human dignity and all its consequences as is spelled out in Catholic social teaching.

In this perspective, the search for and configuration of a new order, which was the aim of the "Constituent Convention" instituted by the Council of Europe at the Laeken Summit in December 2001, should be acknowledged as positive steps in themselves. Indeed, they are geared to that desirable strengthening of the institutional framework of the European Union, which can effectively contribute to the development of peace, justice and solidarity for the whole continent through a freely accepted network of obligations and cooperation.

3. However, if a new European order of this kind is to be adequate for the promotion of the authentic common good, it must recognize and safeguard the values that constitute the most precious heritage of European humanism, which has assured and continues to assure Europe a unique influence in the history of civilization. These values constitute the characteristic intellectual and spiritual contribution that has formed the European identity through the centuries and is part of the valuable cultural treasure of the continent. As I have recalled on other occasions, they concern the dignity of the person; the sacred character of human life; the central role of the family founded on marriage; the importance of education; freedom of thought, of speech and of the profession of personal convictions and religion; the legal protection of individuals and groups; the collaboration of all for the common good; work, seen as a personal and a social good; political power understood as a service, subject to law and reason, and "limited" by the rights of the person and of peoples.

Expressly, it will be necessary to recognize and safeguard the dignity of the human person and the right to religious freedom in its threefold dimension: individual, collective and institutional.

Moreover, one must make room for the horizontal and vertical dimensions of the principle of subsidiarity, as well as for a vision of social and community relations founded on an authentic culture and ethics of solidarity.

4. Multiple are the cultural roots that have contributed to reinforce the values just mentioned: from the spirit of Greece to that of Roman law and virtue; from the contributions of the Latin, Celtic, Germanic, Slav and Hungarian-Finnish peoples, to those of the Jewish culture and the Islamic world. These different factors found in the Jewish-Christian tradition the power that harmonized, consolidated and promoted them. By acknowledging this historical fact in the process leading to a new institutional order, Europe cannot deny its Christian heritage, since a great part of its achievements in the fields of law, art, literature and philosophy have been influenced by the evangelical message. Not giving in to a temptation to be nostalgic or

to be content mechanically to repeat past models, but being open to the new challenges emerging, Europe will need to draw inspiration with creative fidelity from the Christian roots that have defined European history.

Historical memory demands it; but also and above all, it is essential to its mission. Europe is called today to be a teacher of true progress, to spread a globalization of solidarity without marginalization, to take part in building a just and lasting peace within it and in the world, to bring together different cultural traditions to give life to a humanism in which the respect for rights, solidarity and creativity will allow every man and woman to fulfill his/her noblest aspirations.

5. A challenging task lies ahead of European political persons! To be fully equal to it they will need to know how to give to such values the deeply rooted transcendence that is expressed in openness to the religious dimension.

This will also allow them to reaffirm the non-absolute nature of political institutions and public authorities due to the fact that primarily and quintessentially the human being "belongs" to God, whose image is indelibly stamped on the nature of every man and woman. If this were not to take place, there would be a risk of legitimizing the orientations of agnostic and atheist laicism and secularism that lead to the exclusion of God and of the natural moral law from the sectors of human life. The Continent's civil coexistence has suffered from this tragic experience—as the history of Europe has demonstrated.

6. In this whole process the specific identity and social role of the churches and religious confessions must also be recognized and safeguarded. Indeed, they have always played and still play a determining role in many ways, in inculcating the supporting values of coexistence, proposing answers to the fundamental questions about the meaning of life, fostering the culture and identity of peoples, offering Europe what helps to give it a desirable and necessary spiritual foundation.

Moreover, they cannot be reduced to being merely private bodies; they operate with a specific institutional density that deserves to be appreciated and accorded juridical recognition, respecting and not jeopardizing the status that they enjoy in the ordering of the union's various member states.

In other words, it is a question of reacting against the temptation to build a European coexistence that excludes the contribution of the religious communities with the riches of their message, action and witness. Among other things, the process of building Europe would lack important energies for the ethical and cultural foundation of civil coexistence. I hope, therefore—in accord with the logic of a "healthy collaboration" between the ecclesial community and the political community (cf. *Gaudium et Spes*, no. 76)—that in this process the European institutions will be able to enter into dialogue with the churches and religious denominations on regular terms, accepting the contribution they can certainly offer by reason of their spirituality and commitment to the humanization of society.

7. Last, I would like to address the Christian communities and all who believe in Christ to ask them to undertake a vast and coherent cultural action. Indeed, it is urgent to show—with strong convincing arguments and magnetic examples—that founding the new Europe on the values that shaped it in the course of history and

which are rooted in the Christian tradition will benefit all, regardless of their philosophical or spiritual tradition, and serve as the solid foundation of a coexistence that is more human and peaceful because it respects all and each one.

On the basis of these common shared values, it will be possible to achieve the forms of democratic consensus required to outline, even at the institutional level, the program for a Europe that may truly be the home of all, and in which no person and no people feel excluded but all can feel called upon to contribute to the common good, on the Continent and throughout the world.

8. In this perspective it is legitimate to expect a great deal from the Catholic universities of Europe. They will not fail to develop a comprehensive reflection on the various aspects of such a stimulating problematic. Your congress can certainly make a valuable contribution to this research.

As I invoke God's light and comfort upon the involvement of each one, to you I impart a special apostolic blessing.

~

JOHN PAUL II

Message to Archbishop Alberto Giraldo Jaramillo of Medellín, President of the Bishops' Conference of Colombia

1. A century has now passed since 22 June 1902, when the bishops, the civil authorities, and the people of Colombia, stirred by deep sentiments of love and devotion, consecrated the Republic to the Sacred Heart of Jesus, promising to build a votive shrine to beg for peace for the nation. Since then, with constant enthusiasm and hope, this consecration has been renewed every year in parishes, religious houses, and in many families who have confidence in the love and mercy of the Savior who loves and continues to love all men and women, and welcomes them with the gentle words: "Come to me, all who labor and are heavily burdened, and I will give you rest" (Mt 11:28).

THE WATER AND BLOOD SYMBOLIZE THE FLOW
OF ABUNDANT GIFTS TO US TODAY

2. The Gospel reveals to us the unfathomable riches of the Heart of Christ in his attitude of pardon and mercy for all, in his burning love for the Father and for all humanity. At the same time, Jesus shows us the path to new life: "Learn from me

for I am meek and humble of heart" (Mt 11:29). From this heart, a particularly expressive symbol of divine love, pierced by the soldier's spear (cf. Jn 19:33–34), flow abundant gifts for the life of the world: "I have come that they may have life, and have it abundantly" (Jn 10:10). These are the gifts that Pope Pius XII mentioned in his Encyclical *Haurietis acquas:* his own life, the Holy Spirit, the Eucharist, the priest-hood, the Church, his Mother, and his unceasing prayer for us (cf. nn. 36–44).

THE HEART OF JESUS SPEAKS OF THE TRUE VALUES OF THE CIVILIZATION OF LOVE

3. Now that the Catholic faithful of Colombia, presided over by their pastors and the authorities, prepare to renew this centenary consecration of their Nation to the Heart of Jesus, I want to repeat to them the appeal I made at the beginning of my mission as Successor of Peter: "Open wide the doors for Christ!" (*Homily,* 22 October 1978, n. 5; *ORE,* 2 November 1978, p. 12). Listen, dear Brothers, to the voice of Christ who continues to speak to the people of today. As I already wrote on another occasion: "In the Heart of Christ, man's heart learns to know the gen-uine and unique meaning of his life and his destiny, to understand the value of an authentically Christian life, to keep himself from certain perversions of the human heart and to unite the filial love for God with the love of neighbor. The true repa-ration asked by the Heart of the Savior will come when the civilization of love, the Kingdom of the Heart of Christ, can be built upon the ruins heaped up by hatred and violence" (Letter to the Superior General of the Society of Jesus, 5 October 1985; *ORE,* 27 October 1986, p. 7).

RENEWAL OF CONSECRATION ENTAILS PERSONAL CONVERSION AND SOCIAL TRANSFORMATION

4. The consecration of the men and women of Colombia to the Sacred Heart of Jesus, which you prepare to renew in the admirable tradition established now for 100 years, must be a special moment of grace and great dedication. Indeed, it must be a fervent prayer to the Lord to renew the whole of Colombian society, so that it can act with a new heart and a new spirit (cf. Ez 11:19). Thus it will be possible to accept the call for prayer which I made in my Apostolic Letter *Novo Millennio Ineunte* (cf. nn. 32–33), when I asked that each Christian distinguish himself pre-cisely in the art of prayer and contemplation of the face of the Lord (cf. ibid., nn. 16–28), the One whom they pierced (cf. Jn 19:37); at the same time, it will foster an ongoing conversion which is the indispensable foundation for life as the new cre-ation (cf. Col 3:10).

However, this personal conversion must also be accompanied by a profound social change which starts by strengthening the family, the richest school of humanism. Indeed, solid families are the core communities who foster and hand on human and

Christian virtues, who nourish hope and real dedication among their members, who welcome and respect human life in all its stages, from conception to natural death.

A society that listens to and obeys Christ's message, moves on the way to true peace, rejects every kind of violence and conceives of new ways of harmonious living, takes the reliable and sound path of justice, reconciliation and forgiveness, and fosters bonds of unity, fraternity, and respect for each person.

LAUNCHING A NATIONAL MOVEMENT
OF RECONCILIATION AND FORGIVENESS

5. I strongly urge that this centenary that is observed at a time when unfortunately your beloved nation does not yet enjoy stable peace and when violence continues to reap victims at every level of society, including even the pastors of the Church, this event will be an occasion for everyone—priests, religious, and lay faithful—united with their bishops and coming from everywhere in this beloved land, to launch a great national movement of reconciliation and forgiveness. May it also be a moment to implore God for the gifts of peace, and for each one in his own walk of life to commit himself to laying the foundations of the moral and material reconstruction of your national community. You know that in this work Jesus Christ, the Prince of Peace, will give you the necessary strength to re-establish a society based on justice, solidarity, responsibility, and peace.

As I join you in spirit in the Consecration to the Sacred Heart of Jesus, I beg him to pour out his abundant gifts upon the citizens, families, ecclesial communities, the public institutions and their leaders, and at the same time, entrusting these hopes to the motherly intercession of Our Lady of Chiquinquirá, Queen of Colombia, with great love I impart to you my Apostolic Blessing.

BENEDICT XVI

Address to the Delegates of Other Churches and Ecclesial Communities and of Other Religious Traditions

Monday, 25 April 2005

Dear Delegates of the Orthodox Churches, of the Oriental Orthodox Churches and of the Ecclesial Communities of the West, I greet you with joy a few days after my election. I particularly appreciated your presence in St. Peter's Square yesterday, after we had lived together the sorrowful moments of the farewell to our late Pope John Paul II. The tribute of sympathy and affection that you expressed to my unforgettable Predecessor went far beyond a mere act of ecclesial courtesy. Much progress was made during the years of his Pontificate, and your participation in the mourning of the Catholic Church on his departure has shown how true and great the common eagerness for unity is.

In greeting you, I would like to thank the Lord who has blessed us with his mercy and instilled in us sincere willingness to make his prayer our own: *ut unum sint*. He has thus made us increasingly aware of the importance of moving forward towards full communion. With brotherly friendship we can exchange the gifts we have received from the Spirit, and we feel urged to encourage one another so that we may proclaim Christ and his message to the world, which often appears troubled and restless, uninformed and indifferent.

Our meeting today is particularly important. First of all, it enables the new Bishop of Rome, Pastor of the Catholic Church, to repeat to you all with simplicity: *Duc in altum!* Let us go forward with hope. In the footsteps of my Predecessors, especially Paul VI and John Paul II, I feel strongly the need to reassert the irreversible commitment taken by the Second Vatican Council and pursued in recent years, also thanks to the activity of the Pontifical Council for Promoting Christian Unity. The path to the full communion desired by Jesus for his disciples entails, with true docility to what the Spirit says to the Churches, courage, gentleness, firmness and hope, in order to reach our goal. Above all, it requires persistent prayer and with one heart, in order to obtain from the Good Shepherd the gift of unity for his flock.

How can we not recognize in a spirit of gratitude to God that our meeting also has the significance of a gift that has already been granted? In fact, Christ, the Prince of Peace, has acted in our midst: he has poured out friendship by the handful, he has mitigated points of disagreement, he has taught us to be more open to dialogue and in harmony with the commitments proper to those who bear his Name. Over and above what divides us and casts shadows on our full and visible communion, your presence, dear Brothers in Christ, is a sign of sharing and support for the Bishop of Rome, who can count on you to continue the journey in hope and to grow towards the One who is Christ, the Head.

On such a special occasion, when we are gathered together at the very beginning of my ecclesial service, welcomed with respect and trusting obedience to the Lord, I ask you all to join with me in setting an example of that spiritual ecumenism which, through prayer, can bring about our communion without obstacles.

I entrust these intentions and reflections to you together with my most cordial greetings, so that you may pass them on to your Churches and Ecclesial Communities.

I turn now to you, dear friends from different religious traditions, and I thank you sincerely for your presence at the solemn inauguration of my Pontificate. I offer warm and affectionate greetings to you and to all those who belong to the religions that you represent. I am particularly grateful for the presence in our midst of members of the Muslim community, and I express my appreciation for the growth of dialogue between Muslims and Christians, both at the local and international level. I assure you that the Church wants to continue building bridges of friendship with the followers of all religions, in order to seek the true good of every person and of society as a whole.

The world in which we live is often marked by conflicts, violence and war, but it earnestly longs for peace, peace which is above all a gift from God, peace for which we must pray without ceasing. Yet peace is also a duty to which all peoples must be committed, especially those who profess to belong to religious traditions. Our efforts to come together and foster dialogue are a valuable contribution to building peace on solid foundations. Pope John Paul II, my Venerable Predecessor, wrote at the start of the new Millennium that "the name of the one God must become increasingly what it is: a name of peace and a summons to peace" (*Novo Millennio Ineunte,* n. 55). It is therefore imperative to engage in authentic and sincere dialogue, built on respect for the dignity of every human person, created, as we Christians firmly believe, in the image and likeness of God (cf. Gn 1:26–27).

At the beginning of my Pontificate, I address to you and to all believers of the religious traditions that you represent, as well as to all who seek the Truth with a sincere heart, a pressing invitation together to become artisans of peace, in a reciprocal commitment to understanding, respect and love.

My cordial greeting to you all.

~

BENEDICT XVI

Address to the Diplomatic Corps Accredited to the Holy See

Thursday, 12 May 2005

Your Excellencies, Ladies and Gentlemen,

I am pleased to meet you today, a little less than a month after I began my pastoral service as Successor of Peter. I am touched by the words that His Excellency Prof. Giovanni Galassi, Dean of the Diplomatic Corps to the Holy See, has just addressed to me, and appreciate the attention that all the diplomats pay to the Church's mission in the world. I offer my cordial greetings to each one of you and to those who work with you. I thank you for your courtesy during the great events that we lived through this past April, as well as for your daily work.

As I speak to you, I am thinking in addition of the countries you represent and of their Leaders. I am also thinking of the nations with which the Holy See does not yet have diplomatic relations. Some of them took part in the celebrations for the funeral of my Predecessor and for my election to the Chair of Peter.

Having appreciated these gestures, today I would like to thank them and to address a respectful greeting to the civil Authorities of those countries. Moreover, I express the hope that sooner or later I will see them represented at the Holy See.

I have received messages from them, especially those with numerous Catholic communities, which I particularly appreciated. I would like to say that I cherish these communities and all the peoples that belong to them, and assure them all of my remembrance in prayer.

In seeing you, how can I fail to recall the long and fruitful ministry of our beloved Pope John Paul II! An unflagging Gospel missionary in the many countries that he visited, he also rendered a unique service to the cause of the unity of the human family. He pointed out the way to God, inviting all people of good will to sharpen their consciences all the time and to build a society of justice, peace and solidarity, in charity and in mutual forgiveness.

Nor should we forget his countless meetings here in the Vatican with Heads of State, Heads of Government and Ambassadors, at which he devoted himself to defending the cause of peace.

For my part, I come from a Country where peace and brotherhood are treasured by all the inhabitants, especially those who, like myself, lived through the war and the separation of brothers and sisters belonging to the same Nation because of destructive and inhuman ideologies that, beneath a mask of dreams and illusions, burdened men and women with the heavy yoke of oppression. Thus, you will understand that I am particularly sensitive to dialogue between all human beings in order to overcome every kind of conflict and tension and to make our earth an earth of peace and brotherhood.

All together, by combining their efforts, Christian communities, national Leaders, Diplomats and all people of good will are called to achieve a peaceful society, to overcome the temptation of confrontation between cultures, races and worlds that are different. For this, each people must find in its spiritual and cultural patrimony the best values it possesses so that it may advance undaunted to encounter the other, ready to share its own spiritual and material riches for the benefit of all.

In order to continue in this direction, the Church never ceases to proclaim and defend the fundamental human rights, which unfortunately are still violated in various parts of the earth. She is working for recognition of the rights of every human person to life, food, a home, work, health-care assistance, the protection of the family and the promotion of social development, with respect for the dignity of men and of women, created in the image of God.

Rest assured that the Catholic Church will continue to offer to cooperate, in her own province and with her own means, to safeguard the dignity of every person and to serve the common good. She asks no privileges for herself but only the legitimate conditions of freedom to carry out her mission. In the concert of nations, she always seeks to encourage understanding and cooperation between peoples based on loyalty, discretion and friendliness.

Lastly, I ask you to renew my thanks to your Governments for their participation in the celebrations on the occasion of the death of Pope John Paul II and of my election, as well as my respectful and cordial greeting, which I accompany with a special prayer that God will pour out an abundance of his Blessings upon you personally, upon your families, upon your countries and upon all who live in them.

∾

BENEDICT XVI

Address to Carlo Azeglio Ciampi, President of the Italian Republic

Quirinal Palace, Friday, 24 June 2005

Mr. President,

I have the joy today of reciprocating the most cordial visit that you were pleased to pay me as Head of the Italian State last 3 May on the occasion of the new pastoral service to which the Lord has called me. First of all, therefore, I would like to thank you and through you, to thank the Italian People for the warm welcome they have accorded me from the very first day of my pastoral service as Bishop of Rome and Pastor of the universal Church.

For my part, I assure the citizens of Rome and then the whole Italian Nation of my commitment to do my utmost for the religious and civil good of those whom the Lord has entrusted to my pastoral care.

The proclamation of the Gospel which, in communion with the Italian Bishops, I am called to make to Rome and to Italy is not only at the service of the Italian people's growth in faith and in the Christian life but also of its progress on the paths of concord and peace. Christ is the Saviour of the whole person, spirit and body, his spiritual and eternal destiny and his temporal and earthly life. Thus, when his message is heard, the civil community also becomes more responsible and attentive to the needs of the common good and shows greater solidarity with the poor, the abandoned and the marginalized.

Reviewing Italian history, one is struck by the innumerable works of charity that the Church, with great sacrifices, set up for the relief of all kinds of suffering. Today the Church intends to journey on along this same path, without any ambition for power and without requesting social or financial privileges. The example of Jesus Christ, who "went about doing good works and healing all" (Acts 10: 38), remains the Church's supreme norm of conduct among the peoples.

Relations between the Church and the Italian State are founded on the principle spelled out by the Second Vatican Council, which says: "The political community and the Church are autonomous and independent of each other in their own fields. Nevertheless, both are devoted to the personal vocation of man, though under different titles" (*Gaudium et Spes,* n. 76).

This principle was already present in the Lateran Pacts and was subsequently confirmed in the Agreements that modified the Concordat. Therefore, a healthy secularism of the State, by virtue of which temporal realities are governed according to their own norms but which does not exclude those ethical references that are ultimately founded in religion, is legitimate. The autonomy of the temporal sphere does not exclude close harmony with the superior and complex requirements that derive from an integral vision of man and his eternal destiny.

I am eager to assure you, Mr. President, and all the Italian People, that the Church desires to maintain and to foster a cordial spirit of collaboration and understanding at the service of the spiritual and moral growth of the Country; it would be seriously harmful, not only for her but also for Italy, to attempt to weaken or to break these very special ties that bind her to the Country. The Italian culture is deeply imbued with Christian values, as can be seen in the splendid masterpieces that the Nation has produced in all fields of thought and art.

My hope is that the Italian People will not only not deny the Christian heritage that is part of their history but will guard it jealously and make it produce new fruits worthy of the past. I am confident that Italy, under the wise and exemplary guidance of those who are called to govern it, will continue to carry out in the world its civilizing mission in which it has so distinguished itself down the centuries. By virtue of its history and its culture, Italy can make a very worthwhile contribution, particularly to Europe, helping it to rediscover the Christian roots that enabled it to achieve greatness in the past and can still serve to deepen the profound unity of the Continent.

Mr. President, as you can easily understand, I have many concerns at the beginning of my pastoral service on the Chair of Peter. I would like to point out some of them which, because of their universally human character, cannot but also concern those who are responsible for government. I am alluding to the problem of the protection of the family founded on marriage, as it is recognized also in the Italian Constitution (n. 29), the problem of the defence of human life from conception to its natural end and lastly, the problem of education and consequently of school, an indispensable training ground for the formation of the new generations.

The Church, accustomed as she is to scrutinizing God's will engraved in the very nature of the human creature, sees in the family a most important value that must be defended from any attack that aims to undermine its solidity and call its very existence into question.

The Church recognizes human life as a primary good, the premise for all other goods. She therefore asks that it be respected both at its initial and its final stages and stresses the duty to provide adequate palliative treatment that makes death more human.

As for schools, her role is connected with the family as a natural expansion of its task of formation. In this regard, save the competence of the State to dictate the general norms of instruction, I cannot but express the hope that the right of parents to choose education freely will be respected, and that in so doing they will not have to bear the additional burden of further expenses. I trust that Italian legislators, in their wisdom, will be able to find "human" solutions to the problems mentioned here, in other words, solutions that respect the inviolable values implicit in them.

Lastly, expressing my hope that the Nation will continue to advance on the path of spiritual and material well being, I join you, Mr. President, in urging all the citizens and all the members of society always to live and work in a spirit of genuine harmony, in a context of open dialogue and mutual trust, in the commitment to serve and promote the common good and the dignity of every person. I would like to conclude, Mr. President, by recalling the esteem and affection that the Italian People feels for you, as well as its full confidence in fulfilling the duties inherent in your exalted office.

I have the joy of joining in this affectionate esteem and trust, as I entrust you and your Consort, Mrs. Franca Ciampi, the leaders of the life of the Nation and the entire Italian People, to the protection of the Virgin Mary, so intensely venerated in the countless shrines dedicated to her. With these sentiments, I invoke upon you all the Blessing of God, a pledge of every desired good.

4. *Relations with Jews*

YEHEZKEL LANDAU

Pope John Paul II's Holy Land Pilgrimage: A Jewish Appraisal

He came to the Holy Land as a pilgrim, a man of prayer, to bring a message of peace. Earlier in the Jubilee Year 2000, he had identified with Abraham's journey from Ur of the Chaldeans to the land then called Canaan. Afterwards he traveled to Mount Sinai to identify with Moses' journey through the wilderness with the Israelites. At the spot where the Torah was revealed, he affirmed the Ten Commandments as essential for reconsecrating private and public morality in our time. And then, on the first leg of his Holy Land pilgrimage, he stood atop Mount Nebo to view the Promised Land from Moses' final resting place.

As he flew into Ben Gurion Airport on March 21, 2000, John Paul II was making his 91st international trip as pope. For many, this was *the* journey, par excellence, of his long and remarkable pontificate. For Jews, especially Israeli Jews, the papal visit was a watershed in the history of our relations with Christianity, and with Catholicism in particular. For all of humanity, it was, I believe, a metahistorical event in which the combination of person, place, and time produced a *kairos* moment transcending political divisions and offering a glimpse of true holiness. For Jews and Muslims locked in mortal combat over Israel/Palestine, the humble witness of this frail pilgrim pope demonstrated the potential of Christians to be peacemakers, which is to be, in the spirit of the Beatitudes, true "children of God." In his words and deeds along his route, this pope sought, on behalf of Christians everywhere, to make amends for two millennia of persecution toward both Jews and Muslims, the elder and younger siblings in the Abrahamic family of faith.

For Christian-Jewish relations, the pontiff's Holy Land pilgrimage broke new ground, both theologically and politically. To fully understand its impact on both levels, some historical context is needed. But first I offer a vignette from my own life journey. The context for this episode, my only direct encounter with the pope, is my peacebuilding work in the Holy Land over the past twenty-six years. In 1991, shortly after the Gulf War—when I was a reserve soldier serving with my Israeli army unit at Sha'arei Tzedek Hospital in Jerusalem, simulating with the medical staff the intake of hundreds of chemical warfare victims—I attended an interfaith conference in Italy convened by the World Conference on Religion and Peace. The gathering focused on peacebuilding in the Middle East. On July 4, the conference participants were bused from Castel Gandolfo, outside Rome, to the Vatican for an audience with John Paul II. In his prepared remarks before our group, the pontiff expressed his support for our religiously motivated peacemaking efforts.

After his speech, the pope greeted each member of our group. When I was introduced to him by name, with the geographic coordinate "from Jerusalem," I shook his hand and said to him, "Shalom! I hope you grace us with your presence soon." He simply nodded and said nothing in response. Almost nine years later, I was privileged to be in Jerusalem as the pope traversed the land, as Abraham had done, spreading his message of justice, love, and reconciliation and touching the hearts of all who watched and listened in amazement. I recall standing on a rooftop in East Jerusalem, watching the pope's motorcade wind its way through the streets of the city and eventually pass the spot where I stood in order to get to the apostolic delegate's home on the Mount of Olives, where the pontiff was staying. Later in the week I was in the audience at an interfaith event at the Notre Dame Center. This was the one event during the papal visit that deteriorated into political rancor and disarray. (More on that unfortunate incident below.) Given the risks and potential land mines that beset the pope's journey, the fact that only one event turned sour underscored the generally positive, indeed inspirational, nature of his extraordinary pilgrimage.

In the Middle East, memory is both a blessing and a curse. For the Arab Muslims, the Crusades happened yesterday. Israeli Jews, not only Holocaust survivors, cannot forget two millennia of disdain, hatred, and murderous assaults by ostensibly faithful Christians, including popes. For any Jew, a visit to Rome evokes haunting memories: the Jewish ghetto and the Arch of Titus depicting the menorah from the Second Temple carried away as a spoil of war. For centuries, newly elected popes would stop at the Arch of Titus on their way to St. Peter's Basilica for their coronation. At that spot, symbolizing the defeat and humiliation of the Jewish people, the new pope would receive a Torah scroll from a Jewish representative. He would then hand it back, saying, "I receive this book from you, but not your interpretation of it." This custom reflected the supersessionist theology and the "teaching of contempt" that characterized Catholicism until the Second Vatican Council.

During the pontificate of John Paul II, so much has happened to transform that tragic history of persecution and suffering. Indeed, it is safe to say that this pope has done more than anyone else in history to advance the cause of Christian-Jewish reconciliation. His historic visits to the Rome synagogue and the Auschwitz death camp were but two of the landmark events of his tenure as pontiff. The establishment of formal diplomatic relations between the Holy See and the State of

Israel, a revolutionary development awaited by Jews for years, would not have come about without the pope's blessing and encouragement. In his meetings with Jewish leaders, in Rome and elsewhere, he reiterated his condemnation of anti-Semitism and his fraternal solidarity with Jews as "elder brothers." And Jews knew that his words carried the authenticity of his life experience. His childhood friendships with Jews in Wadowice, Poland, helped him to later identify with the indescribable suffering of the Jewish people during the *Shoah* and with their yearning for freedom, dignity, and national renewal in a sovereign Jewish state.

By the time John Paul II came to Israel in March of 2000, much of the foundation for Catholic-Jewish rapprochement had already been laid. And yet Jews, especially in Israel, were still suspicious, wondering what his motives for visiting were. Partly this was because few Jews are aware of the spiritual and theological sea change that many church leaders have undergone in their relationships toward Jews and Judaism in the last half-century. This widespread ignorance made the pope's symbolic pilgrimage all the more astounding to most Jews. To appreciate just how remarkable the papal visit was for Israelis, consider this: In arithmetic classes, Israeli Jewish schoolchildren are taught to make a small inverted T rather than a cross when adding numbers. (One of Christianity's most sacred symbols evokes aversion in many Jews, given the long history of pogroms on Good Friday and following the enactment of passion plays.) Despite this common practice in Israeli schools, when the pope's jubilee journey was covered on Israeli television, the Hebrew words for *pilgrimage (aliyah leregel)* included a small cross instead of the letter *yod*.

Most observers would agree that the historic turning point in Catholic-Jewish relations was the *Nostra Aetate* statement issued on October 28, 1965, by the Second Vatican Council. The council, convened originally by the beloved Pope John XXIII, extended over four years after its inaugural session on October 11, 1962. The document referring to the Jewish people was one of sixteen conciliar texts, and it bears the official title "Declaration on the Relation of the Church to Non-Christian Religions." After centuries of triumphalism, praying for the conversion of the "perfidious Jews" on Good Friday, the Roman Catholic Church changed its official stance. It still affirmed that it is "in duty bound to proclaim without fail Christ who is the way, the truth, and the life" (John 1:6), that in Christ "God reconciled all things to himself [and so] people find the fullness of their religious life" in Christianity, and that the church "believes that Christ who is our peace has through his cross reconciled Jews and Gentiles and made them one in himself." Yet, together with this classical formulation of Christian faith, the council was able to detoxify the most poisonous element in Jewish-Christian relations over the centuries: the accusation that the Jews were guilty of crucifying Christ and were rejected and punished by God for this cosmic crime of deicide. *Nostra Aetate* (the first two words in the Latin version) repudiated this heinous libel once and for all. While it does refer generally to "other religions" in a positive light and states that "the Church looks with esteem" upon Muslims in particular, the declaration is best remembered for its revolutionary statements about the Jews:[1]

As holy Scripture testifies, Jerusalem did not recognize the time of her visitation (cf. Luke 19:44), nor did Jews in large number accept the Gospel; indeed, not a few opposed the spreading of it (cf. Rom 11:28). Nevertheless, according to the Apostle, the Jews still remain most dear to God because of their fathers, for He does not repent of the gifts He makes nor of the calls He issues (cf. Rom 11:28–29). . . .

True, authorities of the Jews and those who followed their lead pressed for the death of Christ (cf. John 19:6); still, what happened in His passion cannot be blamed upon all the Jews then living without distinction, nor upon the Jews of today. Although the Church is the new people of God, the Jews should not be presented as repudiated or cursed by God, as if such views followed from the holy Scriptures. All should take pains, then, lest in catechetical instruction and in the preaching of God's Word they teach anything out of harmony with the truth of the gospel and the spirit of Christ.

The Church repudiates all persecutions against any man. Moreover, mindful of her common patrimony with the Jews, and *motivated by the gospel's spiritual love and by no political considerations,* she deplores the hatred, persecutions, and displays of anti-Semitism directed against the Jews at any time and from any source [emphasis added].[2]

These statements merit some analysis, especially in light of subsequent events. (The recent controversy over Mel Gibson's film *The Passion of the Christ,* for example, serves to underscore how sensitive these issues are, and how Jewish-Christian relations are still adversely affected by the demonization of Jews by Christians over many centuries.) Why the explicit denial of any "political considerations" as a factor in condemning anti-Semitism? Why, instead, the affirmation of a single justification for this theological transformation: "the gospel's spiritual love"? To understand this argument, we need to examine the speech delivered to the participants in Vatican II by Cardinal Augustin Bea, SJ. Cardinal Bea, then president of the Secretariat for Promoting Christian Unity, was the person most responsible for getting the *Nostra Aetate* text adopted. He was commissioned personally for this assignment by Pope John XXIII. In order to overcome opposition to the document as it was being considered, Bea delivered a speech in defense of the new theological stance being promulgated. Here are excerpts from his remarks, part of the "oral tradition" accompanying the *Nostra Aetate* text:[3]

The decree [on the Jews] is very brief, but the material treated in it is not easy. Let us enter immediately into the heart of it and tell what we are talking about. Or rather, since it is so easy to understand it wrongly, before all else let us say what we are not talking about. There is no national or political question here. Especially is there no question of acknowledging the State of Israel on the part of the Holy See. . . . There is only treatment of a purely religious question. . . .

There are those who object: Did not the princes of this people, with the people in agreement, condemn and crucify the innocent Christ, the Lord? Did they not "clamor": "Let his blood be upon us and upon our children" (Matt. 27:25)? Did not Christ himself speak most severely about Jews and their punishment?

I reply simply and briefly: It is true that Christ spoke severely, but only with the intention that the people might be converted and might "recognize the time of its visitation" (Luke 19:42–49). But even as he is dying on the cross he prays: "Father forgive them, for they know not what they do" (Luke 23:34).

Wherefore, since the Lord emphasized before the burial of Lazarus, speaking to the Father: "I know that thou always hearest me" (John 11:42), it is wrong to say that his prayer to the Father was not heard and that God has not only not forgiven the fault of his chosen people but that he has rejected them. . . .

The point, therefore, is not in any way to call into doubt—as is sometimes falsely asserted—the events which are narrated in the Gospels about Christ's consciousness of his dignity and divine nature, or about the manner in which the innocent Lord was unjustly condemned. Rather that, with these things kept fully in mind, it is still possible and necessary to imitate the gentle charity of Christ the Lord and his Apostles with which they excused their persecutors.

Bea then asked his colleagues: "But *why is it so necessary precisely today* to recall these things?" (italics in the original text). He answered that the "propaganda" against the Jews that was spread by the Nazis needed to be rooted out from the minds of Catholics and replaced by the truth of Christianity. He condemned National Socialism's "particularly violent and criminal form" of anti-Semitism, "which through hatred for the Jews committed frightful crimes, extirpating several millions of Jewish people. . . ." And he argued for the application of Christian love and forgiveness: "If Christ the Lord and the Apostles who personally experienced the sorrows of the crucifixion embraced their very persecutors with an ardent charity, how much more must we be motivated by the same charity?"[4] We see here how Bea's thinking informed the text of *Nostra Aetate*.

In his speech, Bea declared that "the Jews of our times can hardly be accused of the crimes committed against Christ, so far removed are they from those deeds. Actually, even in the time of Christ, the majority of the chosen people did not cooperate with the leaders of the people in condemning Christ."[5] Bea combined two arguments: the Jews as a whole, then and now, are not culpable for the crucifixion, and those who *were* guilty, at that time, have been forgiven by God, both the Father and the Son. Consequently, he concludes his remarks by stressing that, for the council, what should be "simply decisive" is "the example of burning charity of the Lord himself on the cross praying 'Father, forgive them, for they know not what they are doing.' This is the example to be imitated by the Church, the bride of Christ. This is the road to be followed by her. This is what the schema proposed by us intends to foster and promote."[6]

From Bea's speech, we get a clearer idea of the theological rationale behind *Nostra Aetate*'s declaration exculpating the Jews from the deicide accusation. And what of the "political considerations" that might otherwise be imputed to the drafters of this historic conciliar document? We saw above that Bea disavowed any recognition of the State of Israel by the Holy See. (That watershed in 1993 was due largely to John Paul II's leadership.) Toward the end of his speech, Bea returned to this thorny subject of statehood and said: "Lastly: since we are here treating a merely religious question, there is obviously no danger that the Council will get entangled in those difficult questions regarding the relations between the Arab nations and the State of Israel, or regarding so-called Zionism."[7]

For most Jews, Judaism and Zionism are so intertwined in their self-understanding that it is impossible to separate the two. The tendency of many Christians, including Catholics, to make that distinction (based on their own tradition of separating God and Caesar) has caused much misunderstanding and ill will in Jewish-Christian relations in recent decades—at least until the Holy See recognized the State of Israel. The political and theological considerations are interrelated, and always were, despite Bea's rhetorical dichotomy.

To fully appreciate the importance of Pope John Paul II's jubilee pilgrimage to Israel/Palestine in 2000, we need, first of all, to recall the two millennia of Christian persecution of Jews and contempt for Judaism. In this light, Cardinal Bea's plea to his colleagues to forgive the Jews as Christ and the Apostles did—for a crime they did not even commit (since it was the Romans who crucified Jesus)—sounds absurd and outrageous to Jewish ears. But this is as far as the Church was ready to go in 1965.

The years following were characterized by further movement away from the notion that the Jews needed to be forgiven, as a gesture of "Christian charity," for anything they might have done. One can cite, as one of many benchmarks, the 1985 speech delivered by Cardinal Johannes Willebrands, who worked under Cardinal Bea at Vatican II and then succeeded him as head of the Secretariat for Promoting Christian Unity. Cardinal Willebrands's presentation at Westminster Cathedral in London was, in fact, the Cardinal Bea Memorial Lecture for that year. In his speech,[8] Willebrands reviewed the progress made in Christian-Jewish relations in the twenty years since *Nostra Aetate*. He noted that "a certain amount of trust has been generated" on the Jewish side, and that "some, if not all, barriers have been torn down." Regarding the Christian side, he said that "we in the Church have become, or are becoming, aware of our historical and our theological responsibilities toward our elder brother, grounded in the link the Council spoke about."

The cardinal stressed the common challenge of combating famine, oppression, and the plight of refugees worldwide. He said that "Jews and Christians, right across the board, are called in the name of their common biblical heritage to stand up and do something together." He understood that such joint action would bring to the surface some underlying tensions in the Christian-Jewish relationship:

> I am not blind to the issues such a decision will raise, or has already raised. The main issue also becomes, once the twenty years of first encounters have elapsed, one of the main challenges we have to face—perhaps the greatest. It thus becomes also a significant part of our task for the future. I refer to the asymmetry between our Catholic and Jewish communities or, better still, between Church and Judaism. The Church is a Church, a worldwide religious community orientated

mainly to the glory of God and the ministry of salvation of those called to her bosom. It has, as such, no particular ethnic or cultural identity; every man and woman from any background should feel at home with her. Judaism is a very different matter. While defined by some as an instrument of redemption, it is at the same time, and almost in the same breath, a people with a definite ethnicity, a culture, with an intrinsic reference to a land and a State. These differences should by now be obvious, but it is an open question whether we are on each side well enough aware of all the implications thereof. It means, at the very least, that agendas do not always coincide, priorities are not necessarily the same and concerns can go very different ways.[9]

These are sound observations. They were confirmed later when Jews and Catholics found themselves on different sides of painful controversies, such as the one that arose over the Carmelite convent at Auschwitz or the mutual misunderstandings around the elevation to sainthood of the Jewish Carmelite nun Edith Stein/Teresa Benedicta. At another point in Willebrands's speech, he asserted:

> Jewish-Christian relations are an unending affair, as are love and brotherhood, but also (regrettably) hatred and enmity. The main point is to change the fundamental orientation, from hatred to love, from enmity to brotherhood. It is not a question only of deploying documents, or of particular actions, however highly placed those who act happen to be. It is a question of people, men and women of flesh and blood. Still more, it is a question of hearts.[10]

This statement surely pertains to the pope's jubilee pilgrimage to the Holy Land: it was obviously a media event with the pope as the central celebrity, and as such it was a public witness on a global stage. But it was, above all, a witness that touched and moved hearts, millions if not billions of human hearts. Love and brotherhood were not just proclaimed; they were embodied in a man of flesh and blood whose flesh was old and weak, but whose spirit was strong and vibrant and radiated compassion for all.

At the Yad Vashem Holocaust Memorial Museum, this frail and elderly pontiff stood next to a youthful and vigorous Israeli prime minister, Ehud Barak, a military commando and commander turned statesman. What a role reversal that iconographic image was, in contrast to the familiar juxtaposition of two female characters representing a feeble, blindfolded Synagogue alongside the Church triumphant. But that visual anomaly at Yad Vashem, which was not lost on Israeli Jews,[11] was reinforced by the genuineness of the pope's solidarity with Jewish suffering. That heartfelt solidarity was evidenced in his words and even more by the affection he displayed toward his survivor friends from Wadowice, who were present for this ceremonial event. One of them was Edith Tzirer, who was liberated from a concentration camp in January 1945, almost paralyzed by tuberculosis and other afflictions. Karol Wojtyla, the present pope, was then a seminarian when he met young Edith and gave her food and drink. He then carried her for almost two miles, from the camp to the local railroad station. Alter regaining her health, Edith later moved to Israel. Aside from this very moving personal dimension, the event at Yad Vashem was laden with deep symbolic meaning, both political and religious—and these two dimensions could not be separated. The two men were the recognized leaders of two communities of faith represented by two sovereign entities, the State of Israel and the Holy See. The agreement establishing diplomatic relations between them, fostered by John Paul II, had put their relations on an unprecedented footing. Ehud Barak, whose grandparents perished at Dachau, represented a Jewish people that had survived genocide, had established its own flourishing state, and was now able to host the Bishop of Rome from a position of strength and pride. It was the ceremony at Yad Vashem, more than any other event during the papal pilgrimage, that symbolized this new, healthier relationship between Jews and Catholics. And it was that historic transformation of power relations, identities, and shared memories that allowed Prime Minister Barak to declare that the Jewish people has a friend in the Vatican.

Despite appeals from other Jews, Barak did not berate his guest for failing to issue an outright apology for the Church's actions during the *Shoah,* including the reticence of Pope Pius XII. Nor did Barak lament the limited access granted to the Vatican archives from that period. Barak understood that magnanimity and fraternal solidarity were the qualities to exhibit on that extraordinary occasion. He praised the Righteous Gentiles who had risked their lives to save Jews, and among them he counted John Paul II. "You have done more than anyone to apply the Church's historic change toward the Jewish people, a change begun by the good Pope John XXIII." Barak called the pope's visit to Yad Vashem "the climax of this historic journey of healing."

The spiritual message of the moment was deepened by John Paul II's expression of deep sadness for the suffering Jews have experienced at the hands of Christians throughout history. In his address he acknowledged that silence spoke more powerfully than words in the face of such horrors and traumatic memories. And those memories, he declared, serve a purpose looking toward the future: "to ensure that never again will evil prevail, as it did for the millions of innocent victims of Nazism. . . . Jews and Christians share an immense spiritual patrimony, flowing from God's self-revelation. Our religious teachings and our spiritual experience demand that we overcome evil with good." The psalmist, in describing the person who savors life, exhorts: "Depart from evil and do good; seek peace, and pursue it" (Ps. 34:15). The good that John Paul II did on his Holy Land trip, with his fervent appeals for peace and justice, served to combat the evils of prejudice, hatred, and war.

The culmination of his six-day sojourn among us, at least in the eyes of Jews, came with his visit to the Western Wall, in Hebrew the *Kotel Ha-Ma'aravi.* Rabbi Michael Melchior, representing the Israeli Government as Minister for Diaspora Affairs, welcomed the pope to that sacred site and presented to him an ornate Bible as a personal gift. When the pontiff shuffled slowly toward those immense stones, placed his prayer of contrition inside a crack in the wall, and remained there to offer his solitary confession before God at the spot that is most holy to our people, Jews everywhere were stunned by this simple yet profound gesture. Ironically, the prayer that he left in the *Kotel* was the same one uttered just days before as part of a litany of penitential confession in St. Peter's Basilica:

> God of our fathers,
> You chose Abraham and his descendants
> to bring your Name to the Nations;
> we are deeply saddened
> by the behaviour of those
> who in the course of history
> have caused these children of yours to suffer
> and asking your forgiveness
> we wish to commit ourselves
> to genuine brotherhood
> with the people of the Covenant.

Some Jews had complained, when this prayer was read out at St. Peter's, that it was not explicit enough in specifying the crimes committed by Christians against Jews or in offering an explicit apology. But the same words took on their true resonance and power when they were brought from Rome to Jerusalem, to be placed by the pope in the Wall which abuts the Temple Mount and the Holy of Holies. This was another iconographic moment, coming near the end of John Paul II's pilgrimage, when person, place, and time converged in historic terms. Instead of gloating triumphantly over the loss of the ancient Temple at the hands of the Romans, instead of rubbing salt in the collective Jewish wound symbolized by the Arch of Titus, this pontiff came from Rome to the Western Wall to ask God's forgiveness for the two millennia of harm that Christians have caused Jews. And through this act of sincere repentance, the pope embodied, in the most direct and powerful way possible, the new era of transformed relations between Christians and Jews. Instead of asking his fellow Catholics to forgive Jews for killing Christ, as Cardinal Bea and *Nostra Aetate* had done, John Paul II acknowledged that it is Christians who are in need of forgiveness for what they have perpetrated against Jews. Jews, in turn, should acknowledge with gratitude this *metanoia* (in Hebrew, *teshuvah:* moral transformation or repentance) on the part of the Church. Only then can we Jews join our Catholic partners in building a more blessed future for everyone, in the spirit of Cardinal Willebrands's remarks in 1985.

Against the backdrop of this appreciative assessment of the pope's pilgrimage, some words should be said about the Jewish-Christian-Muslim trialogue at the Notre Dame Center that turned into a fiasco. The pope was joined for this symbolic occasion by Israeli Ashkenazi Chief Rabbi Lau and Sheikh Tamimi representing the Palestinian Authority.

Rabbi Lau spoke first, delivering a positive message advocating peaceful relations among the religions. But he concluded with a statement of gratitude to the pope for recognizing that Jerusalem is the "eternal, undivided capital" of Israel and the Jewish people. By attributing this political stance to John Paul II, the rabbi sparked a vehement reaction from the Palestinians present. From my seat in the balcony, I could hear my Palestinian Catholic friend Afif Safieh, ambassador to the United Kingdom and the Holy See on behalf of the Palestinian Authority, shouting that the pope never said such a thing.

With the atmosphere now politicized and contentious, Sheikh Tamimi rose to speak. He seemed to speak extemporaneously, without reference to a written text, as he delivered a lengthy tirade in Arabic, scoring political points against Israel and earning the applause of the Palestinians present. The pope sat on the stage with his head in his hands while this belligerent speech was delivered. The moderator for this event, Rabbi Dr. Alon Goshen-Gottstein, tried to restore a sense of decorum and mutual respect by imploring people not to use that interreligious forum for partisan polemics. When John Paul II had his turn to speak, he read his prepared speech calling for harmony and cooperation among the three Abrahamic faith communities. In referring to the Holy City; he declared:

> For all of us Jerusalem, as its name indicates, is the "City of Peace." Perhaps no other place in the world communicates the sense of transcendence and divine election that we perceive in her stones and monuments, and in the witness of the three religions living side by side within her walls. Not everything has been or will be easy in this coexistence. But we must find in our respective religious traditions the wisdom and the superior motivation to ensure the triumph of mutual understanding and cordial respect.

The pope went on to invoke the Golden Rule as a common moral standard. But he urged his listeners to go beyond that guideline to embrace "true love of neighbor," which is "based on the conviction that when we love our neighbor we are showing love for God, and when we hurt our neighbor we offend God." Looking back at history, he said:

> We are all aware of past misunderstandings and conflicts, and these still weigh heavily on relationships between Jews, Christians, and Muslims. We must do all we can to turn awareness of past offenses and sins into a firm resolve to build a new future in which there will be nothing but respectful and fruitful cooperation between us. The Catholic Church wishes to pursue a sincere and fruitful interreligious dialogue with the members of the Jewish faith and the followers of Islam. Such a dialogue is not an attempt to impose our views upon others. What it demands of all of us is that, holding to what we believe, we listen respectfully to one another, seek to discern all that is good and holy in each other's teachings, and cooperate in supporting everything that favors mutual understanding and peace.
>
> The Jewish, Christian, and Muslim children and young people present here are a sign of hope and an incentive for us. Each new generation is a divine gift to the world. If we pass on to them all that is noble and good in our traditions, they will make it blossom in more intense brotherhood and cooperation.

As the pope was uttering these inspiring words, the two youth choirs that were scheduled to sing together at the end of the program were locked in heated arguments in another room, stimulated by the politically oriented remarks of Rabbi Lau and Sheikh Tamimi. In fact, these teenagers only agreed to perform their choral piece on condition that their conductor say, publicly, how distressed they were by the conduct of the two religious leaders. By this time, Sheikh Tamimi had left the stage altogether, leaving the pope and the rabbi and an empty chair.

This event left a sour taste in the mouths of everyone present. Dr. Goshen-Gottstein, who directs the Jerusalem-based Elijah School for the Study of Wisdom in World Religions, drew this lesson from the experience: "In instances where religious personalities are involved in politically sensitive situations, events need to be more tightly controlled and orchestrated." In assessing the overall impact of the pope's visit, he said that it produced a positive change in many Israelis' view of Christianity, especially the nonobservant Jewish majority. Most of the Orthodox Jewish community in Israel simply ignored the visit and excluded themselves from it.

The Notre Dame event reminded us that the ongoing political conflict between Israelis and Palestinians pollutes our spiritualities as Jews, Christians, and Muslims. This was true in 2000 and is even more the case today, as we all suffer the consequences of the horrific violence, death, and destruction that erupted just six months following the pope's jubilee pilgrimage. During his Holy Land visit, the pope did his best to appear politically evenhanded as an apostle of peace and justice. His appearances in Bethlehem and the nearby Dheisheh refugee camp signaled his solidarity with the suffering and the aspirations of Palestinians. All along his route, both sides tried to enlist the pontiff as a champion of their own cause, but he resisted the temptation to take sides. He kept to his self-defined mission, moving about the land and offering its wounded inhabitants the balm of indiscriminate love.

There have been a few encouraging signs of interfaith cooperation since his visit, including the Alexandria Declaration issued in January 2002 by Jewish, Christian, and Muslim clerical leaders from Israel, Palestine, and Egypt, as well as the behind-the-scenes negotiations to resolve the forty-day siege of the Church of the Nativity in Bethlehem in April–May of 2002. But so much more needs to be done by religious leaders and grassroots activists from the various faith communities, to help create a climate more conducive to political discussions between the two peoples.[12] In this context, where the primary antagonists are Jews and Muslims, Christians can and should act as mediating, reconciling agents of peace with justice. John Paul II demonstrated by his example in March 2000 that such a task is possible and beneficial to all, even if there is deeply ingrained hostility and resistance to change on all sides.

In assessing the impact of the pope's visit, the editor of the *Ha'aretz* daily newspaper said: "Mercy has come to the State of Israel this week and has left banal politics to one side." Avraham Burg, then Speaker of the Knesset (the Israeli parliament), wrote an article for the newspaper *Ma'ariv* in which he described how Israeli Jews were now developing a new understanding of Christianity. What had been viewed as "a religion that spilt blood with the Crusades and the Inquisition has become a religion in which its priests are raised to the level of Righteous among the

Nations. It is not possible to understand the fall of totalitarian regimes in Latin America, in South Africa, and in Poland without thinking, in recognition, of the man who yesterday kissed the Western Wall." The most widely read paper in Israel, *Yediot Ahronot,* printed a two-page photo of the pope in prayer before the Wall. Prime Minister Barak told the newspaper, "This historic visit has brought respect for Israel and contributed to *shalom* between Judaism and Christianity."[13]

Four years later, we are trapped in an ongoing political impasse, with its attendant horrors and hardships for both Israelis and Palestinians. The pope still offers prayers for peace from Rome, and religious personalities around the world issue pleas for safeguarding the sanctity of human life and upholding the dignity of every human being.

The political toxicity threatens to overwhelm the spiritual dimension of our lives, in the Holy Land and, after September 11, 2001, everywhere else.

In the midst of political hostility and uncertainty, the relations between the government of Israel and the Christian communities of the land have turned sour during the course of 2003 and 2004. On April 7, 2004, a letter was sent to Israel's ambassador to the United States, Daniel Ayalon, cosigned by the Most Reverend John H. Ricard, SSJ, Bishop of Pensacola-Tallahassee, Florida, and Chairman of the International Policy Committee of the Conference of Catholic Bishops, and by Cardinal William Keeler, Archbishop of Baltimore and Episcopal Moderator for Catholic-Jewish Relations. After referring to the holy festivals of Passover and Easter which overlapped again this year, and to the joy of the U.S. Catholic community in its experience of dialogue with the Jewish people, the two Catholic officials appealed to Ambassador Ayalon to help rectify some festering problems:

> Against the background of this mutual affection, and in the light of the progress made in Catholic-Jewish relations and honest dialogue these past forty years, we are dismayed at the deterioration of relations between your government and the Catholic Church in Israel and the territories under Israel's control. The growing problem of the denial of visas [for church workers and clerics] or indefinite delay in their issuance, the recent cases of mistreatment of clergy and religious awaiting visa renewal, difficulties over taxation, including those of our own Catholic Relief Services, and the suspension of negotiations on treaties regarding fiscal matters and other issues have created the most difficult situation in living memory for the Church in the Holy Land.
>
> In December 1993, we celebrated, with your predecessor, the signing of the Fundamental Agreement [between the Holy See and the government of Israel], which is so important, not just for the Church and the government of Israel, but for freedom and pluralism within Israeli society as a whole. Regrettably, as the agreement's tenth anniversary passed, provisions respecting the Church's right to deploy its own personnel in Israel and for both parties to avoid "actions incompatible" with negotiating an agreement on fiscal matters, including taxation, were being routinely ignored. Despite repeated promises of remedies, the visa problem has grown still more serious, and, the requests of the Holy See notwithstanding, negotiations on a fiscal agreement have been suspended.

With all our affection for the Jewish people and without wavering in our commitment to the state of Israel, the many disappointments and the multiplication of problems are a cause of grave concern.[14]

Another letter was sent on April 13, 2004, this time to President George Bush from the Most Reverend Wilton D. Gregory, President of the U.S. Conference of Catholic Bishops. Bishop Gregory called on the president to be more active in mediating a two-state political accommodation between Israelis and Palestinians. He cited Pope John Paul II's appeal to all parties in the Middle East conflict to "renew dialogue without delay," with the help of "the international community [which] cannot flee from its responsibilities . . . but must assume them courageously." Also in his letter, Bishop Gregory shared his "grave concern about the deteriorating relations between the Israeli government and the Catholic Church in the Holy Land," identifying the same problems specified in the letter to Ambassador Ayalon.[15]

It is clear from these two letters that the inspiration and promise in the pope's jubilee pilgrimage are being challenged by new obstacles to improved relations. Jews and Catholics must join together to guarantee that our bonds of fraternal affection, nurtured by gestures of repentance and forgiveness, are not undermined by reactionary attitudes. Good will must be continually fostered, and honest dialogue on difficult issues must be facilitated by people who are sensitive to the apprehensions and concerns of all parties.

I hope and pray that the present difficulties can be overcome. Against the backdrop of history, they should be seen as temporary setbacks on the long and uphill path toward a blessed future. Just one hundred years ago, in 1904, a historic encounter took place between Theodore Herzl, the father of modern political Zionism, and Pope Pius X. Herzl went to the Vatican shortly before his death to secure the pope's endorsement of his movement's aim to reestablish Jewish sovereignty in the Holy Land. In his diary, Herzl recorded Pope Pius's response:

The Jews have not recognized our Lord; therefore we cannot recognize the Jewish people. . . . We cannot prevent the Jews from going to Jerusalem, but we could never sanction it. If you come to Palestine and settle your people there, our churches and priests will be ready to baptize all of you.[16]

It took another sixty years, and the genocide of European Jewry, for this normative Catholic understanding to be replaced by "Christian charity" toward Jews on the theological level, divorced from international politics. It took yet another twenty-nine years until the Holy See, under Pope John Paul II's direction, established diplomatic relations with the State of Israel, thereby repudiating Pius X's anti-Zionist theology. And it was not until the media spectacular of John Paul II's Jubilee Pilgrimage that the Church's conditioned resistance to Jewish statehood was finally and unequivocally relegated to the history books.

It is now up to us, all Jews and Catholics who care about redeeming the past and ensuring a blessed future for the coming generations, to add our contributions to the betterment of relations between us. As an unforgettable milestone along this sacred path, Pope John Paul II's Jubilee Pilgrimage to the Holy Land will stand out as a beacon of light to illumine our way.

NOTES

1. From *The Documents of Vatican II,* ed. Walter M. Abbott, SJ (New York: The America Press, 1966), 660–68.

2. Ibid., p. 667.

3. "Catholics and Jews," in *Council Speeches of Vatican II,* eds. Hans Küng, Yves Congar, OP, and Daniel O'Hanlon, SJ (New York/Glen Rock, NJ: Paulist Press, 1964), 254–61; here, edited from 254–58.

4. Ibid., 258–59.

5. Ibid., 259.

6. Ibid., 261.

7. Ibid.

8. "Christians and Jews: A New Vision," in *Vatican II Revisited by Those Who Were There,* ed. Alberic Stacpoole (Minneapolis: Winston Press, 1986), 220–36.

9. Ibid., p. 233.

10. Ibid., pp. 229–30.

11. See Yossi Klein Halevi, "Zionism's *Gift,*" *The New Republic,* April 10, 2000, p. 6.

12. See my research report *Healing the Holy Land: Interreligious Peacebuilding in Israel/Palestine,* Peaceworks #51 (Washington, DC: United States Institute of Peace, 2003).

13. All three newspaper quotes reported in "Israeli Press Moved Day After Pope's Farewell," ZENIT.org, dated March 27, 2000, at http://www.zenit.org/english archive/0003/ZE000327.html#item3.

14. Full letter is on the USCCB's web site at http://www.nccbuscc.org/ sdwp/international/ayalon2.htm.

15. Posted on the USCCB web site at http://www.usccb.org/sdwp/international /bush404.htm.

16. Quoted in Sergio I. Minerbi, *The Vatican and Zionism: Conflict in the Holy Land 1895–1925* (New York: Oxford University Press, 1990), 100–101.

BENEDICT XVI

World Youth Day Address to the Jewish Community

Cologne Synagogue, Friday, 19 August 2005

Distinguished Jewish Authorities, Ladies and Gentlemen,
Dear Brothers and Sisters,

I greet all those who have already been mentioned. *Shalom lêchém!*

It has been my deep desire, during my first Visit to Germany since my election as the Successor of the Apostle Peter, to meet the Jewish community of Cologne and the representatives of Judaism in Germany. By this Visit I would like to return in spirit to the meeting that took place in Mainz on 17 November 1980 between my venerable Predecessor Pope John Paul II, then making his first Visit to this Country, and members of the Central Jewish Committee in Germany and the Rabbinic Conference.

Today, too, I wish to reaffirm that I intend to continue with great vigour on the path towards improved relations and friendship with the Jewish People, following the decisive lead given by Pope John Paul II (cf. *Address to the Delegation of the International Jewish Committee on Interreligious Consultations*, 9 June 2005).

The Jewish community in Cologne can truly feel "at home" in this city. Cologne is, in fact, the oldest site of a Jewish community on German soil, dating back to the Colonia of Roman times, as we have come to know with precision.

The history of relations between the Jewish and Christian communities has been complex and often painful. There were blessed times when the two lived together peacefully, but there was also the expulsion of the Jews from Cologne in the year 1424.

And in the 20th century, in the darkest period of German and European history, an insane racist ideology, born of neo-paganism, gave rise to the attempt, planned and systematically carried out by the regime, to exterminate European Jewry. The result has passed into history as the *Shoah*.

The victims of this unspeakable and previously unimaginable crime amounted to 11,000 named individuals in Cologne alone; the real figure was surely much higher. The holiness of God was no longer recognized, and consequently, contempt was shown for the sacredness of human life.

This year, 2005, marks the 60th anniversary of the liberation of the Nazi concentration camps, in which millions of Jews—men, women and children—were put to death in the gas chambers and ovens.

I make my own the words written by my venerable Predecessor on the occasion of the 60th anniversary of the liberation of Auschwitz and I too say: "I bow my head before all those who experienced this manifestation of the *mysterium iniquitatis*." The terrible events of that time must "never cease to rouse consciences, to resolve conflicts, to inspire the building of peace" (*Message for the Liberation of Auschwitz*, 15 January 2005).

Together we must remember God and his wise plan for the world he created. As we read in the Book of Wisdom, he is the "lover of life" (11:26).

This year also marks the 40th anniversary of the promulgation of the Second Vatican Council's Declaration *Nostra Aetate*, which opened up new prospects for Jewish-Christian relations in terms of dialogue and solidarity. This Declaration, in the fourth chapter, recalls the common roots and the immensely rich spiritual heritage that Jews and Christians share.

Both Jews and Christians recognize in Abraham their father in faith (cf. Gal 3:7; Rom 4:11ff.), and they look to the teachings of Moses and the prophets.

Jewish spirituality, like its Christian counterpart, draws nourishment from the psalms. With St. Paul, Christians are convinced that "the gifts and the call of God are irrevocable" (Rom 11:29; cf. 9:6, 11; 11:1ff.). In considering the Jewish roots of Christianity (cf. Rom 11:16–24), my venerable Predecessor, quoting a statement by the German Bishops, affirmed that "whoever meets Jesus Christ meets Judaism" (*Insegnamenti*, Vol. III/2, 1980, p. 1272).

The conciliar Declaration *Nostra Aetate* therefore "deplores feelings of hatred, persecutions and demonstrations of anti-Semitism directed against the Jews at whatever time and by whomsoever" (n. 4). God created us all "in his image" (cf. Gn 1:27) and thus honoured us with a transcendent dignity. Before God, all men and women have the same dignity, whatever their nation, culture or religion.

Hence, the Declaration *Nostra Aetate* also speaks with great esteem of Muslims (cf. n. 3) and of the followers of other religions (cf. n. 2).

On the basis of our shared human dignity the Catholic Church "condemns as foreign to the mind of Christ any kind of discrimination whatsoever between people, or harassment of them, done by reason of race or colour, class or religion" (n. 5).

The Church is conscious of her duty to transmit this teaching, in her catechesis for young people and in every aspect of her life, to the younger generations which did not witness the terrible events that took place before and during the Second World War.

It is a particularly important task, since today, sadly, we are witnessing the rise of new signs of anti-Semitism and various forms of a general hostility towards foreigners. How can we fail to see in this a reason for concern and vigilance?

The Catholic Church is committed—I reaffirm this again today—to tolerance, respect, friendship and peace between all peoples, cultures and religions.

In the 40 years that have passed since the conciliar Declaration *Nostra Aetate*, much progress has been made, in Germany and throughout the world, towards better and closer relations between Jews and Christians. Alongside official relationships, due above all to cooperation between specialists in the biblical sciences, many friendships have been born.

In this regard, I would mention the various declarations by the German Episcopal Conference and the charitable work done by the "Society for Jewish-Christian Cooperation in Cologne," which since 1945 have enabled the Jewish community to feel once again truly "at home" here in Cologne and to establish good relations with the Christian communities.

Yet much still remains to be done. We must come to know one another much more and much better.

Consequently, I would encourage sincere and trustful dialogue between Jews and Christians, for only in this way will it be possible to arrive at a shared interpretation of disputed historical questions, and, above all, to make progress towards a theological evaluation of the relationship between Judaism and Christianity.

This dialogue, if it is to be sincere, must not gloss over or underestimate the existing differences: in those areas in which, due to our profound convictions in faith, we diverge, and indeed, precisely in those areas, we need to show respect and love for one another.

Finally, our gaze should not only be directed to the past, but should also look forward to the tasks that await us today and tomorrow. Our rich common heritage and our fraternal and more trusting relations call upon us to join in giving an ever more harmonious witness and to work together on the practical level for the defence and promotion of human rights and the sacredness of human life, for family values, for social justice and for peace in the world.

The Decalogue (cf. Ex 20; Dt 5) is for us a shared legacy and commitment. The Ten Commandments are not a burden, but a signpost showing the path leading to a successful life.

This is particularly the case for the young people whom I am meeting in these days and who are so dear to me. My wish is that they may be able to recognize in the Decalogue our common foundation, a lamp for their steps, a light for their path (cf. Ps 119:105).

Adults have the responsibility of handing down to young people the torch of hope that God has given to Jews and to Christians, so that "never again" will the forces of evil come to power, and that future generations, with God's help, may be able to build a more just and peaceful world, in which all people have equal rights and are equally at home.

I conclude with the words of Psalm 29, which express both a wish and a prayer: "May the Lord give strength to his people, may he bless his people with peace."

May he hear our prayer!

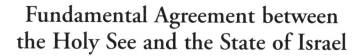

Fundamental Agreement between the Holy See and the State of Israel

December 30, 1993

PREAMBLE

The Holy See and the State of Israel,

Mindful of the singular character and universal significance of the Holy Land;

Aware of the unique nature of the relationship between the Catholic Church and the Jewish people, and of the historic process of reconciliation and growth in mutual understanding and friendship between Catholics and Jews;

Having decided on 29 July 1992 to establish a "Bilateral Permanent Working Commission" in order to study and define together issues of common interest, and in view of normalizing their relations;

Recognizing that the work of the aforementioned Commission has produced sufficient material for a first and Fundamental Agreement;

Realizing that such Agreement will provide a sound and lasting basis for the continued development of their present and future relations and for the furtherance of the Commission's task,

Agree upon the following Articles:

ARTICLE 1

- The State of Israel, recalling its Declaration of Independence, affirms its continuing commitment to uphold and observe the human right to freedom of religion and conscience, as set forth in the Universal Declaration of Human Rights and in other international instruments to which it is a party.
- The Holy See, recalling the Declaration on Religious Freedom of the Second Vatican Ecumenical Council, "Dignitatis humanae," affirms the Catholic Church's commitment to uphold the human right to freedom of religion and conscience, as set forth in the Universal Declaration of Human Rights and in other international instruments to which it is a party. The Holy See wishes to affirm as well the Catholic Church's respect for other religions and their followers as solemnly stated by the Second Vatican Ecumenical Council in its Declaration on the Relation of the Church to Non-Christian Religions, "Nostra aetate."

ARTICLE 2

- The Holy See and the State of Israel are committed to appropriate cooperation in combatting all forms of antisemitism and all kinds of racism and of religious intolerance, and in promoting mutual understanding among nations, tolerance among communities and respect for human life and dignity.
- The Holy See takes this occasion to reiterate its condemnation of hatred, persecution and all other manifestations of antisemitism directed against the Jewish people and individual Jews anywhere, at any time and by anyone. In particular, the Holy See deplores attacks on Jews and desecration of Jewish synagogues and cemeteries, acts which offend the memory of the victims of the Holocaust, especially when they occur in the same places which witnessed it.

ARTICLE 3

- The Holy See and the State of Israel recognize that both are free in the exercise of their respective rights and powers, and commit themselves to respect this principle in their mutual relations and in their cooperation for the good of the people.
- The State of Israel recognizes the right of the Catholic Church to carry out its religious, moral, educational and charitable functions, and to have its own institutions, and to train, appoint and deploy its own personnel in the said institutions or for the said functions to these ends. The Church recognizes the right of the State to carry out its functions, such as promoting and protecting the welfare and the safety of the people. Both the State and the Church recognize the need for dialogue and cooperation in such matters as by their nature call for it.
- Concerning Catholic legal personality [of] canon law the Holy See and the State of Israel will negotiate on giving it full effect in Israeli law, following a report from a joint subcommission of experts.

ARTICLE 4

- The State of Israel affirms its continuing commitment to maintain and respect the "Status quo" in the Christian Holy Places to which it applies and the respective rights of the Christian communities thereunder. The Holy See affirms the Catholic Church's continuing commitment to respect the aforementioned "Status quo" and the said rights.
- The above shall apply notwithstanding an interpretation to the contrary of any Article in this Fundamental Agreement.
- The State of Israel agrees with the Holy See on the obligation of continuing respect for and protection of the character proper to Catholic sacred places, such as churches, monasteries, convents, cemeteries and their like.
- The State of Israel agrees with the Holy See on the continuing guarantee of the freedom of Catholic worship.

ARTICLE 5

- The Holy See and the State of Israel recognize that both have an interest in favouring Christian pilgrimages to the Holy Land. Whenever the need for coordination arises, the proper agencies of the Church and of the State will consult and cooperate as required.

- The State of Israel and the Holy See express the hope that such pilgrimages will provide an occasion for better understanding between the pilgrims and the people and religions in Israel.

ARTICLE 6

The Holy See and the State of Israel jointly reaffirm the right of the Catholic Church to establish, maintain and direct schools and institutes of study at all levels; this right being exercised in harmony with the rights of the State in the field of education.

ARTICLE 7

The Holy See and the State of Israel recognize a common interest in promoting and encouraging cultural exchanges between Catholic institutions worldwide, and educational, cultural and research institutions in Israel, and in facilitating access to manuscripts, historical documents and similar source materials, in conformity with applicable laws and regulations.

ARTICLE 8

The State of Israel recognizes that the right of the Catholic Church to freedom of expression in the carrying out of its functions is exercised also through the Church's own communications media; this right being exercised in harmony with the rights of the State in the field of communications media.

ARTICLE 9

The Holy See and the State of Israel jointly reaffirm the right of the Catholic Church to carry out its charitable functions through its health care and social welfare institutions, this right being exercised in harmony with the rights of the State in this field.

ARTICLE 10

- The Holy See and the State of Israel jointly reaffirm the right of the Catholic Church to property.
- Without prejudice to rights relied upon by the Parties:
  - The Holy See and the State of Israel will negotiate in good faith a comprehensive agreement, containing solutions acceptable to both Parties,

on unclear, unsettled and disputed issues, concerning property, economic and fiscal matters relating to the Catholic Church generally, or to specific Catholic Communities or institutions.
- For the purpose of the said negotiations, the Permanent Bilateral Working Commission will appoint one or more bilateral subcommissions of experts to study the issues and make proposals.
- The Parties intend to commence the aforementioned negotiations within three months of entry into force of the present Agreement, and aim to reach agreement within two years from the beginning of the negotiations.
- During the period of these negotiations, actions incompatible with these commitments shall be avoided.

ARTICLE 11

- The Holy See and the State of Israel declare their respective commitment to the promotion of the peaceful resolution of conflicts among States and nations, excluding violence and terror from international life.
- The Holy See, while maintaining in every case the right to exercise its moral and spiritual teaching-office, deems it opportune to recall that, owing to its own character, it is solemnly committed to remaining a stranger to all merely temporal conflicts, which principle applies specifically to disputed territories and unsettled borders.

ARTICLE 12

The Holy See and the State of Israel will continue to negotiate in good faith in pursuance of the Agenda agreed upon in Jerusalem, on 15 July 1992, and confirmed at the Vatican, on 29 July 1992; likewise on issues arising from Articles of the present Agreement, as well as on other issues bilaterally agreed upon as objects of negotiation.

ARTICLE 13

- In this Agreement the Parties use these terms in the following sense:
    - The Catholic Church and the Church—including, inter alia, its Communities and institutions;
    - Communities of the Catholic Church—meaning the Catholic religious entities considered by the Holy See as Churches sui juris and by the State of Israel as Recognized Religious Communities;
    - The State of Israel and the State—including, inter alia, its authorities established by law.

- Notwithstanding the validity of this Agreement as between the Parties, and without detracting from the generality of any applicable rule of law with reference to treaties, the Parties agree that this Agreement does not prejudice rights and obligations arising from existing treaties between either Party and a State or States, which are known and in fact available to both Parties at the time of the signature of this Agreement.

ARTICLE 14

- Upon signature of the present Fundamental Agreement and in preparation for the establishment of full diplomatic relations, the Holy See and the State of Israel exchange Special Representatives, whose rank and privileges are specified in an Additional Protocol.
- Following the entry into force and immediately upon the beginning of the implementation of the present Fundamental Agreement, the Holy See and the State of Israel will establish full diplomatic relations at the level of Apostolic Nunciature, on the part of the Holy See, and Embassy, on the part of the State of Israel.

ARTICLE 15

This Agreement shall enter into force on the date of the latter notification of ratification by a Party.

Done in two original copies in the English and Hebrew languages, both texts being equally authentic. In case of divergency, the English text shall prevail.

Signed in Jerusalem, this thirtieth day of the month of December, in the year 1993, which corresponds to the sixteenth day of the month of Tevet, in the year 5754.

For the Government of the State of Israel
For the Holy See

ADDITIONAL PROTOCOL

- In relation to Art. 14(1) of the Fundamental Agreement, signed by the Holy See and the State of Israel, the "Special Representatives" shall have, respectively, the personal rank of Apostolic Nuncio and Ambassador.
- These Special Representatives shall enjoy all the rights, privileges and immunities granted to Heads of Diplomatic Missions under international law and common usage, on the basis of reciprocity.
- The Special Representative of the State of Israel to the Holy See, while residing in Italy, shall enjoy all the rights, privileges and immunities defined

by Art. 12 of the Treaty of 1929 between the Holy See and Italy, regarding Envoys of Foreign Governments to the Holy See residing in Italy. The rights, privileges and immunities extended to the personnel of a Diplomatic Mission shall likewise be granted to the personnel of the Israeli Special Representative's Mission. According to an established custom, neither the Special Representative, nor the official members of his Mission, can at the same time be members of Israel's Diplomatic Mission to Italy.

- The Special Representative of the Holy See to the State of Israel may at the same time exercise other representative functions of the Holy See and be accredited to other States. He and the personnel of his Mission shall enjoy all the rights, privileges and immunities granted by Israel to Diplomatic Agents and Missions.
- The names, rank and functions of the Special Representatives will appear, in an appropriate way, in the official lists of Foreign Missions accredited to each Party.

Signed in Jerusalem, this thirtieth day of the month of December, in the year 1993, which corresponds to the sixteenth day of the month of Tevet, in the year 5754.

FOR THE GOVERNMENT OF THE STATE OF ISRAEL
FOR THE HOLY SEE

5. *Relations with Muslims*

Ibrahim M. Abu-Rabi
John Paul II and Islam

Christians and Muslims in general . . . have badly understood each other, and sometimes, in the past, have opposed and even exhausted each other in polemics and in wars. I believe that today, God invites us to change our old practices. We must respect each other, and also we must stimulate each other in good works on the path to God.

—John Paul II

This essay offers a critical reading of John Paul II's ideas on Islam as they have developed from the time he assumed the papacy in 1978. In order to attain a clear view of his position, I will follow three courses of analysis: (1) I will focus on his understanding of Islam, as both a theological system and a sociohistorical phenomenon, with all that these two dimensions imply; (2) I will discuss his ideas against the recent engagement of the Catholic Church in the life of the international Catholic community, especially in the Muslim world; and (3) I will compare his ideas on Islam to those of a selected number of modern Muslim theologians and thinkers on Christianity.

At the outset, I should like to state that my choice of terminology reflects a complex world in transition, one in which such terms as "Muslims" and "Christians" must be understood in the context of the recent triumph of the Western, that is, capitalist, system both culturally and economically, and in the Muslim world as well as in the West. In other words, the reader must not take the "religious terms" employed here at face value, but must understand them as part of the major intellectual mutations taking place in the world in the wake of the collapse of the Soviet Union, the triumph of the capitalist system, and the attempt of different contemporary religious movements, including the Islamic ones, to reorganize themselves and revitalize their activism.[1]

As a universal monotheistic religion, Islam is a complex religious phenomenon that has given rise to all sorts of ideas, forces, and conditions over its long history. Regardless of their political motivations and ideological positions, Western scholars, often called "orientalists,"[2] have carried out serious research over the past five hundred years in the field of Islamic studies, including the Arabic language, the Qur'an, *Hadith, Fiqh,* Sufism, and various Muslim social and political institutions.[3] Especially since the 1979 Islamic revolution in Iran, the Western scholarly community has preoccupied itself with "Islamic fundamentalism"—its nature, history, and the menace it may pose to Western interests and to the nation-states in the Muslim world. Very often, and even in respected Western intellectual circles, Islam and Muslims are treated as the dangerous "other." It is heartening to realize, as will be amply illustrated below, that the Western religious community, especially the Catholic community under the guidance of its religious leadership, does not share these negative views of Islam and Muslims.

Whether Western scholars consider it an object of fascination, or a pirated copy of either Christianity or Judaism, Islam remains a unique religion, possessing an autonomous *Weltanschauung* that defines its place in the world of ideas and events through dialogue and openness. From this perspective, it should not be surprising that nineteenth-century Muslim thinkers, such as 'Abd al-Rahman al-Jabarti, Hassan al-'Attar, Rifa'a R. Tahtawi, al-Saffar, Jamal al-Din al-Afghani, and Muhammad 'Abduh, accepted, at least in principle, the concept of appropriating the scientific and intellectual spirit of Western civilization, although they were opposed to its political and military agenda, that is, expansion to the Muslim world under the guise of modernity.[4]

Therefore, in dealing with the position of John Paul II on Islam, one must be attentive to both the evolution of the Catholic position on interreligious dialogue, and especially that with Islam, and the complex manifestations of Islam in the modern Muslim world as well. Furthermore, one must not ignore the nature of coexistence among Muslims and Catholics in different parts of the Muslim world, especially in the Arab Middle East, and in such countries as Indonesia, Nigeria, Sudan, Bangladesh, and the Philippines.

It is clear that the Pope is cognizant of the nature of Islam as a universal tradition, and understands its theological and spiritual dimensions. He appreciates the impact of Western modernity on the Muslim people, the rise of the nation-states in the Muslim world, the intellectual Islamic response to the Western onslaught, and the appropriation of selected Western concepts. In other words, in treating the Pope's position on Islam, I take Islam to mean both theology and history: These two dimensions, multilayered as they are, define the meaning and identity of Islam in the modern world. Furthermore, I think that to appreciate the position of Islam in the modern world and, more specifically, in the Arab Middle East and North Africa, one must note the adaptation of the mainstream Islamic tradition to the modern world, the new relationship forged between Islam and society, and the newly acquired Muslim historical consciousness of the position that Islam must (or must not) take in the new nation-state.

The Catholic Church began to acknowledge the need for understanding the Muslim world and appreciating the religious impact of Islam on modern Muslim lives with the Second Vatican Council (1962–65). It emphasized unequivocally that

> [t]he Church has also a high regard for the Muslims. They worship God, who is one, living and subsistent, merciful and mighty; the Creator of heaven and earth, who has also spoken to humankind. . . . Over the centuries, many quarrels and dissensions have arisen between Christians and Muslims. The sacred council now pleads with all to forget the past, and urges that a sincere effort be made to achieve mutual understanding; for the benefit of all, let them together preserve and promote peace, liberty, social justice and moral values. *(Nostra Aetate* 3)[5]

With Vatican II, the Church began to stress the common spiritual and moral bonds binding all peoples of faith, including Muslims and Catholics. Religion promotes progress and must be in the business of protecting human rights. According to one observer, the Church is preoccupied with promoting "a doctrine of dialogue."[6] John Paul II, elected in 1978, accelerated the process of dialogue with people of other faiths. He has since encouraged the followers of the Catholic Church to investigate, with both wisdom and intelligence, the spiritual treasures of other faith-traditions, the worship aspects of other religions, and the belief in the one Unseen God. In an address to religious and government leaders in Karachi, Pakistan, in 1981, the Pope stated: "I pray this mutual understanding and respect between Christians and Muslims, and indeed between all religions, will continue and grow deeper, and that we will find still better ways of cooperation and collaboration for the good of all."[7] The Pope's tone is universal, and the spirit of his message is highly reconciliatory.

Both Muslims and Christians constitute the same nation in many countries. The Pope urges both to coexist in peace. In addressing Muslims on a visit to the Philippines in 1981, he stated: "My dear friends, I wish you to be convinced of the fact that your Christian brothers and sisters need you and they need your love. And the whole world, with its longing for greater peace, brotherhood and harmony, *needs to see fraternal coexistence between Christians and Muslims in a modern, believing and peaceful Philippine nation*" (emphasis added).[8] It is interesting to note that the Pope highlights dialogue between Catholics and all believers of other faiths as a method of reconciliation, understanding, safeguarding human dignity, and protecting the rights of the underprivileged—both the poor and minorities. His concept of human rights derives from the inalienable rights given by God to human beings, and this leads me to conclude that the Pope's thinking on the matter of social justice, equality, and human rights is motivated by a new theological understanding of the human being—any human being regardless of his/her social, educational, and religious background and, above all, regardless if s/he is a believer or not. Humans must be protected, respected, and encouraged to do the right thing. The Pope's ethos of universality is to be commended in a world that is getting smaller day by day and in a context that permits the rich to dominate the poor, both intellectually and culturally.

During his visit to Indonesia in 1989, John Paul II stated:

> One of the principal challenges facing modern Indonesia is that of building a harmonious society from the many diverse elements which are the source of the nation's present promise and future greatness. Indonesia's Catholics find a deep motivation for their contributions to this enterprise in the vision of universal harmony which the Christian faith offers them. By our belief in one God who is the creator of heaven and earth, of all that is seen and unseen, we who follow Christ are inspired to work for the advancement of peace and harmony among all people.[9]

In a sense, the Pope agrees wholeheartedly with *Pancasila,* the official philosophy or ideology of Suharto's Indonesia. From the perspective of the state, *Pancasila* guarantees the freedom of all religions, namely, Islam, Catholicism, Protestantism, Hinduism, and Buddhism. Although Indonesia has the largest Muslim population in the world, it has stressed the necessity of separating religion from politics while respecting, if not encouraging, the religious wishes of all groups in society. In his response to the Pope's remarks, Dr. H. Munawir Sjadzali, the Minister of Religious Affairs in the Republic of Indonesia (in 1989), stressed that "[i]t is true that the Muslims in Indonesia are a majority. But for us, there is no majority and minority. We are all sons and daughters of Indonesia who have the human right to adhere to a religion according to one's own conviction."[10] In order to clarify the Pope's position on Islam, the following treatment of Muslim-Christian relations, especially Muslim-Catholic relations, in Indonesia is in order.

A main contention of this essay is that both John Paul II and the Catholic Church prefer a secular and democratic system of government in the Muslim world to an Islamist one (that is, a type of government that preaches the slogan, "Islam and politics are one"). It is in this context, one may argue, that the interests of the Christians, as equal citizens of the same state, can be safeguarded. To an objective observer, Indonesia has been a secular country since the proclamation of its independence from the Dutch in 1945.[11] In other words, the political elite governing the country has refused to associate itself with "Islamism" or Islamic revivalism of the type which governs in Iran and the Sudan. In the words of President Suharto, *Pancasila* is based on the rejection of poverty, backwardness, conflicts, exploitation, capitalism, feudalism, dictatorship, colonialism, and imperialism. That is to say, *Pancasila* is based on the conviction that Indonesia must follow an independent foreign policy and a cohesive nationalist policy that preserve the religious, ethnic, and linguistic balance and integrity of the country.

Like any Third World country after independence, Indonesia has faced the "question of religion" (that is, Are religion and politics one?) with an eye to the long legacy of Dutch colonialism and to new, creative ways to imagine the future of the nascent Indonesian nation. Taking into account the different religious, social, economic, and intellectual forces at play after independence, Indonesia opted to create a secular, although theistic, state system while maintaining a clear separation between religion and state. Within this system is a guarantee that all people have the freedom to practice the religion of their choice.

Although Islam has been a potent political and social force in Indonesian society since 1945, various Islamic voices have arisen to express a variety of religious positions and trends. Indeed, one may distinguish four main currents of Muslim thought in contemporary Indonesia: modernism, neomodernism, Islamic social democracy, and internationalism-universalism. Such "neomodernist" Muslim thinkers as Abdurrahman Wahid,[12] Nurcholish Madjid,[13] Ahmad Wahib, Djohan Effendi, and, to a limited extent, Amien Rais stress the democratization of Indonesian society and reject placing religion at the service of politics, since both deal with different arenas of life. This latter current is very much appreciated by the Indonesian Catholics and the Catholic Church, especially as Catholics voice their concern about the burning of churches in certain regions in Indonesia.[14] Other "internationalist" Islamic voices, although paying lip service to *Pancasila,* would prefer to establish an Islamic state, and warn of the threat of Christian missionaries to the Islamic foundations of Indonesian society.[15]

The way the contemporary Indonesian state is imagined differs somewhat from that of Muslim revivalists within and outside of Indonesia. The Pope seems to support the spirit of *Pancasila,* which is the state's official ideology, and he distances himself from Islamists and their attempt to seize political control. While addressing the Indonesian bishops in 1996, the Pope states that "[w]hen the laity receive a solid Christian formation, they are equipped to play a constructive role in the life of the Nation, with a distinctive motivation and force. . . . This is the attitude which inspires support for *Pancasila,* the body of principles which fosters national unity, religious tolerance and justice among all various communities of your vast country."[16] In one sense, one may argue that the Pope is for the nationalist imagining of the contemporary nation-state in the Muslim world, which is, in the case of Indonesia, based on instilling pride in all Indonesians of their common historical and cultural experience and values, the nationalist fight against Dutch colonialism in the first half of the twentieth century, creating an atmosphere of religious harmony and tolerance within the country, supporting the modernization process, and abhorring all external intervention that is threatening to the political and social fabric of society.[17] The Pope seems to be saying that the rights of the Christian community in Muslim countries can be best served in the context of a democracy and deepening understanding of each other's faith.[18]

In spite of a greater presence of Islamic values and symbols in the contemporary Indonesian public and social space, the Indonesian elite is far more conservative in its Islamic pronouncements than its neighbor, the Malaysian elite. The nationalist imagining of Indonesia stresses the importance of cultural and social integration while shying away from religious tension and disintegration. The message of *Pancasila* as conceived by the writers of the Indonesian constitution is clear: let us keep the multifaith and multicultural composition of society, since pluralism, with its flexible and creative interaction with society, is an important element for the progress and modernization of society.[19] In other words, the vision of those who believe in the nation-state differs substantially from that of the Muslim revivalists. In normative terms, revivalists would like to see the Muslim world linked together by the power of the Muslim doctrine, whereas the nation is linked together by language, common heritage, and past experience. Since this type of nationalist imagining is more suitable to the religious minorities than the revivalist one, religious minorities fear the possibility of the revivalists' ascendance to power in the future Indonesia.

To elaborate John Paul II's understanding of the relationship between Catholics, as a minority in a Muslim society, and Muslims, it is imperative that we take an additional example to that of Indonesia, the Sudan. Since the coming to power of General Omar al-Bashir in 1989, the Sudan has declared itself an Islamic state, meaning that the *Shari'ah* is the supreme law in the land.[20] By and large, the Christian community in the Sudan, be it Protestant or Catholic, has opposed the implementation of the *Shari'ah* since, in their view, it infringes upon their rights to worship and lead a peaceful life. The Sudan is thus a different case from Indonesia. In his visit to the Sudan in 1993, John Paul II was particularly concerned with the unique situation facing the Christian community there. In addressing the President of the Sudan, he maintained that "[t]he inalienable dignity of every human person, irrespective of racial, ethnic, cultural or national origin or religious belief, means that when people coalesce in groups they have a right to enjoy a collective identity. Thus, minorities [that is, Christians] within a country have a right to exist, with their own language, culture and traditions, and *the State is morally obliged to leave room for their identity and self-expression*" (emphasis added).[21] In other words, the Pope believes that the Sudanese state has no right to impose ready-made rules, especially *Shari'ah* rules, on the minority groups in the Sudan. Although the Pope recognizes that especially in the Sudan, religion permeates all society, it is clear that he prefers a secular state to an Islamist one.[22] That is, John Paul II's notion of religious liberty, especially for Catholics in the Muslim context, diverges somewhat from that of the Muslim notion,[23] however variously defined. From a Catholic standpoint, the rule of the *Shari'ah* does not guarantee Christian religious liberty, and old legal formulations do not suffice to protect the rights of the Christians in the Muslim world. Likewise, although not mentioned explicitly by the Pope or any official in the Catholic Church, it is clear that there is a feeling on the side of the Catholic leadership that the application of the *Shari'ah* may lead to religious fanaticism on the Muslim side. The official position of the Church is that "[r]eligious fanaticism or extremism, which sometimes manifests itself in intolerance and even violence and murder, is a major obstacle to dialogue."[24] The closest John Paul II comes to condemning the type of government ruling in the Sudan or Iran is when he maintains that "[i]n countries where fundamentalist movements come to power, human rights and the principle of religious freedom are unfortunately interpreted in a very one-sided way—religious freedom comes to mean freedom to impose on all citizens the 'true religion.' In these countries the situation of Christians is sometimes terribly disturbing. Fundamentalist attitudes of this nature make reciprocal contacts very difficult."[25] For their part, Muslim revivalists argue that they are the only organized group in Muslim society who take the issue of religious dialogue with Christians seriously and who respect the freedom of the "People of the Book" to worship and to express their ideas.

Likewise, John Paul II takes up another issue that has proven problematic to Palestinians and Israelis: the question of Jerusalem and the rights of the Palestinians. He encourages all, especially Israelis, to preserve the sacred character of Jerusalem as a holy city to Jews, Christians, and Muslims and supports the right of the Palestinians to self-determination by creating their own state.[26]

Besides being preoccupied with the presence of Catholics in Muslim societies, John Paul II is also concerned with the human dignity and social well-being of the Muslim community, especially Muslim workers and their families, in Europe. In addressing the Muslims in France in 1980, he said that "[w]hile the motive which led you to leave your own countries, whether it be work or study, gives your departure a character of undoubted dignity, it is no less true that your condition as immigrants causes serious social, cultural and religious problems both for you and for the country which has received you."[27] It is clear that John Paul II is conscious of the fact that there must be a thorough conversation between Muslims and Europeans about cultural and religious values. He is tireless in his encouragement, not just of Christians, but of Muslims to adhere to their sublime spiritual and cultural values, especially in a Westernized context. Also, one may argue, John Paul II implores the Muslims to reaffirm their authentic values in a secular environment as a way of leading a spiritually fulfilling life. Furthermore, he seems to defend the right of the Muslims to preserve and enhance their cultural values in the face of the encroachment of the atheist values of the secular West.[28] What that means is that John Paul II could be in agreement with a number of leading contemporary Muslim intellectuals, such as Hasan Hanafi,[29] Muhammad 'Abid al-Jabiri,[30] and Mahdi Elmandjara,[31] that the affluent North, that is, Western Europe and North America, refuses to embark upon a thorough conversation on cultural values with the South on the supposition that occidental values are the norm—that is, they are universal values—and that adopting them will mean the solution to the social and economic problems of the Third World.[32] John Paul II believes that cultural diversity protects human dignity and human rights,[33] and that religious and spiritual norms, which are essentially neither occidental nor oriental but human, are the norm.

The Muslim world, like most of the Third World, suffers from the absence of democracy, a crisis in human rights, and a lack of democratic channels that enable people to express their ideas freely. All of this takes place without a major outcry from the West.

Further, another dilemma facing the Muslim world is how to safeguard universal cultural diversity and pluralism in the face of the mounting hegemony of the United States of America! The answer lies in achieving major changes in the thinking of both North and South. The North must recognize cultural diversity, and the South must affirm its cultural independence.[34] Also, the Muslim world suffers from a continuous "intellectual hemorrhage," identified as the "brain drain," which is the exodus of competent people, professionals and intellectuals, from South to North.

Many emigrate, not just in search of better economic and social standards, but because the development process in their native countries lacks the appropriate vision to incorporate them productively. Very often, this lack of vision is complicated by blind imitation of the modernized North, leading to transfer of technology with no creative contribution from the South. In other words, the South can purchase technology, but it must create its own forms of modernity and modernization. These forms, however, cannot be created in the context of the continuous exodus of skilled professionals. Therefore, the Muslim world suffers from three major problems: (1) illiteracy; (2) lack of scientific research; and (3) lack of democratic values. In reading the official pronouncements of the Pope, it is clear that these issues have not escaped his attention.

It is possible to argue that John Paul II is for cultural and religious interchange between the Muslim world and the West. In addressing Muslims, he said, "When you are not embarrassed to pray publicly, you thereby give us Christians an example worthy of respect. Live your faith aloud in this foreign land and do not let it be misused for any worldly or political interest."[35] The emigration of Muslim populations to the West can produce positive cultural and religious results. In addition to expanding the cultural horizons of the host country and population, it teaches Christians the viability of piety and prayer in a modern setting.

One perplexing issue that the Pope deals with in various speeches is "political Islam" or Islamic political revival. It seems to me that his concern about this issue stems from the fact that the majority of the Christians in the Muslim world are uncomfortable with an Islamic political system and the application of the *Shari'ah*. John Paul II has stated:

> A particular set of problems arises for the Christian because of the Islamic revival and reform movements in Islam. Catholics who are committed to the new impetus of the spirit which the Second Vatican Council has brought our Christian community can readily understand the desire of Muslim reformers to purify Islamic society. . . . However, we confess apprehension about the direction which Islamic reform can take and the possible consequences which it might have on our own Christian communities. In particular, we note concern about the status of Christians when Islamic states are created. . . . Christians cannot limit their contacts to particular segments within the Islamic community. Christians must realize that reformist, traditionalist, mystical, militant, quietist, and still other tendencies are to be found among Muslims. It is not necessary to determine which of these represents "true Islam."[36]

In other words, the Pope maintains correctly that "Islam is a complex religious and historical phenomenon" which has given rise to all sorts of forces and tendencies and which cannot be confined to one particular trend or expression. Furthermore, Islamic revivalism, though a viable tendency on the contemporary Islamic scene, cannot claim the allegiance of all Muslims. In the view of Islamic revivalism, "true Islam" must be practiced only within the confines of an Islamic political system.

The Pope seems not to want to challenge Muslim revivalists to implement a societal ethos in which they would be open to treating the Christians as equal citizens within an Islamist state. John Paul II seems, instead, to prefer a modern nation-state to an Islamist state, mainly because he does not want to see the mixing of religion and politics in Islam.

I think that this discussion of John Paul II's treatment of Islam cannot be entirely satisfactory or complete without a discussion of the basic theoretical outlines of the modern Muslim discussion of Christianity. Over the past century, Muslim scholars and religious thinkers have advanced a number of positions on Christianity. The Muslim religious leadership does not enjoy the same hierarchical organization as the Catholic Church. That is to say, Muslims lack a clear-cut "official" position on Christianity, and hence Muslim intellectuals have provided a variety of interesting opinions on Christianity, especially since the nineteenth century. These intellectuals were faced with the dual problem of Muslim stagnation and Western progress, a reality brought about by the Western penetration of the Muslim world during the colonialist era. The Egyptian thinker Muhammad 'Abduh (d. 1905) did not treat Christianity as the antithetic other, but considered Islam, as a monotheistic phenomenon and a divine religion, to be highly intertwined with Christianity; that is, he saw the essence of Islam to be that of Christianity. This is what one also gets from John Paul II's official statements on Islam.

'Abduh analyzes Christianity in response to two major critiques leveled at Islam by Farah Antoun, a Syrian émigré to Egypt and the founder of the secularist journal *al-Jami'ah*.[37] Antoun maintains that Islam, as opposed to Christianity, is intolerant of science and liberalism for two reasons: (1) Islam does not distinguish between "civil regime" *(sultah madaniyah)* and "religious regime" *(sultah diniyah)*. According to Antoun, this fusion between the political and religious has had a negative impact on tolerance and civil freedoms in general. Christianity, on the other hand, has known of a distinction between the political and religious, and, as a result, modern Western civilization has come to appreciate freedom and democracy. (2) In the West, science and philosophy have escaped the oppression of the Church. Progress has been but a normal fruit of this. In Islam, however, religious oppression has stifled progress and the freedom of both science and philosophy.[38]

In response to these accusations, 'Abduh decides to tackle the "nature of the Christian religion" *(tabi'at al-din al-masihi)* in order to prove that Islam does not oppose science, philosophy, or the freedom of all religions and minorities to coexist. He argues that Christianity derives its authenticity from the Unseen (the idea of one God), miracles, and the transience of this world. Islam's strong connection to Christianity is based on the strong Muslim belief in Christ as "God's spirit, God's word [or Logos], and His messenger to the people of Israel. Jesus did invite people to follow the correct maxims of the *Tawrah*, and practice a righteous life, and to use reason, as a human faculty, in a righteous fulfillment of life."[39]

In a sense, 'Abduh celebrates the pristine vision of Christianity as a bridge-builder, as an affirming message, not as dividing element or epistemological rupture. He argues that "[r]eligion, [in a generic sense], is God's. It is essentially one religion in past and present. In spirit and fact, religion has never changed: it is the sincere belief in one God and the lending [of] a helpful hand to people in life."[40] This last position is in full agreement with John Paul II's understanding of the rapprochement that has to evolve between Islam and Christianity. One cannot but argue that to both the Pope and 'Abduh, both Christianity and Islam are of the same essence. It is human history which has given rise to theological and doctrinal differences, applications, and results. In the final analysis, 'Abduh argues that Islam's identity is highly intertwined with that of Christianity and the "other" has no theological foundations; it has only social, political, and historical reality.

But a major divergence may exist between 'Abduh's ideas and the Pope's. In his discussion of the relationship between Christianity and "current civilization" *(al-madaniyah al-hadirah)*, 'Abduh argues that

> it is my opinion that there is no connection whatsoever between the Christian religion and the current civilization. Here is the New Testament, before our eyes, and its latent and hidden meanings do not escape us. The New Testament commands the believers to disentangle themselves from this transient life and be oblivious to its transient glory. . . . This civilization, on the other hand, is the civilization of power, glory, luxury, arrogance, and hypocrisy, and its supreme ruler is money and business.[41]

In other words, the material side of this civilization opposes the ideals of Christianity as stipulated in the New Testament. It is clear from the different statements of John Paul II and the official pronouncements of the Catholic Church that modern Christianity is part and parcel of modern civilization and that the evolution in the Church's position on dialogue, from no dialogue to dialogue, is predicated on the complex nature of modern Christianity and its connection to Muslims all over the world.

Some of 'Abduh's ideas were translated into practice by the pioneering work of Hasan al-Banna, the founder of the Ikhwan, or the Muslim Brotherhood Movement, in the Arab world. Al-Banna agrees with some of 'Abduh's basic premises, since his ideas reflect the legacy of the reform school of both 'Abduh and his disciple, Shaykh Rashid Rida.[42] Al-Banna's solution to the question of stagnation and to the problematic of Westernization and direct colonialism was to build a mass-oriented organization in which he translated the ideas of the reform movement into a sociopolitical program that aims, in principle, at altering the social and political state of affairs. In a sense, he was both a thinker and an organizer. It is against this background that one must assess his views of the "other."

Al-Banna builds upon the arguments of 'Abduh, but goes beyond him in two significant areas: first, he does not equate Christianity, as does 'Abduh, with the European "other," since there is an indigenous Egyptian Christian community which, to him, "is indigenous to Egyptian soil and is not part of the Western conquest." Second, unlike Muhammad 'Abduh, who was somewhat soft on colonialism, al-Banna criticizes European Christianity because, in his view, it was used by the secular West to colonize the rest of the world: "Europe retained its Christianity only as an historical heritage, as one factor among others for educating the simple-minded and naive among the masses, and as a means for conquest, colonization, and the suppression of political aspirations."[43]

Therefore, to al-Banna, the strange "other" is to be found in the realm of European education exporting itself to the Muslim world. That is where colonialism and missionary activities coincide. Western powers were able to found educational and scientific schools in the heart of Islam "which cast doubt and heresy into the souls of Muslims and taught them how to demean themselves, disparage their religion and their fatherland, divest themselves of their traditions and beliefs, and to regard as sacred anything Western, in the belief that only that which had a European source could serve as a model to be emulated in this life."[44]

What is even more harmful is that education was a tool used by the colonial powers to create an indigenous mercenary intellectual class made up of "the sons of the upper class alone," and consequently the masses were deprived of basic education in religious and secular sciences. Al-Banna goes on to cite *"mental colonization,"* which was a "well-organized campaign with a tremendous success, since it was rendered most attractive to the mind, and would continue to exert a strong intellectual influence on individuals over a long period of time. For this reason, it was more dangerous than the political and military campaigns so far."[45] The majority of the modern Muslim intelligentsia follow, to varying degrees, the line of argument provided by al-Banna and other Islamic leaders vis-à-vis mental colonization and the role of the Christian mission in effecting such a colonization in the modern Muslim mind. In that sense, it is very important to discuss the Pope's position on the issue of mission, since this has proven to be very controversial from both the Islamic and Christian sides.

The Islamic position is more or less clear that *da'wah,* or mission, is an integral part of Islam and that there are many methods to spread Islamic *da'wah,* one of which is through "kind debate" *(jidal bilati hiya ahsan).*[46] The Catholic Church, under the leadership of John Paul II, considers mission as an integral part in its vision of a better relationship between the Church and the followers of other faith-traditions. The Church sees itself as "the universal sacrament of salvation."[47] In other words, the mission of the Church is totally embedded in the "mystery of Christ," and Christians need to be more aware of this mystery. Love is one of the principal foundations of the mystery of Christ, and, in that sense, the Catholic Church "is a messianic people, a visible assembly and spiritual community, and a pilgrim people who go forward together with all of mankind with whom they share the human experience. . . . The pilgrim Church is therefore 'missionary by its nature.' . . . For every Christian, the missionary duty is the normal expression of his lived faith."[48] Therefore, in its approach toward other traditions, in our case Islam, the Catholic Church is guided by its need to carry out its vision through mission and love. In theological terms, the Church is fully convinced of the validity of its theological pronouncements (God is love, the mystery of Christ, and so on). Thus, preaching the Gospel of Christ to Muslims and non-Muslims alike and building churches as a means of embodying Christian teachings are in line with the theological vision of the Church. Theoretically, building churches and spreading Christian mission emanate from the position of the Church on peaceful coexistence and dialogue between Christians and Muslims. Practically, however, in areas of political tension in the Muslim world, the Catholic understanding of mission might backfire and jeopardize the relationship between the Catholic community and the Muslims.

The issue becomes complicated from a Muslim theological standpoint when the Pope preaches the concept of Christ as the Redeemer: "Man—every man without any exception whatever—has been redeemed by Christ. And with man—with each man without any exception, whatever—Christ is in a way united, even when man is unaware of it. Christ, who died and was raised up for all, provides man, each and every man, with the light and strength to measure up to his supreme calling."[49] Theologically, even the most open-minded Muslims cannot accept the claim that Christ, and not God, is the Redeemer and that Christ, "the Redeemer, is present with grace in every human encounter, to liberate us from our selfishness and to make us love one another as he has loved us."[50] In addition, Muslims cannot accept the claim, however positively made, that "no salvation exists outside of the Catholic Church."[51]

Also, the Pope, as the highest representative of the Catholic Church, does not believe that the Islamic perspective of revelation is as true as that of Christianity. He argues that "[i]n Islam all the richness of God's self-revelation, which constitutes the heritage of the Old and New Testaments, has been definitely set aside."[52] He further says that although the Qur'an addresses God in the most beautiful of names, God "is ultimately . . . outside of the world, a God who is only Majesty, never Emmanuel, God-with-us. Islam is not a religion of redemption."[53] What that means in effect is that both Christianity and Islam, according to the Pope, have two clashing religious and theological visions. Whether the preceding statements are the Pope's personal opinion on Islam or represent part of the Catholic teachings on Islam is not the point here. There are many Catholics who believe in these statements, and the Pope seems to sympathize with these views personally.

John Paul II's view that God in Islam is outside the world and distant from humanity does not accurately represent the Qur'anic view of God as being close to man: "It was We Who created man, and We know what dark suggestions his soul makes to him: for We are nearer to him than (his) jugular vein."[54] Also, this position, which is polemical at best, does not reflect the rich history of Islamic spirituality, or *tassawuf,* that has always emphasized the nearness of God to humans.[55]

Finally, it is possible to advance the following conclusions about John Paul II's position on Islam and the Muslim world:

First, one may argue that his position on Islam is politically and socially open, but theologically conservative. Salvation is to be sought inside the Church, and the only true Redeemer is Jesus Christ.

Second, "a doctrine of dialogue," as a reflection of the political openness of the Catholic Church as understood by Pope John Paul II, is far from static. It means engagement, appreciation, sacrifice, patience, spiritual enrichment, and fighting on behalf of the underprivileged in society. Dialogue means a comprehensive and deep reconciliation between Muslims and Catholics in public life. This colossal project of reconciliation entails "a common will [between Christians and Muslims] to build a better world for future generations."[56] In a sense, he encourages both Muslims and Catholics to go beyond dialogue to engagement in the true sense of the word.[57] He sees many common challenges and dangers.

Third, John Paul II does not encounter Islam and the Muslim world, especially in his latest pronouncements, as the estranged other, like the secular press, but as a spiritual community that has deep religious roots and whose fate is highly intertwined with that of the Catholics. This is especially heartening if one deeply examines the great cultural and political mutations taking place in the world in the wake of the New World Order following the defeat of Iraq in the second Gulf War and the collapse of the Soviet system. The Pope does not treat Islam and Muslims as a new universal enemy to the Western civilization. Far from that, he thinks that contemporary Christians have a lot to learn from the Muslim religious experience.

Fourth, the Pope prefers a democratic nation-state to an Islamist state in the Muslim world, the type of state that is committed to treating Christians as equal citizens by protecting their cultural and religious rights as a minority.

Fifth, John Paul II defends human rights—those of the Muslims and the Christians—and in this he challenges the modern Muslim world to come up with its own version of human rights that is congruent with both the lofty principles of Islam and the current situation in the Muslim world. In other words, he is critical of most of the military regimes in the Muslim world that do not promote genuine democracy in civil society. One may also argue that the Pope is implicitly critical of the Western support given to those military regimes that are afraid of democracy.

Sixth, to the Pope's mind, Muslims, especially those who live in Europe, can serve as a religious model for the Christians to emulate. The Pope seems to be concerned about the loss of spiritual and religious values in the contemporary Western world. Although he does not oppose modernity in principle, he would like the modern world to open its arms to basic traditional values, such as worship, transcendence, and belief in the afterlife. The erosion of religious values in modern life is not the answer.

Seventh, although John Paul II has encouraged the Catholic community to be open to Jews and Judaism, he does not support the Zionist attempt at Judaizing Jerusalem. In addition to being a central city in the religious imagination of the Muslims, Jerusalem is sacred to Christians and Jews as well.[58] The Pope emphasizes the uniqueness of Jerusalem as a spiritual treasure to the three monotheistic traditions. He argues for preserving its sacred character and being open to all people.

These ideas summarize Pope John Paul II's religious position on Islam and the Muslim world. At heart, the Pope comes to the conclusion that Islam is a different religion than Christianity and that it has to be treated as such, especially in light of the fact that he does not call openly for the conversion of Muslims to Christianity. Dialogue, and not conversion, is the only true method to reach out to Muslims and peoples of other faiths. Let us hope that both Catholics and Muslims practice the art of dialogue as a way to know about each other and, above all, to know about one's own religious and spiritual treasures and values.

NOTES

1. See M. Arkoun, "Emergences et problèmes dans le monde musulman contemporain," *Islamochristiana* 12 (1986): 135–61; and M. Watt, "Muslims and Christians after the Gulf War," *Islamochristiana* 17 (1991): 35–51.

2. See Edward Said, *Orientalism* (New York: Vintage Books, 1978).

3. See Albert Hourani, *Islam in European Thought* (New York: Cambridge University Press, 1991).

4. See A. Hourani, *Arabic Thought in the Liberal Age: 1798–1939* (Cambridge: Cambridge University Press, 1970); H. Sharabi, *Arab Intellectuals and the West: The Formative Years* (Baltimore: Johns Hopkins University Press, 1970); and I. Abu-Rabi', *Intellectual Origins of Islamic Resurgence in the Modern Arab World* (Albany: State University of New York Press, 1986).

5. Thomas Michel and Michael Fitzgerald, eds., *Recognize the Spiritual Bonds Which Unite Us: Sixteen Years of Christian-Muslim Dialogue* (Vatican City: Pontifical Council for Interreligious Dialogue, 1994), 3. For an elaboration on the views of Pope Paul VI on Islam, consult M. Borrmans, "Le pape Paul VI et les musulmans," *Islamochristiana* 4 (1978): 1–10.

6. Lucie Provost, "From Tolerance to Spiritual Emulation: An Analysis of Official Texts in Christian-Muslim Dialogue," in K. Rousseau, ed., *Christianity and Islam* (Scranton, Pa.: Ridge Row Press, 1985), 204. For a discussion of the activities of the Vatican in the field of Christian-Muslim relations, consult M. L. Fitzgerald, "Twenty-Five Years of Dialogue: The Pontifical Council for Inter-Religious Dialogue," *Islamochristiana* 15 (1989): 109–20.

7. *Recognize the Spiritual Bonds Which Unite Us,* 21.

8. Ibid., 23.

9. Ibid., 25.

10. Ibid. According to a contemporary Catholic scholar: "Au nom de la philosophie *Pancasila,* les représentants de l'Etat estiment qu'ils doivent préserver l'harmonie à l'intérieur de chaque religion, entre toutes les religions, et entre les religions et le Gouvernement" (F. Raillon, "Chrétiens et Musulmans en Indonésie: Les voies de la tolérance," *Islamochristiana* 15 [1989]: 162–63).

11. The official position of the Indonesian government on this matter is as follows: "Indonesia is neither a secular state nor a theistic one" (see H. Tarmizi Taher, *Aspiring for the Middle Path: Religious Harmony in Indonesia* [Jakarta: Center for the Study of Islam and Society, 1997], especially 55).

12. "Abdurrahman [Wahid] and his followers are social democrats and religious liberals" (K. William Liddle, "The Islamic Turn in Indonesia: A Political Explanation," *Journal of Asian Studies* 55 [1996]: 617).

13. Nurcholish Madjid, *Islam, Kemoderna dan Keindonesiaan* (Islam, Modernity, and Indonesianness) (Bandung, Indonesia: Mizan, 1987).

14. To get the view of some people in the Christian community on religious tension in contemporary Indonesia, consult Indonesia Christian Communication Forum, "The Closing, Damage and Burning of 374 Church Buildings in Indonesia from 1945 to 1997," *ICCF Publications* (Surabaya, Indonesia, 1997).

15. See T. Michel, "Militant Islam in Asia," *Pro Dialogo* 88 (1995): 50–53.

16. "Discourse of the Pope to the Bishops of Indonesia on 'Ad Limina' Visit," *Pro Dialogo* 95 (1997): 177.

17. On the differences between the "nationalist imagination" and the "Islamist imagination" in the Muslim world, see Ibrahim M. Abu-Rabi', *Intellectual Origins of Islamic Resurgence in the Modern Arab World* (Albany: State University of New York Press, 1996), especially chapter 3.

18. See F. Machado, "Harmony among Believers of the Living Faiths: Christians and Muslims in Southeast Asia," *Pro Dialogo* 87 (1994): 214–16.

19. See Nurcholish Madjid, "Islamic Roots of Modern Pluralism: [The] Indonesia Experience," *Studia Islamika: Indonesian Journal for Islamic Studies* 1, 1 (1994): 57–77.

20. See A. W. El-Affendi, *Turabi's Revolution: Islam and Power in Sudan* (London: Grey Seal Books, 1991).

21. In *Recognize the Spiritual Bonds Which Unite Us,* 136.

22. The Pope does not express this notion quite explicitly. He, however, says that "[r]eligion permeates all aspects of life in [Sudanese] society, and citizens need to accept one another, with all the differences of language, customs, culture and belief, if civic harmony is to be maintained. Religious leaders play an important role in fostering that harmony" (Pope John Paul II in addressing the leaders of the various religions of Sudan in Khartoum, February 10, 1993; in F. Gioia, ed., *Interreligious Dialogue: The Official Teaching of the Catholic Church (1963–1995)* [Boston: Pauline Books, 1997], 509).

23. See M. Talbi, "Religious Liberty: A Muslim Perspective," in L. Swidler, ed., *Religious Liberty and Human Rights in Nations and Religions* (Philadelphia: Ecumenical Press, 1986), 175–87.

24. F. Arinze, "The Engagement of the Catholic Church in Interreligious Dialogue since Assisi 1986," *Pro Dialogo* 95 (1997): 211. See also K. Etchegaray, "Comment assurer le succès des processus de réconciliation et les soustraire aux contrecoups d'extrémistes?" *Pro Dialogo* 89 (1995): 140–42.

25. John Paul II, *Crossing the Threshold of Hope* (New York: Alfred A. Knopf, 1994), 94.

26. In *Recognize the Spiritual Bonds Which Unite Us,* 56.

27. Ibid., 29.

28. "Mais la libération du Sud passe d'abord par une décolonisation culturelle car un des principaux objectifs du post-colonialisme est l'hégémonie culturelle et la propagation des valeurs occidentales. Les conflits à venir seront des conflits de valeurs et il y a une très grande urgence a développer une communication culturelle entre le Nord et le Sud" (Mahdi Elmandjara, *La décolonisation culturelle: Défi majeur du 21ième siècle* [Marrakech, Morocco: Editions Walili, 1996; and Paris: Futuribles, 1996], 214).

29. Hasan Hanafi is a leading Egyptian philosopher at the University of Cairo. See I. Boullata, "Hasan Hanafi," in *The Oxford Encyclopedia of the Modern Islamic World,* vol. 2, ed. John L. Esposito (New York: Cambridge University Press, 1995), 97–99.

30. Muhammad 'Abid al-Jabiri is the leading Arab philosopher today. See I. Abu-Rabi', *On the Threshold of Modernity: Studies in Post-1967 Arab Thought* (Albany: State University of New York Press, forthcoming).

31. Mahdi Elmandjara is at the University of Muhammad V at Rabat, Morocco.

32. "Le Nord a déployé jusqu'à présent très peu d'efforts pour comprendre et encore moins pour parler le langage du Sud. Il faut accorder une priorité aux systèmes de valeurs

pour se rendre compte que la crise actuelle entre le Nord et le Sud est une crise du système total" (Mahdi Elmandjara, *Rétrospective des futurs* [Casablanca: Ouyoun, 1992], 164).

33. Not counting its nuclear and military prowess or economic and political influence, "post-colonialism is a weapon that aims at destroying cultural diversity" (ibid., 215).

34. Ibid., 15.

35. In *Recognize the Spiritual Bonds Which Unite Us,* 30.

36. Ibid., 113.

37. See F. Antoun, *Ibn Rushd wa falsafatuhu,* ed. Tayyib Tizine (Beirut: Dar al-Farabi, 1988).

38. M. 'Imarah, ed., *al-'Amal al-Kamilah li'l Shaykh Muhammad 'Abduh,* vol. 3 (Cairo: Dar al-Shuruq, 1993), 263–64.

39. Ibid., 295.

40. Ibid.

41. Ibid., 222–23.

42. See A. al-Abyad, *Rashid Rida: Tarikh wa Sirah* (Tripoli: Gross Press, 1983); E. Shahin, *Through Muslim Eyes: M. Rashid Rida and the West* (Herndon, Va.: International Institute of Islamic Thought, 1993); and A. al-Sharabasi, *Rashid Rida* (Cairo: Matabi' al-Ahram, 1970).

43. H. Banna, *Five Tracts of Hasan al-Banna,* trans. C. Wendell (Berkeley: University of California Press, 1978), 26.

44. Ibid., 28.

45. Ibid., 29.

46. The Qur'an states the following: "Invite (all) to the Way of thy Lord with wisdom and beautiful preaching; and argue with them in ways that are best and most gracious" (16:125).

47. Gioia, ed., *Interreligious Dialogue,* 566.

48. Ibid., 568.

49. Ibid., 573–74.

50. Ibid., 573.

51. See M. Fitzgerald, "Other Religions in the Catechism of the Catholic Church," *Islamochristiana* 19 (1993): 29-41.

52. John Paul II, *Threshold,* 92.

53. Ibid.

54. *The Holy Qur'an,* trans. Abdullah Yusuf Ali (Brentwood, Md.: Amana Corporation, 1989), 50:16.

55. See A. Schimmel, *Mystical Dimensions of Islam* (Chapel Hill: University of North Carolina Press, 1975); and I. M. Abu-Rabi', ed., *The Mystical Teachings of al-Shadhili* (Albany: State University of New York Press, 1993).

56. M. Borrmans, "Les dimensions culturelles et spirituelles du dialogue islamo-chrétien," *Islamochristiana* 22 (1996): 1.

57. On the conditions of dialogue, see H. Teissier, "Pour un renouveau du dialogue islamo-chrétien," *Islamochristiana* 15 (1989): 95-107. According to the contemporary Algerian thinker Ali Merad, Christian-Muslim amity is eternal: "[L]'amitié des Chrétiens est une donnée permanente et précieuse pour les musulmans. Elle est inscrite dans leur Livre: V, 83. Et parce qu'ils trouvent son fondement dans la Parole divine, les Musulmans se sentent personnellement responsables de la sauvegarde et de la perennité de cette amitié, comme s'il s'agissait pour eux de faire en sorte que la réalité vivante de l'Histoire réponde comme un

écho à la vérité toujours actuelle de l'Ecriture" (A. Merad, "Dialogue islamo-chrétien: Pour la recherche d'un langage commun," *Islamochristiana* 1 [1975]: 9).

58. See G. Irani, *The Papacy and the Middle East: The Role of the Holy See in the Arab-Israeli Conflict 1962–1984* (Notre Dame, Ind.: University of Notre Dame Press, 1986); A. Kreutz, *Vatican Policy on the Palestinian-Israeli Conflict: The Struggle for the Holy Land* (Westport, Conn.: Greenwood Press, 1990); R. Etchegaray, "De Jérusalem aux extremités de la terre, le défi de la paix: Juifs, chrétiens, musulmans," *Pro Dialogo* 91 (1996): 33–35; and Roger Friedland and Richard Hecht, *To Rule Jerusalem* (New York: Cambridge University Press, 1996).

Benedict XVI

World Youth Day Address to the Muslim Community

Cologne, Saturday, 20 August 2005

Dear Muslim Friends,

It gives me great joy to be able to be with you and to offer you my heartfelt greetings.

As you know, I have come here to meet young people from every part of Europe and the world. Young people are the future of humanity and the hope of the nations. My beloved Predecessor, Pope John Paul II, once said to the young Muslims assembled in the stadium at Casablanca, Morocco: *"The young can build a better future if they first put their faith in God and if they pledge themselves to build this new world in accordance with God's plan, with wisdom and trust"* (*Insegnamenti*, VIII/2, 1985, p. 500).

It is in this spirit that I turn to you, dear and esteemed Muslim friends, to share my hopes with you and to let you know of my concerns at these particularly difficult times in our history.

I am certain that I echo your own thoughts when I bring up one of our concerns as we notice the spread of terrorism. I know that many of you have firmly rejected, also publicly, in particular any connection between your faith and terrorism and have condemned it. I am grateful to you for this, for it contributes to the climate of trust that we need.

Terrorist activity is continually recurring in various parts of the world, plunging people into grief and despair. Those who instigate and plan these attacks evidently wish to poison our relations and destroy trust, making use of all means, including religion, to oppose every attempt to build a peaceful and serene life together.

Thanks be to God, we agree on the fact that terrorism of any kind is a perverse and cruel choice which shows contempt for the sacred right to life and undermines the very foundations of all civil coexistence.

If together we can succeed in eliminating from hearts any trace of rancour, in resisting every form of intolerance and in opposing every manifestation of violence, we will turn back the wave of cruel fanaticism that endangers the lives of so many people and hinders progress towards world peace.

The task is difficult but not impossible. The believer—and all of us, as Christians and Muslims, are believers—knows that, despite his weakness, he can count on the spiritual power of prayer.

Dear friends, I am profoundly convinced that we must not yield to the negative pressures in our midst, but must affirm the values of mutual respect, solidarity and peace. The life of every human being is sacred, both for Christians and for Muslims. There is plenty of scope for us to act together in the service of fundamental moral values.

The dignity of the person and the defence of the rights which that dignity confers must represent the goal of every social endeavour and of every effort to bring it to fruition. This message is conveyed to us unmistakably by the quiet but clear voice of conscience. It is a message which must be heeded and communicated to others: should it ever cease to find an echo in people's hearts, the world would be exposed to the darkness of a new barbarism.

Only through recognition of the centrality of the person can a common basis for understanding be found, one which enables us to move beyond cultural conflicts and which neutralizes the disruptive power of ideologies.

During my Meeting last April with the delegates of Churches and Christian Communities and with representatives of the various religious traditions, I affirmed that "the Church wants to continue building bridges of friendship with the followers of all religions, in order to seek the true good of every person and of society as a whole" (*L'Osservatore Romano*, 25 April 2005, p. 4).

Past experience teaches us that, unfortunately, relations between Christians and Muslims have not always been marked by mutual respect and understanding. How many pages of history record battles and wars that have been waged, with both sides invoking the Name of God, as if fighting and killing the enemy could be pleasing to him. The recollection of these sad events should fill us with shame, for we know only too well what atrocities have been committed in the name of religion.

The lessons of the past must help us to avoid repeating the same mistakes. We must seek paths of reconciliation and learn to live with respect for each other's identity. The defence of religious freedom, in this sense, is a permanent imperative, and respect for minorities is a clear sign of true civilization. In this regard, it is always right to recall what the Fathers of the Second Vatican Council said about relations with Muslims.

"The Church looks upon Muslims with respect. They worship the one God living and subsistent, merciful and almighty, creator of heaven and earth, who has spoken to humanity and to whose decrees, even the hidden ones, they seek to submit themselves whole-heartedly, just as Abraham, to whom the Islamic faith readily relates itself, submitted to God. . . . Although considerable dissensions and enmities between Christians and Muslims may have arisen in the course of the centuries, the Council urges all parties that, forgetting past things, they train themselves towards sincere mutual understanding and together maintain and promote social justice and moral values as well as peace and freedom for all people" (Declaration *Nostra Aetate*, n. 3).

For us, these words of the Second Vatican Council remain the *Magna Carta* of the dialogue with you, dear Muslim friends, and I am glad that you have spoken to us in the same spirit and have confirmed these intentions.

You, my esteemed friends, represent some Muslim communities from this Country where I was born, where I studied and where I lived for a good part of my life. That is why I wanted to meet you. You guide Muslim believers and train them in the Islamic faith.

Teaching is the vehicle through which ideas and convictions are transmitted. Words are highly influential in the education of the mind. You, therefore, have a great responsibility for the formation of the younger generation. I learn with gratitude of the spirit in which you assume responsibility.

Christians and Muslims, we must face together the many challenges of our time. There is no room for apathy and disengagement, and even less for partiality and sectarianism. We must not yield to fear or pessimism. Rather, we must cultivate optimism and hope.

Interreligious and intercultural dialogue between Christians and Muslims cannot be reduced to an optional extra. It is in fact a vital necessity, on which in large measure our future depends.

The young people from many parts of the world are here in Cologne as living witnesses of solidarity, brotherhood and love.

I pray with all my heart, dear and esteemed Muslim friends, that the merciful and compassionate God may protect you, bless you and enlighten you always.

May the God of peace lift up our hearts, nourish our hope and guide our steps on the paths of the world.

Thank you!

6. *Social and Moral Issues*

JOHN PAUL II
Introduction to *The Gospel of Life*

1. The Gospel of life is at the heart of Jesus' message. Lovingly received day after day by the Church, it is to be preached with dauntless fidelity as "good news" to the people of every age and culture.

At the dawn of salvation, it is the Birth of a Child which is proclaimed as joyful news: "I bring you good news of a great joy which will come to all the people; for to you is born this day in the city of David a Saviour, who is Christ the Lord" (Lk 2:10–11). The source of this "great joy" is the Birth of the Saviour; but Christmas also reveals the full meaning of every human birth, and the joy which accompanies the Birth of the Messiah is thus seen to be the foundation and fulfilment of joy at every child born into the world (cf. Jn 16:21).

When he presents the heart of his redemptive mission, Jesus says: "I came that they may have life, and have it abundantly" (Jn 10:10). In truth, he is referring to that "new" and eternal life which consists in communion with the Father, to which every person is freely called in the Son by the power of the Sanctifying Spirit. It is precisely in this "life" that all the aspects and stages of human life achieve their full significance.

2. Man is called to a fullness of life which far exceeds the dimensions of his earthly existence, because it consists in sharing the very life of God. The loftiness of this supernatural vocation reveals the *greatness* and the *inestimable value* of human life even in its temporal phase. Life in time, in fact, is the fundamental condition, the initial stage and an integral part of the entire unified process of human existence. It is a process which, unexpectedly and undeservedly, is enlightened by the promise and renewed by the gift of divine life, which will reach its full realization in eternity (cf. 1 Jn 3:1–2). At the same time, it is precisely this supernatural calling which highlights the *relative character* of each individual's earthly life. After all, life on earth is not an "ultimate" but a "penultimate" reality; even so, it remains a

sacred reality entrusted to us, to be preserved with a sense of responsibility and brought to perfection in love and in the gift of ourselves to God and to our brothers and sisters.

The Church knows that this *Gospel of life,* which she has received from her Lord,[1] has a profound and persuasive echo in the heart of every person—believer and non-believer alike—because it marvelously fulfils all the heart's expectations while infinitely surpassing them. Even in the midst of difficulties and uncertainties, every person sincerely open to truth and goodness can, by the light of reason and the hidden action of grace, come to recognize in the natural law written in the heart (cf. Rom 2:14–15) the sacred value of human life from its very beginning until its end, and can affirm the right of every human being to have this primary good respected to the highest degree. Upon the recognition of this right, every human community and the political community itself are founded.

In a special way, believers in Christ must defend and promote this right, aware as they are of the wonderful truth recalled by the Second Vatican Council: "By his incarnation the Son of God has united himself in some fashion with every human being."[2] This saving event reveals to humanity not only the boundless love of God who "so loved the world that he gave his only Son" (Jn 3:16), but also the *incomparable value of every human person.*

The Church, faithfully contemplating the mystery of the Redemption, acknowledges this value with ever new wonder.[3] She feels called to proclaim to the people of all times this "Gospel," the source of invincible hope and true joy for every period of history. *The Gospel of God's love for man, the Gospel of the dignity of the person and the Gospel of life are a single and indivisible Gospel.*

For this reason, man—living man—represents the primary and fundamental way for the Church.[4]

NEW THREATS TO HUMAN LIFE

3. Every individual, precisely by reason of the mystery of the Word of God who was made flesh (cf. Jn 1:14), is entrusted to the maternal care of the Church. Therefore every threat to human dignity and life must necessarily be felt in the Church's very heart; it cannot but affect her at the core of her faith in the Redemptive Incarnation of the Son of God, and engage her in her mission of proclaiming the *Gospel of life* in all the world and to every creature (cf. Mk 16:15).

Today this proclamation is especially pressing because of the extraordinary increase and gravity of threats to the life of individuals and peoples, especially where life is weak and defenceless. In addition to the ancient scourges of poverty, hunger, endemic diseases, violence and war, new threats are emerging on an alarmingly vast scale.

The Second Vatican Council, in a passage which retains all its relevance today, forcefully condemned a number of crimes and attacks against human life. Thirty years later, taking up the words of the Council and with the same forcefulness I repeat that condemnation in the name of the whole Church, certain that I am interpreting the genuine sentiment of every upright conscience: "Whatever is opposed to life itself, such as any type of murder, genocide, abortion, euthanasia, or wilful self-destruction, whatever violates the integrity of the human person, such as mutilation, torments inflicted on body or mind, attempts to coerce the will itself; whatever insults human dignity, such as subhuman living conditions, arbitrary imprisonment, deportation, slavery, prostitution, the selling of women and children; as well as disgraceful working conditions, where people are treated as mere instruments of gain rather than as free and responsible persons; all these things and others like them are infamies indeed. They poison human society, and they do more harm to those who practise them than to those who suffer from the injury. Moreover, they are a supreme dishonour to the Creator."[5]

4. Unfortunately, this disturbing state of affairs, far from decreasing, is expanding: with the new prospects opened up by scientific and technological progress there arise new forms of attacks on the dignity of the human being. At the same time a new cultural climate is developing and taking hold, which gives crimes against life a *new and—if possible—even more sinister character,* giving rise to further grave concern: broad sectors of public opinion justify certain crimes against life in the name of the rights of individual freedom, and on this basis they claim not only exemption from punishment but even authorization by the State, so that these things can be done with total freedom and indeed with the free assistance of health-care systems.

All this is causing a profound change in the way in which life and relationships between people are considered. The fact that legislation in many countries, perhaps even departing from basic principles of their Constitutions, has determined not to punish these practices against life, and even to make them altogether legal, is both a disturbing symptom and a significant cause of grave moral decline. Choices once unanimously considered criminal and rejected by the common moral sense are gradually becoming socially acceptable. Even certain sectors of the medical profession, which by its calling is directed to the defence and care of human life, are increasingly willing to carry out these acts against the person. In this way the very nature of the medical profession is distorted and contradicted, and the dignity of those who practise it is degraded. In such a cultural and legislative situation, the serious demographic, social and family problems which weigh upon many of the world's peoples, and which require responsible and effective attention from national and international bodies, are left open to false and deceptive solutions, opposed to the truth and the good of persons and nations.

The end result of this is tragic: not only is the fact of the destruction of so many human lives still to be born or in their final stage extremely grave and disturbing, but no less grave and disturbing is the fact that conscience itself, darkened as it were by such widespread conditioning, is finding it increasingly difficult to distinguish between good and evil in what concerns the basic value of human life.

IN COMMUNION WITH ALL THE BISHOPS OF THE WORLD

5. The *Extraordinary Consistory* of Cardinals held in Rome on 4–7 April 1991 was devoted to the problem of the threats to human life in our day. After a thorough and detailed discussion of the problem and of the challenges it poses to the entire human family, and in particular to the Christian community, the Cardinals unanimously asked me to reaffirm with the authority of the Successor of Peter the value of human life and its inviolability, in the light of present circumstances and attacks threatening it today.

In response to this request, at Pentecost in 1991 I wrote a *personal letter* to each of my Brother Bishops asking them, in the spirit of episcopal collegiality, to offer me their cooperation in drawing up a specific document.[6] I am deeply grateful to all the Bishops who replied and provided me with valuable facts, suggestions and proposals. In so doing they bore witness to their unanimous desire to share in the doctrinal and pastoral mission of the Church with regard to the *Gospel of life.*

In that same letter, written shortly after the celebration of the centenary of the Encyclical *Rerum Novarum,* I drew everyone's attention to this striking analogy: "Just as a century ago it was the working classes which were oppressed in their fundamental rights, and the Church very courageously came to their defence by proclaiming the sacrosanct rights of the worker as a person, so now, when another category of persons is being oppressed in the fundamental right to life, the Church feels in duty bound to speak out with the same courage on behalf of those who have no voice. Hers is always the evangelical cry in defence of the world's poor, those who are threatened and despised and whose human rights are violated."[7]

Today there exists a great multitude of weak and defenceless human beings, unborn children in particular, whose fundamental right to life is being trampled upon. If, at the end of the last century, the Church could not be silent about the injustices of those times, still less can she be silent today, when the social injustices of the past, unfortunately not yet overcome, are being compounded in many regions of the world by still more grievous forms of injustice and oppression, even if these are being presented as elements of progress in view of a new world order.

The present Encyclical, the fruit of the cooperation of the Episcopate of every country of the world, is therefore meant to be a *precise and vigorous reaffirmation of the value of human life and its inviolability,* and at the same time a pressing appeal addressed to each and every person, in the name of God: *respect, protect, love and serve life, every human life!* Only in this direction will you find justice, development, true freedom, peace and happiness!

May these words reach all the sons and daughters of the Church! May they reach all people of good will who are concerned for the good of every man and woman and for the destiny of the whole of society!

6. In profound communion with all my brothers and sisters in the faith, and inspired by genuine friendship towards all, I wish to *meditate upon once more and*

proclaim the Gospel of life, the splendour of truth which enlightens consciences, the dear light which corrects the darkened gaze, and the unfailing source of faithfulness and steadfastness in facing the ever new challenges which we meet along our path.

As I recall the powerful experience of the Year of the Family, as if to complete the *Letter* which I wrote "to every particular family in every part of the world,"[8] I look with renewed confidence to every household and I pray that at every level a general commitment to support the family will reappear and be strengthened, so that today too—even amid so many difficulties and serious threats—the family will always remain, in accordance with God's plan, the "sanctuary of life."[9]

To all the members of the Church, *the people of life and for life,* I make this most urgent appeal, that together we may offer this world of ours new signs of hope, and work to ensure that justice and solidarity will increase and that a new culture of human life will be affirmed, for the building of an authentic civilization of truth and love.

NOTES

1. The expression "Gospel of life" is not found as such in Sacred Scripture. But it does correspond to an essential dimension of the biblical message.

2. Pastoral Constitution on the Church in the Modern World *Gaudium et Spes,* 22.

3. Cf. John Paul II, Encyclical Letter *Redemptor Hominis* (4 March 1979), 10: *AAS* 71 (1979), 275.

4. Cf. *ibid.,* 14; *loc. cit.,* 285.

5. Pastoral Constitution on the Church in the Modern World *Gaudium et Spes,* 27.

6. Cf. Letter to all my Brothers in the Episcopate regarding the "Gospel of Life" (19 May 1991): *Insegnamenti* XIV, 1 (1991), 1293–1296.

7. *Ibid., loc. cit.,* p. 1294.

8. Letter to Families *Gratissimam sane* (2 February 1994), 4: *AAS* 86 (1994), 871.

9. John Paul II, Encyclical Letter *Centesimus Annus* (1 May 1991), 39; *AAS* 83 (1991), 842.

JOHN PAUL II

Recognize Identity of Human Embryo

Dear Brothers and Sisters,

1. Today, the first Sunday of February, Italy is celebrating *"Pro-Life Day,"* a wonderful occasion to reflect on the fundamental value of human life.

RECOGNIZE MEANS TO GUARANTEE THE RIGHT
OF THE HUMAN PERSON TO LIFELONG DEVELOPMENT

The subject that the bishops proposed this year is: *"Recognize Life."* To recognize means, above all, to rediscover with renewed wonder what reason itself and science do not hesitate to call a "mystery." Life, especially human life, inspires a fundamental question that the Psalmist expresses so well: "What is man that you are mindful of him; the son of man that you care for him?" (Ps 8, 5). Moreover, to recognize means to *guarantee* to every human being the right to *develop* according to his own potential, ensuring his *inviolability* from conception until natural death. No one is master of life; no one has the right to manipulate, oppress, or even take life, neither that of others nor his own. Much less can he do so in the name of God, who is the only Lord and the most sincere lover of life. The *martyrs* themselves *do not take their own lives* but, in order to remain faithful to God and to his commandments, they allow themselves to *be killed.*

RECOGNIZE THE IDENTITY OF THE HUMAN EMBRYO

2. To recognize the value of life implies *consistent measures from the legal point of view,* especially the protection of human beings who are unable to defend themselves, such as the unborn, the mentally handicapped, and the most critically or terminally ill. In particular, in the study of the *human embryo,* science has now demonstrated that it is a human individual who possesses his own identity from the moment of fertilization. Therefore, it is logical to call for this identity to be legally recognized, above all, in its fundamental right to life, as the Italian "Pro-Life Movement" demands with praiseworthy initiative.

3. We entrust to the Holy Mother of Christ and of all human beings the commitment in Italy and the whole world in favour of life, especially wherever it is despised, marginalized or violated. May Mary teach us to "recognize life" as a mystery and responsibility, remembering that *"gloria Dei vivens homo,"* the glory of God is living man (St. Irenaeus).

[After the Angelus, the Holy Father greeted in Italian and in English special groups who were present. Here is the English greeting and a further pro-life greeting.]

I warmly greet the group of families of the Diocese of Rome with the Auxiliary Bishop in charge of family life concerns, and I give a special blessing to the mothers who are expecting a child. I am pleased that in Rome the Pro-Life Day has taken the form of a *Diocesan Week for Life and for the Family,* at the end of which next Sunday, parishes will reflect on the welcome they give to new families who have come to live in their neighborhood.

I am particularly pleased with the initiative of some university professors, who these days at the University of Rome, *"La Sapienza,"* have been studying in depth the theme "The embryo as patient," putting into a "declaration" the conclusions they reached about the dignity of the human being in the first phase of his existence.

I welcome all the English-speaking visitors, especially the pilgrims from St. Pius the Tenth Parish in Tachikawa, Japan. Upon you and your families I cordially invoke God's blessings of joy and peace.

∿

Angelo Sodano

After Iraq: Holy See Supports UN

Dear Mr. Secretary General,

The recent Security Council Resolution 1483 (2003) regarding the rebuilding of the institutions and the economy of Iraq can be considered the beginning of a reconfirmation of the validity of the mission of the United Nations Organization as stipulated by the Charter of 1945.

Pope John Paul II, recognizing the importance of the United Nations, has directed me to express to Your Excellency the Holy See's support for the fundamental role of the United Nations Organization at the present time. As you know, the Popes have spoken on various occasions of the need for an international and independent Authority capable of serving not only as a mediator in potential conflicts but also as a guide for all humanity, leading the human family in peace towards the rule of law. A particular sign of this interest is the presence of the Permanent Observer Mission of the Holy See at the United Nations.

Forty years ago, Pope John XXIII, in his Encyclical Letter *Pacem in Terris* (11 April 1963), clearly stated that the moral order itself calls for the establishment of a universal public Authority (n. 137). Pope John Paul II himself, in his Address to the General Assembly on 5 October 1995 expressed the hope that *"the United Nations Organization . . . become a moral center where all the nations of the world feel at home and develop a shared awareness of being, as it were, a 'family of nations'"* (*ORE,* 11 October 1995, p. 10, n. 14).

The recent Iraqi crisis has drawn attention to the need for a greater commitment to the principles set forth in the United Nations Charter in order to avoid unilateral actions which could lead to the weakening of international law and existing agreements.

The Holy See is confident that the United Nations Organization will be able to develop more efficient and concerted forms of cooperation which will enable world leaders to join in combating situations of injustice and oppression, leading to hostility between people, rather than building that "family of nations" of which Pope John Paul II spoke in 1995.

In seconding the sentiments of His Holiness, I wish to convey the recognition of the Holy See for your own commitment and that of all those who daily work for peace in the world, especially those associated with the efforts of the United Nations to foster international peace, dialogue, and cooperation.

Renewing the Holy See's esteem for this important international body, please accept, Your Excellency, the assurance of my highest consideration.

CARDINAL ANGELO SODANO

~

ROBERT GRANT

The Roman Catholic Hierarchy: Putting the Squeeze on Politicians

When Pope John Paul II annually addresses the ambassadors to the Vatican in his New Year's "state of the world" speech, he sets forth his priority concerns for the coming year. In his 2005 address, given January 10 and followed by a posting of its English translation on the Vatican website, the pope maintains that the greatest challenge facing humanity "is *the challenge of life*" and that "the State has as its primary task precisely the safeguarding and promotion of human life." In this the pope specifically refers, first, to "the *beginning of human life*," declaring: "the human embryo is a subject identical to the human being, which will be born at the term of its development." In this context he speaks against both abortion and embryonic stem cell research. Second, the pope refers to "the very sanctuary of life: *the family,*" which he says is, in some countries, "threatened by legislation which—at times directly—challenges its natural structure, which is and must necessarily be that of a union between a man and a woman founded on marriage." He adds that the family "must never be undermined by laws based on a narrow and unnatural vision of man"—in other words, by laws recognizing gay marriage.

Though he takes up other issues in this speech, such as war and natural disasters, it's only in these matters that he argues in terms of government action. This is part of a pattern. The current leadership of the Roman Catholic Church has moved in recent years from pastoral persuasion to political pressure, using intimidation, coercion, and force to achieve obedience to its teachings on contraception, abortion, euthanasia, divorce, same-sex marriage, and a range of other issues. The church seeks not merely to discipline recalcitrant church members but to require that church teachings on these subjects be imposed by coercive measures upon entire nations.

This is particularly clear in a Vatican statement issued in January 2003 by the authoritative Congregation for the Doctrine of the Faith and signed by the pope. In this statement, Roman Catholic politicians are told they aren't being faithful to church teaching if they vote against the church's position on issues such as abortion. "A well-formed Christian conscience does not permit one to vote for a political program or an individual law which contradicts the fundamental contents of faith and morals." This reiterates church teaching that no division of public and private morality can be allowed. "There cannot be two *parallel* lives in their existence; on the one hand, the so-called spiritual life, with its values and demands; and on the other, the so-called secular life; that is life in a family, at work, in social responsibilities, in the responsibilities of public life, and in culture." The statement goes on to say, "No Catholic can appeal to the principle of pluralism or to the autonomy of lay involvement in political life to support policies affecting the common good which compromise or undermine fundamental ethical requirements."

In 2004 the Vatican released another strongly worded directive demanding that Catholic politicians vote against the legalization of same-sex marriages, marriages that the pope had declared immoral. And, as reported in the May 1, 2004, *New York Times*, Cardinal Francis Arinze, head of the Vatican office of worship and sacraments, declared that "any Catholic politician who supports abortion rights is 'not fit' to receive the Eucharist."

This viewpoint was stated as American Catholic policy on June 18, 2004, when the Roman Catholic bishops of the United States, at their spring meeting outside of Denver, Colorado, approved a statement on "Catholics in Political Life" that brands Catholic politicians who support abortion rights for non-Catholics as "cooperating in evil." The statement insists that Catholic leaders are obligated to demonstrate their "fidelity to the moral teaching of the church in personal and public life." The bishops declare, "The separation of church and state does not require division between belief and public action, between moral principles and political choices, but protects the right of believers and religious groups to practice their faith and act on their values in public life."

Consistent with this, in the middle of the recent presidential campaign, Bishop Raymond Burke of St. Louis, Missouri, declared that he would refuse communion to Senator John Kerry, the Democratic presidential candidate, because of the latter's views on abortion. And most shocking of all, on October 9, 2004, just three weeks before the election, Archbishop Charles J. Chaput of Denver, Colorado, declared that to be a faithful Catholic one had to vote against Kerry (although he didn't explicitly endorse George W. Bush). Chaput was joined by Burke, Archbishop John J. Meyers of Newark, New Jersey, and many others. Never before have so many Catholic bishops interfered in a presidential election by explicitly warning Catholics that to vote a certain way was to commit a mortal sin requiring confession before receiving communion. In sum, agents of the last remaining absolute monarch in Europe interfered with the presidential election of a self-governing democracy.

And Kerry hasn't been the only target of such attacks. In April 2004 Bishop John Smith of Trenton, New Jersey, expressed his partisanship by declaring that New Jersey Governor James E. McGarvey was "not a devout Catholic" because, in the words of a May 1 *New York Times* article, "he held the view, common among Democratic politicians, of being personally opposed to abortion but feeling compelled to support abortion rights in his public life." Nor is abortion the only matter at issue. The new bishop of Camden, New Jersey, Joseph A. Galante, declared at his installation that he would deny communion to Governor McGarvey since the governor has remarried without obtaining a church annulment. A decade earlier, both former New York governor Mario Cuomo and former Democratic vice-presidential candidate Geraldine Ferraro incurred the wrath of church leaders for refusing to impose church abortion views on non-Catholics.

Developments like these force us to ask to what extent a large and powerful church, synagogue, or mosque has the right to coerce its members in order to influence public debate on issues of public morality. Every time a dominant church group does this, it is turning to the power of the state to enforce its religious or sectarian values, doing so because persuasion of a free people failed. This naturally violates the religious freedom of those of differing faith or no faith. The Virginia Constitutional Convention of 1788 that ratified the U.S. Constitution stated the principle best. That convention called for a Bill of Rights, including the right of religious freedom, to be added to the new constitution, saying:

> That religion or the duty which we owe to our Creator, and the manner of discharging it can be directed only by reason and conviction, not by force or violence, and therefore all men have an equal, natural, and unalienable right to the free exercise of religion according to the dictates of conscience, and that no particular religious sect or society ought be favored or established by Law in preference to others.

Roger Williams, a Baptist minister and the founder of Rhode Island, advanced the right of religious freedom, teaching in his famous "ship letter" of 1654 that compulsion may be exercised by officials of the state in the area of the secular but not of the sacred. James Madison, while a member of the Virginia legislature in 1785, wrote in his *Memorial and Remonstrance Against Religious Assessments* that religion and its practice must be left to the conviction and conscience of each person. Every individual and every religious body owes the duty of tolerance to all others with whom it disagrees, supporting the freedom of religion and conscience of everyone.

Beyond this principle, the American Catholic Church has a special duty to be tolerant to non-Catholics because it was a beneficiary of the tolerance of others when it was a small immigrant church. Now that it's the largest private organization in the United States—claiming to represent 63 million people, or one of every five Americans—it should set a positive example.

Moreover, intolerance violates the early tradition of the American church. One of the finest examples of Catholic tolerance was provided by the first American bishop, John Carroll of Carrollton, the brother of Charles Carroll who was a signer of the Declaration of Independence from Maryland. Canon Anson Phelps Stokes, in his definitive history, *Church and State in the United States*, observed:

> Carroll's consecration as the first American bishop of the Roman Catholic Church was the occasion of an act highly significant of his tolerance. He was chosen to this office in 1789 but not consecrated until the following year. The delay was due partly . . . to Carroll's desire to have the objectionable medieval phrase *exterminare haereticos* omitted from the enumeration of the bishop's duties in his oath of consecration. That he succeeded in accomplishing his aim was highly important for the whole future of the Church in America.

Stokes quoted a 1787 letter by Carroll written in response to a magazine article critical of Catholicism. In it Carroll wrote:

> Thanks to genuine spirit and Christianity, the United States have banished intolerance from their system of government, and many of them have done the justice to every denomination of Christians, which ought to be done to them in all, of placing them on the same footing of citizenship, and conferring an equal right of participation in national privileges.

Archbishop Gibbons, who presided over the third plenary council of bishops in the United States in 1884, frequently declared that the democratic provisions of the U.S. Constitution and the Bill of Rights were principles to which devout Catholics could give their loyal assent. In an article published in 1909 he declared:

> American Catholics rejoice in our separation of Church and State, and I can conceive no combination of circumstances likely to arise which would make a union desirable to either Church or State.

In the 1950s Archbishop McNicholas of Cincinnati said:

> No group in America is seeking union of church and state; and least of all the Catholics. We deny absolutely and without any qualification that the Catholic Bishops of the United States are seeking a union of church and state by any endeavors whatsoever, either proximate or remote. If tomorrow Catholics constituted a majority of our country, they would not seek a union of church and state. They would then, as now, uphold the constitution and all its Amendments, recognizing the moral obligation imposed on all Catholics to observe and defend the Constitution and its Amendments.

In 1960 at Loyola University, Archbishop Egidio Vagnazzi, apostolic delegate to the United States, said:

In practice, the Church will not interfere, and has not interfered, in local situations where the separation between Church and State may be considered the greater and more general good. . . . As far as the United States is concerned, I feel that it is a true interpretation of the feelings of the Hierarchy and of American Catholics in general to say that they are well satisfied with their Constitution and pleased with the fundamental freedom enjoyed by their Church; in fact, they believe that this freedom is to a large extent responsible for the expansion and consolidation of the Church in this great country.

Historically, Catholic politicians, from Al Smith to John F. Kennedy, have promised not to let the pope dictate to American Catholics on matters of secular public policy.

Contrary to that history and tradition, however, there has now been an enormous and conscious shift in policy by Catholic Church officials to move from persuasion to the use of coercive tactics to enforce certain official teachings. Make no mistake about it: by this change in policy, the Catholic Church is using its power not merely to enforce church teachings among its members but to engage the coercive power of the state to establish crimes and thus to impose its doctrines and view of morality upon the entire community.

The method used by the current leadership is to specifically target and intimidate Catholic politicians. The goal is to force them to vote for and support the church's views on a wide range of subjects including abortion, contraception, same-sex marriage, and assisted suicide. The church intimidates nonconforming Catholic politicians by withholding communion and threatening excommunication. It denies them the opportunity to speak at Catholic churches, colleges, and universities.

Such efforts force Catholic political leaders to choose between their duty to all the people whom they represent and the coercive mandates of a misguided church leadership. To achieve the goal of religious freedom for all, political leaders are required to treat their religious values as personal morality and define crime only according to principles of public, secular morality. But the current Catholic hierarchy doesn't want Catholics who are politicians to think this way.

Though it is true that every person, organization, and religious sect in the United States, including the Catholic Church, has the right to free speech and is thus entitled to express an opinion on any subject and to likewise attempt to persuade nonadherents to its views, this right doesn't logically extend to the use of coercion and intimidation of members and nonmembers through religious sanctions. And though every religious organization has the right to set its own standards for membership and its own rules of member conduct, this doesn't logically extend to imposing conflicts of interest upon those members democratically elected to serve a broad public constituency.

It's difficult for nonbelievers to understand just how intimidating and coercive such measures can be. For a true believer, the loss of the ability to receive the body and blood of Christ, and the peace and comfort that such a union brings at times of stress and spiritual need, is devastating. The separation from spiritual friends, the public castigation of one as a sinner, is a true loss, a powerful duress, and a public humiliation. Though everyone has the right to persuade another to his or her view of truth, this doesn't extend to the use of such intimidation, coercion, or force. And these activities aren't protected as either free speech or the free exercise of religion.

This acceptance of what is tantamount to force then crosses the line and is extremely dangerous. One could ask, if refusal of communion doesn't work, would the church escalate to excommunication, interdict, inquisition, or even burning at the stake? Once the use of force is accepted, it is only a matter of degree as to just how much force will be applied until obedience is achieved.

Ultimately then, the most recent Vatican statements and ecclesiastical misdeeds aren't about taking a principled stand for Catholic doctrines. (Otherwise, why does the church threaten politicians only in opposition to abortion, euthanasia, and same-sex marriage but not in opposition to capital punishment, preemptive war, and the use of atomic weapons?) Rather they are about power and the abuse of power. By setting itself up—through coercion, intimidation, and religious sanctions—as the final arbiter of the morality of legislation enacted by the United States Congress and the legislatures of the several states, the Catholic Church is attempting to become nothing less than the *de facto* established church of the United States. It is admitting that it has been unable to persuade the majority of its faithful, let alone the general public, to some of its demands. After listening to church teaching and considering these matters thoughtfully, a large majority of American Catholics now ignore the church's teaching on contraception and divorce; Catholic women have abortions at about the same rate as other Americans, and a strong majority support a woman's right to choose for herself whether or not to have an abortion. Furthermore, many thoughtful and informed Catholics support the right to die with dignity and the equality of gays and lesbians to choose caring relationships without government or church interference.

The times are clearly changing and the hierarchy has grown desperate in its efforts to hold back the tide. But this desperation could backfire. The church's interference in the recent U.S. presidential election, for example, wasn't only contrary to the principles of freedom and democracy but it was also unwise, since it puts the church in a lose-lose situation. If Kerry had won the election, church officials risked an unfriendly White House. Although Kerry lost for a variety of reasons, authoritarian church leaders have taken the risk that many Catholics who supported him will blame the American bishops for the loss of such a close election. Forcing Catholics and Catholic politicians to choose between their duty to their country and their commitment to the church is a sure recipe for internal dissension, anticlericalism, and perhaps schism. Just such a conflict is what caused English Catholics in the sixteenth century to flock to the Anglican Church.

For these and other reasons, then, it would be of benefit to everyone if American Catholics worked to cleanse the American church of this current intolerance that is inconsistent with the American church's earlier history, the tradition of the

American people, and the demands of nonbelievers for freedom of religion and conscience. In this connection, the American bishops need to be encouraged to advise the Vatican that the Catholic Church in the United States is different from the church in Europe and elsewhere.

There is no official church in the United States. And in our time there are no interdicts or inquisitions.

The complaint, then, isn't with citizens who are Catholics but with the current church leadership. Nor is the complaint to be taken as an excuse for Catholic bashing or religious bigotry. It is simply part of a healthy debate toward restoring tolerance. The United States was founded on that idea and can't survive, values intact, without it.

$\sim$

John Paul II

Human Sexuality in God's Original Plan

Message to the Bishop of Albano for the centenary of the death of St. Maria Goretti (July 6, 2002)

To my venerable brother Bishop Agostino Vallini of Albano:

1. A hundred years ago, on July 6, 1902, Maria Goretti died in the hospital at Nettuno, brutally stabbed the day before in the little village of Le Ferriere, in the Pontine Marshes. Her spiritual life, the strength of her faith, her ability to forgive her murderer have placed her among the best-loved saints of the 20th century. Appropriately, therefore, the Congregation of the Passion (C.P.), entrusted with the care of the shrine where the saint's remains repose, wanted to celebrate the anniversary with special solemnity.

St. Maria Goretti was a girl whom God's spirit endowed with the courage to stay faithful to her Christian vocation even to the point of making the supreme sacrifice of her life. Her tender age, her lack of education and the poverty of the environment in which she lived did not prevent grace from working its miracles in her. Indeed, it was precisely in these conditions that God's special love for the lowly appeared. We are reminded of the words with which Jesus blesses the heavenly Father for revealing himself to children and the simple, rather than to the wise and learned of the world (cf. Mt 11:25).

It was rightly observed that St. Maria Goretti's martyrdom heralded what was to be known as the century of martyrs. It was in this perspective that at the end of the Great Jubilee of the Year 2000, I stressed that "this lively sense of repentance . . . has not prevented us from giving glory to the Lord for what He has done in every century, and in particular during the century that we have just left behind, by granting his Church a great host of saints and martyrs" *(Novo Millennio Ineunte,* no. 7).

2. Maria Goretti, born in Corinaldo in The Marches on Oct. 16, 1890, was soon obliged to emigrate with her family, and after some time they arrived at Le Ferriere di Conca in the Pontine Marshes. Despite the hardships of poverty that even prevented her from going to school, little Maria lived in a serene and united family atmosphere, enlivened by Christian faith, in which the children felt welcomed as a gift and were taught by their parents self-respect and respect for others, as well as a sense of duty based on love of God. This enabled the little girl to grow up peacefully, nourishing her simple but deep faith. The Church has always recognized the role of the family as the first and fundamental place for the sanctification of its members, starting with the children.

In this family environment, Maria assimilated steadfast trust in God's provident love, which she showed in particular at the death of her father, who died of malaria. "Mother, be brave, God will help us," the little girl was in the habit of saying in those difficult times, bravely reacting to her deep feeling of loss at her father's death.

3. In the homily for her canonization, Pope Pius XII of venerable memory pointed to Maria Goretti as "the sweet little martyr of purity" (cf. *Discorsi e Radiomessaggi,* XII [1950–1951], 121), because she did not break God's commandment in spite of being threatened by death.

What a shining example for young people! The noncommittal mind-set of much of our society and culture today sometimes has a struggle to understand the beauty and value of chastity. A high and noble perception of dignity, her own and that of others, emerges from the behavior of this young saint, which was mirrored in her daily choices, giving them the fullness of human meaning. Is not there a very timely lesson in this? In a culture that idolizes the physical aspect of the relations between a man and a woman, the Church continues to defend and to champion the value of sexuality as a factor that involves every aspect of the person and must therefore be lived with an interior attitude of freedom and reciprocal respect, in the light of God's original plan. With this outlook, a person discovers he or she is being given a gift and is called, in turn, to be a gift to the other.

In the apostolic letter *Novo Millennio Ineunte,* I noted that "in the Christian view of marriage, the relationship between a man and a woman—a mutual and total bond, unique and indissoluble—is part of God's original plan, obscured throughout history by 'hardness of heart,' but which Christ came to restore to its pristine splendor, disclosing what had been God's will 'from the beginning' (Mt 19:8). Raised to the dignity of a sacrament, marriage expresses the 'great mystery' of Christ's nuptial love for His Church (cf. Eph 5:32)" (no. 47).

It cannot be denied that today the threats to the unity and stability of the family are many. However, at the same time there is a renewed awareness of the child's right to be raised in love, protected from every kind of danger and educated so as to be able to set out in life with confidence and fortitude.

4. In the heroic testimony of the saint of Le Ferriere, her forgiveness of the man who killed her and her desire to be able to meet him one day in heaven deserve special attention. This spiritual and social message is of extraordinary relevance in our time.

The recent Great Jubilee of the Year 2000, among other aspects, was marked by a profound appeal for pardon in the context of the celebration of God's mercy. The divine indulgence for human shortcomings is a demanding model of behavior for all believers. Forgiveness, in the Church's opinion, does not mean moral relativism or permissiveness. On the contrary, it demands the full recognition of one's sin and the assumption of one's responsibilities as a condition for rediscovering true peace and for confidently resuming the journey to evangelical perfection.

May humanity start out with determination on the way of mercy and forgiveness! Maria Goretti's murderer recognized the sin he had committed. He asked forgiveness of God and of the martyr's family, conscientiously expiated his crime and lived the rest of his life in this spiritual frame of mind.

The saint's mother, for her part, pardoned him on behalf of the family in the hall of the tribunal where his trial was taking place. We do not know whether it was the mother who taught her daughter to forgive or the martyr's forgiveness on her deathbed that determined her mother's conduct. Yet it is certain that the spirit of forgiveness motivated relations within the whole Goretti family, and for this reason could be so naturally expressed by both the martyr and her mother.

5. Those who were acquainted with little Maria said on the day of her funeral: "A saint has died!" The devotion to her has continued to spread on every continent, giving rise to admiration and a thirst for God everywhere. In Maria Goretti shines out the radical choice of the Gospel, unhindered, indeed strengthened by the inevitable sacrifice that faithful adherence to Christ demands.

I am especially holding up this saint as an example to young people who are the hope of the Church and of humanity. As we are now so close to the 17th World Youth Day, I would like to remind young people of what I wrote in the message I addressed to them in preparation for this longed-for ecclesial event: "In the heart of the night we can feel frightened and insecure, and we impatiently await the coming of the light of dawn. Dear young people, it is up to you to be the watchmen of the morning (cf. Is 21:11–12) who announce the coming of the sun who is the Risen Christ!" (no. 3).

Walking in the footsteps of the divine Teacher always means standing up for Him and committing oneself to follow Him wherever He goes (cf. Rv 14:4). However, on this path, young people know that they are not alone. St. Maria Goretti and the many adolescents who down through the centuries paid the price of martyrdom for their allegiance to the Gospel are beside them, to instill in their hearts the strength to remain firm in fidelity. Thus they will be able to become watchmen of a radiant dawn, illumined by hope. May the Blessed Virgin, Queen of Martyrs, intercede for them!

In raising this prayer, I am united in spirit with everyone who will be taking part in the Jubilee celebrations during this centenary year, and I send a special apostolic blessing, the pledge of an abundance of heavenly favors, to you, venerable diocesan bishop, to the worthy Passionist Fathers in charge of the shrine at Nettuno, to the devotees of St. Maria Goretti and especially to the young people.

❧

BENEDICT XVI

Address to the Participants in the Ecclesial Diocesan Convention of Rome

Basilica of St. John Lateran, Monday, 6 June 2005

Dear Brothers and Sisters,

I very willingly accepted the invitation to introduce our Diocesan Convention with a Reflection, first of all because it gives me the chance to meet you, of having direct contact with you, and then too, because I can help you acquire a deeper understanding of the sense and purpose of the pastoral journey the Church of Rome is making.

I greet with affection each one of you, Bishops, priests, deacons, men and women religious, and in particular you lay people and families who consciously take on those duties of responsibility and Christian witness that have their root in the sacrament of Baptism and, for those who are married, in the sacrament of Marriage. I cordially thank the Cardinal Vicar and the couple, Luca and Adriana Pasquale, for their words on behalf of you all.

This Convention and the guidelines it will provide for the pastoral year are a new stage on the journey begun by the Church of Rome, based on the Diocesan Synod, with the "City Mission," desired by our deeply loved Pope John Paul II in preparation for the Great Jubilee of 2000.

In that Mission all the components of our Diocese—parishes, religious communities, associations and movements—were mobilized, not only for a mission to the people of Rome, but to be themselves "a people of God in mission," putting into practice John Paul II's felicitous expression: "The parish must seek itself outside itself" and find itself, that is, in the places where the people live. So it was that during the City Mission thousands of Christians of Rome, mainly lay people, became missionaries and took the word of faith first to the families in the various districts of the city, and then to the different workplaces, hospitals, schools and universities, and the environments of culture and leisure time.

After the Holy Year, my beloved Predecessor asked you not to stop on this journey and not to lose the apostolic energies kindled or the fruits of grace gathered. Therefore, since 2001, the fundamental pastoral policy of the Diocese has been to give the mission a permanent form, and to impress a more decidedly missionary approach on the life and activities of the parishes and of every other ecclesial situation.

I want to tell you first of all that I fully intend to confirm this decision: indeed, it is proving to be more and more necessary. There are no alternatives to it in a social and cultural context in which many forces are working to distance us from the faith and from Christian life.

For two years now the missionary commitment of the Church of Rome has focused above all on the family. This is not only because today this fundamental human reality is subjected to a multitude of problems and threats and is therefore especially in need of evangelization and practical support, but also because Christian families constitute a crucial resource for education in the faith, for the edification of the Church as communion and for her ability to be a missionary presence in the most varied situations of life, as well as to act as a Christian leaven in the widespread culture and social structures.

We will also continue along these lines in the coming pastoral year, and so the theme of our Convention is "Family and Christian community: formation of the person and transmission of the faith."

The assumption from which it is necessary to set out, if we are to understand the family mission in the Christian community and its tasks of forming the person and transmitting the faith, is always that of the meaning of marriage and the family in the plan of God, Creator and Saviour. This will therefore be the focus of my Reflection this evening and I will refer to the teaching of the Apostolic Exhortation *Familiaris Consortio* (Part II, nn. 12–16).

Marriage and the family are not in fact a chance sociological construction, the product of particular historical and financial situations. On the other hand, the question of the right relationship between the man and the woman is rooted in the essential core of the human being and it is only by starting from here that its response can be found.

In other words, it cannot be separated from the ancient but ever new human question: Who am I? What is a human being? And this question, in turn, cannot be separated from the question about God: Does God exist? Who is God? What is his face truly like?

The Bible gives one consequential answer to these two queries: the human being is created in the image of God, and God himself is love. It is therefore the vocation to love that makes the human person an authentic image of God: man and woman come to resemble God to the extent that they become loving people.

This fundamental connection between God and the person gives rise to another: the indissoluble connection between spirit and body: in fact, the human being is a soul that finds expression in a body and a body that is enlivened by an immortal spirit.

The body, therefore, both male and female, also has, as it were, a theological character: it is not merely a body; and what is biological in the human being is not merely biological but is the expression and the fulfilment of our humanity.

Likewise, human sexuality is not juxtaposed to our being as person but part of it. Only when sexuality is integrated within the person does it successfully acquire meaning.

Thus, these two links, between the human being with God and in the human being, of the body with the spirit, give rise to a third: the connection between the person and the institution.

Indeed, the totality of the person includes the dimension of time, and the person's "yes" is a step beyond the present moment: in its wholeness, the "yes" means "always"; it creates the space for faithfulness. Only in this space can faith develop, which provides a future and enables children, the fruit of love, to believe in human beings and in their future in difficult times.

The freedom of the "yes," therefore, reveals itself to be freedom capable of assuming what is definitive: the greatest expression of freedom is not the search for pleasure without ever coming to a real decision; this apparent, permanent openness seems to be the realization of freedom, but it is not true. The true expression of freedom is the capacity to choose a definitive gift in which freedom, in being given, is fully rediscovered.

In practice, the personal and reciprocal "yes" of the man and the woman makes room for the future, for the authentic humanity of each of them. At the same time, it is an assent to the gift of a new life.

Therefore, this personal "yes" must also be a publicly responsible "yes," with which the spouses take on the public responsibility of fidelity, also guaranteeing the future of the community. None of us, in fact, belongs exclusively to himself or herself: one and all are therefore called to take on in their inmost depths their own public responsibility.

Marriage as an institution is thus not an undue interference of society or of authority. The external imposition of form on the most private reality of life is instead an intrinsic requirement of the covenant of conjugal love and of the depths of the human person.

Today, the various forms of the erosion of marriage, such as free unions and "trial marriage," and even pseudo-marriages between people of the same sex, are instead an expression of anarchic freedom that are wrongly made to pass as true human liberation. This pseudo-freedom is based on a trivialization of the body, which inevitably entails the trivialization of the person. Its premise is that the human being can do to himself or herself whatever he or she likes: thus, the body becomes a secondary thing that can be manipulated, from the human point of view, and used as one likes. Licentiousness, which passes for the discovery of the body and its value, is actually a dualism that makes the body despicable, placing it, so to speak, outside the person's authentic being and dignity.

The truth about marriage and the family, deeply rooted in the truth about the human being, has been actuated in the history of salvation, at whose heart lie the words: "God loves his people." The biblical revelation, in fact, is first and foremost the expression of a history of love, the history of God's Covenant with humankind.

Consequently, God could take the history of love and of the union of a man and a woman in the covenant of marriage as a symbol of salvation history. The inexpressible fact, the mystery of God's love for men and women, receives its linguistic form from the vocabulary of marriage and the family, both positive and negative: indeed, God's drawing close to his people is presented in the language of spousal love, whereas Israel's infidelity, its idolatry, is designated as adultery and prostitution.

In the New Testament God radicalizes his love to the point that he himself becomes, in his Son, flesh of our flesh, a true man. In this way, God's union with humankind acquired its supreme, irreversible form.

Thus, the blue-print of human love is also definitely set out, that reciprocal "yes" which cannot be revoked: it does not alienate men and women but sets them free from the different forms of alienation in history in order to restore them to the truth of creation.

The sacramental quality that marriage assumes in Christ, therefore, means that the gift of creation has been raised to the grace of redemption. Christ's grace is not an external addition to human nature; it does not do violence to men and women but sets them free and restores them, precisely by raising them above their own limitations. And just as the Incarnation of the Son of God reveals its true meaning in the Cross, so genuine human love is self-giving and cannot exist if it seeks to detach itself from the Cross.

Dear brothers and sisters, this profound link between God and the human being, between God's love and human love, is also confirmed in certain tendencies and negative developments that have weighed heavily on us all. In fact, the debasement of human love, the suppression of the authentic capacity for loving, is turning out in our time to be the most suitable and effective weapon to drive God away from men and women, to distance God from the human gaze and heart.

Similarly, the desire to "liberate" nature from God leads to losing sight of the reality of nature itself, including the nature of the human being, reducing it to a conglomeration of functions so as to have them available at will to build what is presumed to be a better world and presumed to be a happier humanity. Instead, the Creator's design is destroyed, and so is the truth of our nature.

Even in the begetting of children marriage reflects its divine model, God's love for man. In man and woman, fatherhood and motherhood, like the body and like love, cannot be limited to the biological: life is entirely given only when, by birth, love and meaning are also given, which make it possible to say yes to this life.

From this point it becomes clear how contrary to human love, to the profound vocation of the man and the woman, are the systematic closure of a union to the gift of life and even more, the suppression or manipulation of newborn life.

No man and no woman, however, alone and single-handed, can adequately transmit to children love and the meaning of life. Indeed, to be able to say to someone "your life is good, even though I may not know your future," requires an authority and credibility superior to what individuals can assume on their own.

Christians know that this authority is conferred upon that larger family which God, through his Son Jesus Christ and the gift of the Holy Spirit, created in the story of humanity, that is, upon the Church. Here they recognize the work of that eternal, indestructible love which guarantees permanent meaning to the life of each one of us, even if the future remains unknown.

For this reason, the edification of each individual Christian family fits into the context of the larger family of the Church, which supports it and carries it with her and guarantees that it has, and will also have in the future, the meaningful "yes" of the Creator. And the Church is reciprocally built up by the family, a "small domestic church," as the Second Vatican Council called it (*Lumen Gentium,* n. 11; *Apostolicam Actuositatem,* n. 11), rediscovering an ancient Patristic expression (cf. St. John Chrysostom, *In Genesim Serm.* VI, 2; VII, 1).

In the same sense, *Familiaris Consortio* affirms that "Christian marriage . . . constitutes the natural setting in which the human person is introduced into the great family of the Church" (n. 15).

There is an obvious consequence to all this: the family and the Church—in practice, parishes and other forms of Ecclesial Community—are called to collaborate more closely in the fundamental task that consists, inseparably, in the formation of the person and the transmission of the faith.

We know well that for an authentic educational endeavour, communicating a correct theory or doctrine does not suffice. Something far greater and more human is needed: the daily experienced closeness that is proper to love, whose most propitious place is above all the family community, but also in a parish, movement or ecclesial association, in which there are people who care for their brothers and sisters because they love them in Christ, particularly children and young people, but also adults, the elderly, the sick and families themselves. The great Patron of educators, St. John Bosco, reminded his spiritual sons that "education is something of the heart and that God alone is its master" (*Epistolario,* 4, 209).

The central figure in the work of educating, and especially in education in the faith, which is the summit of the person's formation and is his or her most appropriate horizon, is specifically the form of witness. This witness becomes a proper reference point to the extent that the person can account for the hope that nourishes his life (cf. I Pt 3: 15) and is personally involved in the truth that he proposes.

On the other hand, the witness never refers to himself but to something, or rather, to Someone greater than he, whom he has encountered and whose dependable goodness he has sampled. Thus, every educator and witness finds an unequalled model in Jesus Christ, the Father's great witness, who said nothing about himself but spoke as the Father had taught him (cf. Jn 8: 28).

This is the reason why prayer, which is personal friendship with Christ and contemplation in him of the face of the Father, is indispensably at the root of the formation of the Christian and of the transmission of the faith. The same is, of course, also true for all our missionary commitment, and particularly for the pastoral care of families: therefore, may the Family of Nazareth be for our families and our communities the object of constant and confident prayer as well as their life model.

Dear brothers and sisters, and especially you, dear priests, I am aware of the generosity and dedication with which you serve the Lord and the Church. Your daily work forming the new generations in the faith, in close connection with the sacraments of Christian initiation, as well as marriage preparation and offering guidance to families in their often difficult progress, particularly in the important task of raising children, is the fundamental way to regenerating the Church ever anew, and also to reviving the social fabric of our beloved city of Rome.

Continue, therefore, without letting yourselves be discouraged by the difficulties you encounter. The educational relationship is delicate by nature: in fact, it calls into question the freedom of the other who, however gently, is always led to make a decision. Neither parents nor priests nor catechists, nor any other educators can substitute for the freedom of the child, adolescent or young person whom they are addressing. The proposal of Christianity in particular challenges the very essence of freedom and calls it to faith and conversion.

Today, a particularly insidious obstacle to the task of educating is the massive presence in our society and culture of that relativism which, recognizing nothing as definitive, leaves as the ultimate criterion only the self with its desires. And under the semblance of freedom it becomes a prison for each one, for it separates people from one another, locking each person into his or her own "ego."

With such a relativistic horizon, therefore, real education is not possible without the light of the truth; sooner or later, every person is in fact condemned to doubting in the goodness of his or her own life and the relationships of which it consists, the validity of his or her commitment to build with others something in common.

Consequently, it is clear that not only must we seek to get the better of relativism in our work of forming people, but we are also called to counter its destructive predominance in society and culture. Hence, as well as the words of the Church, the witness and public commitment of Christian families are very important, especially in order to reassert the inviolability of human life from conception until its natural end, the unique and irreplaceable value of the family founded on marriage and the need for legislative and administrative measures that support families in the task of bringing children into the world and raising them, an essential duty for our common future. I also offer you my heartfelt thanks for this commitment.

I would like to entrust to you a last message concerning the care of vocations to the priesthood and to the consecrated life: we all know the Church's great need of them!

First of all, prayer is crucial in order that these vocations be born and reach maturity, and that those called will always continue to be worthy of their vocation; prayer should never be lacking in any family or Christian community.

However, the life witness of priests and men and women religious and their joy in having been called by the Lord are also fundamental.

Equally so is the essential example that children receive in their own family and the conviction of families themselves that for them too, the vocation of a child of theirs is a great gift from the Lord. Indeed, the choice of virginity for the love of God and the brethren, which is required for priesthood and for consecrated life, goes hand in hand with the estimation of Christian marriage: both, in two different and complementary ways, make visible in a certain way the mystery of God's Covenant with his people.

Dear brothers and sisters, I consign these thoughts to you as a contribution to your work in the evening sessions of the Convention, and later, during the coming pastoral year. I ask the Lord to give you courage and enthusiasm, so that our Church of Rome, each parish, religious community, association or movement, may participate more intensely in the joy and labours of the mission; thus, each family and the entire Christian community will rediscover in the Lord's love the key that opens the door of hearts and makes possible a true education in the faith and people's formation.

My affection and my Blessing go with you today and in the future.

≈

GRETCHEN VOGEL

Abstentions Scuttle Drive to Liberalize Italy's Embryo Laws

An attempt to loosen tight restrictions on in vitro fertilization (IVF) in Italy failed when only 26% of the electorate turned out to vote in a referendum on 12 and 13 June, missing a required 50% quorum. The result was precisely what Catholic Church leaders sought; it means Italy will continue to forbid research using embryos from IVF procedures. Italian scientists are still allowed to work with any imported human embryonic stem (hES) cells—although funding is scarce—but they cannot derive new ones.

The Catholic Church campaigned strongly to persuade voters to stay away from the polls. Under Italian law, a referendum is invalid if fewer than half the eligible voters participate. The abrupt fade-out marked the end of a bitterly fought campaign. Referendum opponents accused proponents of overstating the promise of embryo research, comparing it to Nazi experiments. Many scientists and referendum supporters accused the government of dirty tricks and distortions.

Until January, Italy had no laws on IVF treatments or embryo research, enabling the infamous claims of gynecologist Severino Antinori, who said he was trying to create the first cloned human. But a law passed in February 2004 put tight restrictions into effect 6 months ago. It forbids the creation of more than three embryos per IVF attempt, all of which must be implanted in the potential mother, and it outlaws the donation of sperm or eggs. It also imposes a fine of more than $1 million for any attempt at human cloning. The law was controversial from the start: Members of Parliament offered more than 350 amendments. But none were allowed, and the law passed 277 to 222.

Before the law took effect, Italy's far-left Radical Party collected nearly twice as many signatures as the 500,000 required for a petition to put four parts of the law up for review in a referendum—the ban on embryo research; giving legal rights to the human embryo; the ban on gamete donation; and the requirement that only three IVF embryos can be created, all of which must be implanted.

In the weeks leading up to the vote, the campaign intensified, with researchers and patient groups staging several days of hunger strikes to protest what they called an unfair attack on the referendum. Opponents, including Pope Benedict XVI and Catholic bishops, calculated that a combination of voter apathy, summer vacations, and deliberate abstentions would nullify the vote.

Scientists were active on both sides, with several researchers, including Angelo Vescovi of the Stem Cell Research Institute at the University of Milan–Bicocca, saying new hES lines were not necessary to advance stem cell research. Vescovi appeared on campaign posters saying he planned not to vote. On the other side, more than 130 scientists from around the world signed a letter urging Italians to change the law.

Elena Cattaneo of the University of Milan, one of a handful of researchers working with hES cells in Italy, says she is bitterly disappointed by the vote. "It is a pity for science," she says. "The scientific community wasn't able to express itself the way we should have done."

Marco Cappato, a member of the Radical Party and a leading campaigner for the referendum, says he and his colleagues will try to make the law an issue in the next elections, expected next spring, and win enough votes to change it in Parliament.

~

MICHAEL GRIFFIN

New Pope Benedict XVI a Strong Critic of War

The election of Benedict XVI as pope brings hope for the continuation of peacemaking as central to the papacy. Just as John Paul II cried out again and again to the world, "War never again!" the new pope has taken the name of the one who first made that cry, Benedict XV, commonly known as "the peace pope."

The name is no coincidence. In fact, Cardinal Justin Rigali, Archbishop of Philadelphia, said Tuesday that the new pope told the cardinals he was selecting Benedict because "he is desirous to continue the efforts of Benedict XV on behalf of peace . . . throughout the world."

As a Cardinal, the new pope was a staunch critic of the U.S.-led invasion of Iraq. On one occasion before the war, he was asked whether it would be just. "Certainly not," he said, and explained that the situation led him to conclude that "the damage would be greater than the values one hopes to save."

"All I can do is invite you to read the *Catechism*, and the conclusion seems obvious to me. . . ." The conclusion is one he gave many times: "the concept of preventive war does not appear in *The Catechism of the Catholic Church*."

Even after the war, Cardinal Ratzinger did not cease criticism of U.S. violence and imperialism: "it was right to resist the war and its threats of destruction. . . . It should never be the responsibility of just one nation to make decisions for the world."

Yet perhaps the most important insight of Ratzinger came during a press conference on May 2, 2003. After suggesting that perhaps it would be necessary to revise the *Catechism* section on just war (perhaps because it had been used by George Weigel and others to endorse a war the Church opposed), Ratzinger offered a deep insight that included but went beyond the issue of war in Iraq:

"There were not sufficient reasons to unleash a war against Iraq. To say nothing of the fact that, given the new weapons that make possible destructions that go beyond the combatant groups, today we should be asking ourselves if it is still licit to admit the very existence of a 'just war'."

Along with his actual criticism of war, we take heart in the theological principle behind such criticism. While many Catholics, most notably Weigel, have advocated deference to the heads of state in determining issues such as war and peace, the new pope has consistently taught that the Church "cannot simply retreat into the private sphere."

He is skeptical of the view that politics can be done without reference to the Gospel. Appeals to neutral language that does not refer to religion—popular as they are among many neoconservative Catholics—forget some of the "hard sayings" of Jesus that don't seem quite "rational" enough for public discourse. Sayings like "Love your enemies" and "turn the other cheek" and "put away the sword," these are dismissed as impractical at best, sectarian at worst.

Not by our new pope . . . He signals an invigorated continuance of the Church speaking the truth to power. In a talk on "Church, Ecumenism, and Politics," he insisted that "The Church must make claims and demands on public law. . . . Where the Church itself becomes the state freedom becomes lost. But also when the Church is done away with as a public and publicly relevant authority, then too freedom is extinguished, because there the state once again claims completely for itself the jurisdiction of morality."

He follows his namesake in refusing to let the Gospel become irrelevant to politics. Elected directly after the outbreak of WWI, Benedict XV sent a representative to each country to press for peace. On August 1, 1917, he delivered the Plea for Peace, which demanded a cessation of hostilities, a reduction of armaments, a guaranteed freedom of the seas, and international arbitration.

Interestingly, on August 15, 1917, the Vatican sent a note to James Cardinal Gibbons, leader of the Church in the U.S. The request was that Gibbons and the U.S. Church "exert influence" with President Wilson to endorse the papal peace plan to end the war. Cardinal Gibbons never contacted Wilson. (Nor does he seem to have lobbied on behalf of Benedict XV's call for a boycott on any nation that had obligatory military conscription.) On August 27, President Wilson formally rejected Benedict's plan.

But Gibbons and the U.S. Catholic archbishops were not about to reject Wilson's war plans. They had promised the president "truest patriotic fervor and zeal" as well as manpower: "our people, as ever, will rise as one man to serve the nation," and exhorted young men to "be Americans always." Cardinal Gibbons had even written when war was declared that "the duty of a citizen" is "absolute and unreserved obedience to his country's call."

Such unreserved obedience was not endorsed by Benedict XV, nor is it by Benedict XVI. This was perhaps what upset U.S. neoconservatives most, that John Paul II and Cardinal Ratzinger did not show more deference to the state. Perhaps because of their own experience with violent regimes, they seemed to grasp the biblical axiom from the Acts of the Apostles: "we must obey God rather than men" (Acts 5:29).

Such a decision to not obey men nearly cost the young Jospeh Ratzinger his life. In 1945 he made the decision to desert his post in the German army. When he was spotted and stopped by SS troops, he could have been shot on the spot. They did not, using his wound (his arm was in a sling) as an excuse. Yet in his memoir, *Milestones*, Ratzinger gives the deeper reason for his escape from death. Those soldiers, he wrote, "had enough of war and did not want to become murderers."

Our world, Pope Benedict XVI knows well, has had enough of war. We join the chorus of hopes that his ministry as pope will help put an end to war and hasten along God's kingdom of peace.

Index

Credits

Formicola, Jo Renee. 2005. "The Political Legacy of John Paul II." *Journal of Church and State* 47, no. 2 (Spring): 235–242. Reprinted by permission.

Allen, John L., Jr. 2005. "Who Is Joseph Ratzinger?" Pp. 143–164 in *The Rise of Benedict XVI: The Inside Story of How the Pope Was Elected and Where He Will Take the Catholic Church* by John Allen, Jr. Copyright © John L. Allen, Jr. Used by permission of Doubleday, a division of Random House, Inc.

Pope John Paul II. "Was God at Work in the Fall of Communism?" In *Crossing the Threshold of Hope*, by His Holiness Pope John Paul II, translated by Vittorio Messori. Copyright © 1994 by Alfred A. Knopf. Used by permission of Alfred A. Knopf, a division of Random House, Inc.

Bernstein, Carl, and Marco Politi. "John Paul II and the Fall of Communism." Pp. 449–483 in *His Holiness: John Paul II and the Hidden History of Our Time,* by Carl Bernstein. Copyright © 1996 by Carl Bernstein and Marco Politi. Used by permission of Doubleday, a division of Random House, Inc.

Evans, Ernest. 1998. "Observations: The Vatican and Castro's Cuba." *World Affairs* 161, no. 2: 112–115. Copyright © American Peace Society, 1319 18th St. NW, Washington DC 20036.

Ratzinger, Cardinal Joseph. 1998. "War Service and Imprisonment." Pp. 30–40 in *Milestones: Memoirs 1927–1977,* by Cardinal Joseph Ratzinger. Reprinted by permission of Ignatius Press.

Pope John Paul II. 1995. "Address of His Holiness Pope John Paul II to the Fiftieth General Assembly of the United Nations Organization." Reprinted courtesy of the Vatican.

Jeffreys, Derek S. 2004. "John Paul II and Participation in International Politics." Pp. 147–188 in *Defending Human Dignity: John Paul II and Political Realism,* by Derek S. Jeffreys. Grand Rapids, MI: Brazos Press. Reprinted by permission of the Baker Publishing Group.

Coste, René, and Rosemary A. Peters. 1993. "View from the Vatican." *Harvard International Review* 16, no. 1 (Fall): 28–32. Reprinted by permission.

Pope John Paul II. 2003. "Solidarity Is Essential in the Fight on World Hunger." *The Pope Speaks* 48, no. 1 (January–February): 1–2. Reprinted by permission.

Pope John Paul II. 1991. *Centesimus Annus* (encyclical). Reprinted courtesy of the Vatican.

Pope John Paul II. 2002. "The Role of Religion in a Uniting of Europe." *The Pope Speaks* 47: 40–43. Reprinted by permission.

Pope John Paul II. 2002. "To Archbishop Alberto Giraldo Jaramillo of Medellín, President of Bishops' Conference of Colombia." *L'Osservatore Romano* 25 (19 June): 4. Reprinted courtesy of the Vatican.

Pope Benedict XVI. 2005. "Address to the Delegates of Other Churches and Ecclesial Communities and of Other Religious Traditions." Reprinted courtesy of the Vatican.

Pope Benedict XVI. 2005. "Address to the Diplomatic Corps Accredited to the Holy See." Reprinted courtesy of the Vatican.

Pope Benedict XVI. 2005. "Address to Carlo Azeglio Ciampi, President of the Italian Republic." Reprinted courtesy of the Vatican.

Landau, Yehezkel. 2005. "Pope John Paul II's Holy Land Pilgrimage: A Jewish Appraisal." Pp. 129–156 in *John Paul II in the Holy Land: In His Own Words, with Christian and Jewish Perspectives by Yehezkel Landau and Michael McGarry, CSP,* edited by Lawrence Boadt, CSP, and Kevin di Camillo. Copyright © Paulist Press. Used with permission of Paulist Press.

Pope Benedict XVI. 2005. "World Youth Day Address to the Jewish Community." Reprinted courtesy of the Vatican.

Fundamental Agreement between the Holy See and the State of Israel 1994. Reprinted courtesy of the Vatican.

Abu-Rabi, Ibrahim M. 1999. "John Paul II and Islam." Pp. 185–204 in *John Paul II and Interreligious Dialogue,* edited by Byron L. Sherwin and Harold Kasimow. Maryknoll, NY: Orbis Books. Reprinted by permission of Orbis Books.

Pope Benedict XVI. 2005. "World Youth Day Address to the Muslim Community." Reprinted courtesy of the Vatican.

Pope John Paul II. 1995. "Introduction." *The Gospel of Life (Evangelium Vitae).* Reprinted courtesy of the Vatican.

Pope John Paul II. 2002. "Recognize Identity of Human Embryo." *L'Osservatore Romano* 6 (February 6): 1. Reprinted courtesy of the Vatican.

Pope John Paul II. 2003. "After Iraq: Holy See Supports UN." *L'Osservatore Romano* 26 (25 June): 2. Reprinted courtesy of the Vatican.

Grant, Robert. 2005. "The Roman Catholic Hierarchy: Putting the Squeeze on Politicians." *Humanist* 65, no. 2 (March–April): 18–22. Reprinted by permission of the author.

Pope John Paul II. 2003. "Human Sexuality in God's Original Plan." *The Pope Speaks* 48, no. 1 (January–February): 44–46. Reprinted by permission.

Pope Benedict XVI. 2005. "Address to the Participants in the Ecclesial Diocesan Convention of Rome." Reprinted courtesy of the Vatican.

Vogel, Gretchen. 2005. "Abstentions Scuttle Drive to Liberalize Italy's Embryo Laws." *Science* 308: 1722a. Copyright © 2005 AAAS. Reprinted by permission of AAAS.

Griffin, Michael. 2005. "New Pope Benedict XVI a Strong Critic of War." *Houston Catholic Worker* XXV, no. 4. Reprinted by permission of the author.